HOPE AND DESPAIR

MICHAEL A. HOROWITZ

Hope and Despair

Israel's Future in the New Middle East

HURST & COMPANY, LONDON

First published in the United Kingdom in 2024 by
C. Hurst & Co. (Publishers) Ltd.,
New Wing, Somerset House, Strand, London WC2R 1LA
Copyright © Michael A. Horowitz, 2024
All rights reserved.

The right of Michael A. Horowitz to be identified as the author of this publication is asserted by him in accordance with the Copyright, Designs and Patents Act, 1988.

A Cataloguing-in-Publication data record for this book is available from the British Library.

ISBN: 9781911723196

www.hurstpublishers.com

Printed in Great Britain by Bell & Bain Ltd, Glasgow

CONTENTS

Introduction 1

PART 1
A NEW MIDDLE EAST

1. Arab Springs and Arab Winters 9
2. The Return of Great Power Competition 17
3. Palestinian Fatigue? 33

PART 2
BREAKING ISRAEL'S ISOLATION

4. A Deep Desire for Engagement 51
5. Aligning the Stars 57
6. Security Ties 67
7. The Crown Jewel 85
8. Building Roads, Hoping People Will Use Them 103

PART 3
MANAGING DESPAIR IN THE ISRAELI–PALESTINIAN ARENA

9. Trading Peace for Quiet 119
10. The Palestinian Authority 125
11. Chaos in the Post-Abbas Era 141

12. Israel's Identity Crisis	155
13. The Path of Despair and Disillusion	179
14. The Space for Hope in a Shrinking 'Universe of Possibles'	195
15. Jumping into the Unknown after the 7 October Massacre	201

PART 4
ISRAEL'S COLD WAR

16. Failed States, Successful Iran?	207
17. A Not-So-Distant Enemy	215
18. An Inevitable Collision?	231
19. An Empire at Risk of Collapsing Upon Itself	247

| Conclusion: Thinking about the Future | 251 |

Acknowledgements	255
Notes	257
Index	261

INTRODUCTION

When I looked up at the screen, I couldn't help but feel dizzy, excited and truly amazed. I generally avoid looking out of airplane windows, but the view was worth repressing my fear of flying for a moment: below the plane was a view of the Qatari peninsula, shining in the night.

Just an hour ago, we had flown above northern Saudi Arabia, crossing the kingdom's airspace from Jordan. Moments after, we began our descent towards Dubai, above the shipping lanes and offshore platforms of one of the most strategic chokepoints in the world. We were just a few kilometers from Iran.

The quiet here is often deceptive. A few days before, Iran's Islamic Revolutionary Guard Corps (IRGC) had released a video showing naval forces storming a tanker in the latest in a series of incidents pitting Iran against the United States. And yet days after, a plane that took off from Tel Aviv was flying towards Dubai, mere kilometers from this geopolitical fault-line.

Most of the passengers appeared unfazed—it felt normal to most, perhaps except me. But the route we took was the result of a transformative event. That we flew above Jordan, Saudi Arabia, the Gulf, to land in Dubai was nothing short of a small miracle. It was a sign of deeper changes that have contributed to shaping a new Middle East. In a region that's often caricatured as repeating the same old feuds again and again, two countries had opted for peace.

This was not unprecedented: Israel made peace with Egypt, its longtime enemy, in 1979. In the wake of the Oslo Accords (1993), it also made peace with the Hashemite Kingdom of Jordan.

But decades later, those agreements feel cold and distant. Neither Jordan nor Egypt truly embraced the deals: in 2022, Jordan would sign a 'water-for-energy' agreement that led to notable protests both in Amman and in the Jordanian parliament. It later refused to sign the agreement due to the war that broke out the following year following Hamas's 7 October attacks in Israel. It also took decades for Egypt's state-owned flag carrier, EgyptAir, to offer flights to Tel Aviv. These flights stopped as a result of the war.

That's not to say that the Abraham Accords—the agreement that led to the normalization of relations between Israel and the United Arab Emirates (UAE)—suddenly turned all Emiratis into friends of Israel. But the agreement did feel different, in a concrete way: as I walked towards Burj Khalifa, crowds of Orthodox Jews wearing kippah ran through the crowd to see the famous fountain show. Just before, I had heard Farsi in the crowd—the UAE was Iran's second trade partner in 2020—took a cab with a driver from Pakistan and heard Lebanese dialect spoken behind me. This seemed like the fantasy of a Middle East that had moved past previous divides.

And, in many ways, it is very much a fantasy.

Whereas Israelis have certainly embraced Dubai, the opposite isn't necessarily true. Emiratis have not visited in large numbers. More broadly, the region has changed: it has certainly evolved, but old feuds die hard. Diplomatic agreements don't necessarily make for true friendship, and new friends don't necessarily appease old enemies. Hamas's brutal massacre of 1,200 Israelis on 7 October 2023, and the deluge of fire that followed and killed thousands in Gaza, are a cruel reminder of that. What appear to be diplomatic breakthroughs often fail to solve pre-existing issues. The Abraham Accords did not make the conflict disappear, nor were they meant to.

Still, the Abraham Accords did bring something that felt completely new to the Israeli scene when it comes to geopolitics:

hope. Hope that perhaps, for once, the region was changing for the better—for Israel at least. It suddenly broke the image of Israel as a fortress surrounded by enemies, walls and Iron Domes.

To many Israelis I speak with, the notion of a 'new Middle East' immediately evokes the Abraham Accords. But the region is going through bigger changes, with the accords being only a small part of the transformation taking place. Those changes are less overt, and perhaps also less concrete for Israelis and more difficult to define. But they are here, and Israel will need to contend with them.

The normalization agreements are not the only thing that has changed in the region, nor are they the only development that will affect Israel. This was a new Middle East even before the historic signing of those agreements.

The region itself has changed. It is now more than a decade since the Arab Spring of 2011. Some consider the Arab Spring to be dead, as even countries like Tunisia that seemed to be the most promising have failed to transition towards democracy. I'd instead say it's unfinished: the Arab Spring was the opening stage of a much larger struggle that may well define the region in the decades to come. This new Middle East is one that's in the making.

As pleasant as it was to consider the view from the Tel Aviv–Dubai flight, one also eventually comes back to the ground, where old problems can only be ignored for so long. A taste of hope is new, but despair—a despair that has become a central fixture of the Israeli–Palestinian conflict on both sides—is enduring. Some have pointed to the growing radicalization of the conflict. There is clear evidence of such a trend. Yet, I am just as worried by the lack of hope that can be felt on both sides. The hope that peace between Israelis and Palestinians can be achieved has vanished. Peace has been replaced by the concept of 'quiet.' In the words of Israeli leaders, the main goal of any interaction with Palestinians is to 'restore the quiet.' In the words of Hamas, 'quiet will be answered by quiet.'

Yet quiet is not peace. Quiet is the pause between wars. Quiet, by essence, doesn't last.

This book explores this tension between hope and despair. On the one hand, the hope generated by normalization agreements, as well as the optimism that often defines Israeli society, a society characterized by innovation, adaptability and 'disruptions'—a word often associated with startups and information technology. The despair and disillusion, on the other hand, comes with decades of status quo, violence and entrenchment, both physical and mental. We've rolled back so far from the years of peace and hope that the mere idea that peace is not only possible but also desirable can no longer be taken for granted. Peace is not a consensual goal anymore for either of the two sides.

With Hamas's 7 October attacks and the broad Israeli response, Israelis and Palestinians have jumped into an existential unknown. One can hope that most recognize the absolute necessity to stop doing the same thing again and again. But I also fear that this natural inclination towards change is already matched by a far greater force of fear and hatred, one that prevents us from doing anything differently. One that leads us back to the illusory comfort that comes from ignoring the plight of the other side. An approach that mostly focuses on returning to endless debates over who is to blame, who started it and who is the victim of whom. Decades of tired arguments on both sides have not only failed to help; they've also become a lazy replacement for a much-needed discussion on how to solve the conflict. We've focused so much of our attention on who is to blame for the past that we're forgetting to discuss how to make sure the past does not repeat itself in the future.

My aim is to discuss these topics in a rational and dispassionate way. Anything that touches Israel, and the Israeli–Palestinian conflict, often comes with charged statements and righteous and moral discourse that often serve to narrow the debate. It pains me to see that space for rational and perhaps dispassionate debate on the conflict is shrinking. In a conflict seemingly without end, and where both sides have a hard time imagining or accepting what could be a solution, it is, after all, easier to pander to one side or the other—to say 'to hell with solutions.'

The conflict has been ongoing for so long that it is met with indifference by most but adamant conviction by others. Those who have not tuned out of the conversation are convinced, zealots of a cause. They don't want solutions as much as confirmation of the righteousness of their belief. This is as much a problem outside of Israel and the Palestinian territories as it is within. There is a saying in Israel: 'Don't try to be right, try to be smart.' In many ways, Israeli and Palestinian decision-makers are trying to 'be right' after failing time and time again to be smart.

This tension between hope and despair requires calm and sometimes painful examination. The purpose of the story I told about the first flight I took to Dubai also serves another goal: to highlight where I am coming from. As much as I try, I am not a neutral observer. I am Israeli, and this should certainly be highlighted first, for true neutrality doesn't exist—the closest thing to it is awareness of your own biases, honesty and straightforwardness.

What helps me is that I do this for a living: as a geopolitical analyst, I advise clients—governments, NGOs, corporations—on how to navigate the region and what may happen next. I've unfortunately misplaced my crystal ball, and the next best thing is to seek truth beyond narratives. To look at things coldly, on one hand, while still putting yourself in the shoes of those involved, even those who may hate you for good or bad reasons. Being an analyst is weird. It requires cynicism at times but also great amounts of empathy.

As such, I have come to keep great distance from the narrative debates that surround the Israeli–Palestinian conflict and anything related to Israel. This book is not meant to be a rhetorical debate, a dissertation or an academic essay. Each of those formats has failed us, Israelis and Palestinians, in many ways. This book—to the extent I've succeeded at least—is an examination of this tension between tremendous hope and deep despair and an attempt to see what future challenges may lie ahead for Israel, both in terms of security and beyond.

The Middle East has so much past that we often forget to speak about its future. This book aims to serve as a reminder to do so from time to time. After all, ideally, the future first exists in our heads.

PART 1

A NEW MIDDLE EAST

1

ARAB SPRINGS AND ARAB WINTERS

Israel's security and regional environment has rarely seen as drastic a change as in the 2010s and early 2020s: the Middle East has seen dictators fall and rise again, new civil wars tear through the region and new opportunities present themselves. Even by the standard of other transformative events, the region has seen changes that are unique in regional history and for Israel. All of the previous changes that affected the country, be it the peace treaty with Egypt and later Jordan, or the Oslo Accords, were either gradual or limited to one specific issue of concern for Israel's security. The Arab Spring was not: it was an all-encompassing event that shook the region to its core—perhaps only comparable to the aftermath of the 7 October Hamas attacks that put the region on the verge of a regional war. This is a 'New Middle East' in which Israel has to find its footing, being presented with opportunities and risks that match the unprecedented nature of the change and the scope of transformation.

But what exactly is 'new' in this new Middle East?

The 2010s were first and foremost marked by the Arab Spring and the following wave of revolutions, counter-revolutions and unrest. Calls for dignity that began in Tunisia after the self-immolation of Mohamed Bouazizi shaped the 2010s far more than any other ideology, be it pan-Arabism, Nasserism or Islamism, ever could.

And yet, ten years later, the Arab Spring has faded away, purportedly killed by the 'Arab Winter,' a series of counter-revolutions and clampdowns on democratic aspirations that have effectively rolled most of those changes back. The region in which Israel evolves is one reeling from both of those two 'seasons.'

One can easily argue that, overall, the Arab Spring brought nothing new. A decade later, it's back to square one. Ten years ago, a military strongman, Hosni Mubarak, ruled Egypt with an iron fist. Ten years later, a new military strongman, President Abdel Fattah al-Sisi, is doing the same. Even Tunisia—the Arab Spring's success story—is seeing its moment of reckoning with the rise of a new authoritarian leader, President Kais Saied. More than ten years after the Arab Spring, one could easily consider it a failure. That is, of course, if you believe that the 'story' of the Arab Spring is over.

It is not.

The emergence of the Arab street, not as a mere concept that can be summoned as a scarecrow by the region's strongmen but as a force of its own, cannot be ignored. The Arab Spring cannot be viewed as just a 'moment' that has now passed. Looking at other waves of revolutions, such as the ones in Europe during the eighteenth and nineteenth centuries, it is clear that democratic transitions and aspirations rarely win the day in their first fight. It took a century for France to become a stable republic. One could have easily been tempted to pronounce the French Revolution dead and yet would have ended up wrong.

It is telling that the expression 'Arab Spring' itself comes from two 'moments' of freedom in history that were followed by decades of repression. The first is the European people's spring of 1848, marked by a wave of revolutions that shook the old European order. This 'spring' would soon be followed by a set of monarchist and imperial counter-revolutions. The second, closer to us, is the Prague Spring of 1968, referring to the brief period of liberalization in Soviet-controlled Czechoslovakia that ended up being crushed by the Soviet army and preceded decades of oppression in Eastern Europe. Both moments passed, but both were signs of things to come.

The Arab Spring should be viewed in the same way: not as a lone moment but as part of a process, one that is unlikely to go in a straight line, but the direction of which is clear. The Arab Spring deserves its seasonal name, for it will most likely come back, and so will the Arab Winter that followed it. There may be no guarantee that the hope the movement bears will succeed, but the chance that aspirations to dignity will come back is high.

This changes how Israel views the region. The Arab Spring cemented a shift in Israel's threat perception. During the first thirty years of its existence, the Jewish state feared 'Arab strength.' The young Jewish state was faced with the prospect of military annihilation by its neighbors, being pitted against much larger and more populous states. This threat has all but disappeared following the peace treaty with Egypt and later Jordan.

Israel now faces threats tied to 'Arab weakness' or fragilities and the instability that comes with it. As the prospect of a conventional conflict with one of its neighbors faded, the vulnerabilities that made Israel so successful in fighting its neighbors became liabilities and vectors of conflicts.

This became evident soon after the Arab Spring. In August 2011, a series of attacks shook southern Israel. A shooting attack against a bus on Highway 12 in the Negev, the explosion of a roadside bomb near an Israeli patrol along the border with Egypt and an anti-tank missile attack against a civilian vehicle that killed four all served as the first signs that instability was knocking on Israel's door. These attacks were carried out by Ansar Bayt al-Maqdis, an al-Qaeda-inspired group whose name refers to the holy sites in Jerusalem. Three years later, the same group would pledge allegiance to the Islamic State (ISIS) and become 'Wilayat Sinai'—the group's so-called Sinai Province.

As early as November 2012, the war in Syria also shattered the quiet Israel had enjoyed in the Golan Heights. Clashes broke out between rebels and forces loyal to the Assad regime.

These were the premises of a new Middle East. In this new Middle East, change is the only permanent variable.

These transformational changes are far less likely to be predicted or preempted by the tools at Israel's disposal. Though Israel possesses one of the world's finest intelligence services, the level of uncertainty is so high that it is almost impossible to envisage a way to chart a course through to the future. Transformative events such as the Arab Spring are too fickle to predict. They are tied to limited economic opportunities, lack of representation, a daily feeling of injustice and the sinking feeling that comes with the perception that political change is either impossible or will bring more chaos. While the factors behind those events can be visible for years, if not decades, their triggers—the self-immolation of a street vendor in Tunisia, for instance—are far less likely to be predicted.

In many ways, the same factors that led to the 2011 Arab Spring are still prevalent today and could easily trigger a new wave of revolutions. In fact, in many ways they already are: people in Lebanon and Iraq have risen up to call for an overhaul of their political systems; the relative quiet of countries like Egypt or Jordan barely masks deep political and economic divisions and grievances. The Arab Spring was articulated around the demand for dignity.

The death of a street vendor after facing the weight of arbitrary authority in Tunisia resonated in the region because it felt all too familiar. Before that, the Egyptian police killed Khaled Saeed, beating him to death after snatching him from a cybercafé where he was sitting. Pictures of his deformed face helped launch the 25 January Revolution, a revolution that started on a holiday celebrating the police. Protests in the southern Syrian city of Daraa in March 2011 were also triggered by the arbitrary detention of local students for writing graffiti that criticized the regime. The feeling of proximity between Arab nations played a key role in making the Arab Spring viral but so too did shared experiences of not only limited liberty but despair at the unchecked power of arbitrary government and lack of basic human dignity.

Could the same incidents that prompted the Arab Spring still happen today? The answer is yes, and in fact they regularly do. Why they do not trigger another wave of revolution is a mystery that needs to be addressed as they happen. The lines between tactical and strategic incidents have been blurred, as 'smaller' incidents have the potential to trigger dramatic strategic changes.

With the Arab Spring also came new geopolitical fault-lines. The 2010s and early 2020s in the Middle East have been marked by a divide between those seeking to take advantage of the Arab Spring and those seeking to defeat it. Out of the decade-long struggle, four main camps have emerged. The Islamist camp is led by the Muslim Brotherhood and countries like Turkey and Qatar. They initially stood to benefit most from the revolutions, as the Islamist group was best placed to climb to power after the fall or fragilization of several secular authoritarian regimes. Ten years later, the Muslim Brotherhood and its allies have largely been defeated, including in the countries where they once held power, be it in Egypt, Libya or Tunisia. This has forced their two main backers, Turkey and Qatar, to take stock of the defeat and move on—for now at least.

The second camp is that of the 'Axis of Resistance,' the Iranian-led network of proxies that follows the ideology of the Iranian Islamic Revolution. Against all odds, this camp has prospered both as a result of the collapse of its main rival, the Baathist regime of Saddam Hussein, and its ability to empower local minorities. The Axis of Resistance draws its name directly from the resistance against both the United States and Israel, with the latter viewed as a colonial extension of the former. Despite its 'revolutionary' ideology, the Axis of Resistance is very much a counter-revolutionary and anti-democratic camp: one of its main 'successes' has been to fight off the Syrian Revolution, putting a stop to the wave of regime changes in the region.

The third camp is made up of the various jihadist groups that have prospered in the region, be it ISIS, al-Qaeda-tied groups or other radical Islamist groups operating in the region. ISIS has suffered a defeat with the collapse of its 'Caliphate,' but the jihadist ideology still influences segments of the region. It would be presumptuous, and dangerous, to think the group died with its 'Caliphate.' Some groups have also proven more resilient and shifted away from global jihad to focus on local issues in an effort to entrench themselves in the region.

Finally, the fourth camp comprises what Israeli commentators tend to call the 'pragmatic' or moderate states, like Saudi

Arabia, the UAE, Egypt, Jordan and Morocco. In practice, this camp consists of those that resisted the Arab Spring. They view democratic transition as dangerous, whether because it would bring Islamists to power or simply because those regimes do not derive their legitimacy from the people. A decade after the Arab Spring, this camp has emerged victorious, though it is not without its own fragilities.

The Gulf offers perhaps the most sustainable counter-model to the revolution. The petro-monarchies offer their citizens a different 'social contract' from the one common among most Western democracies. According to this unwritten social contract, citizens in the Gulf should not expect to be part of political decision-making, or at least not in the way the average citizen of a democracy does. They are expected to be 'apolitical' and to fully delegate those rights to the monarch. In exchange, the government ensures that their economic needs will always be taken care of. Government subsidies, salaries and programs giving houses to newlywed couples are more than just 'economic perks': they are part of this unwritten social contract.

To an extent, this social contract represents a viable counter-model to the aspiration for freedom of people of the Middle East. Some young people in the region may look to Dubai and the possibility of economic achievement as their personal dream rather than the freedom and dignity others have demanded and paid for in blood. This is particularly the case after so many of the burgeoning revolutions took a dark turn. Freedom and dignity have a cost that may be viewed as too high, whereas this 'social contract' offers stability and the chance for some form of individual fulfillment, without the risks associated with the pursuit of dignity and freedom. This model requires economic stability and prosperity if it is to be successful.

Missing from this regional divide is a credible and audible 'pro-democracy' or 'pro-reform' camp. All four camps have acted in various degrees against democracy, and it would be wrong to think that one or the other is somehow 'better' for democracy. Israel often touts itself as the 'only democracy in the Middle East,' but that does not make it a defender of democracy. Iran proclaims its intent to export its 'Islamic Revolution,' but this ideology is not one that cares for the will of the people. The Muslim Brotherhood camp has shown that it cared for elections only once: to grab power.

***

In this divide, Israel finds itself firmly in the camp of 'pragmatic' Arab states. Segments of the Israeli public may have sympathized with the pro-democracy protests, but among Israeli decision-makers, the Arab revolutions were viewed through the prism of the 1979 Revolution in Iran. It was a leap into the unknown: a revolution kicked off by pro-democratic and moderate youths, but one that could just as easily be hijacked by fundamentalists—whose views of Israel are rarely positive. Unfortunately, in many ways, those predicting impending doom were proven right. But it would be wrong to think that this 'moment' is over, and that the people in this region no longer seek dignity and freedom.

There is little Israel can do to stir the region one way or the other. On the strategic level, Israel is a ship in the storm. It has very little sway over what the future of this emerging and immense struggle for freedom that started a decade ago entails. Israel can't dictate the direction of the wind.

Israel's rare attempts at political engineering in the Arab world have all failed. The most significant such attempt was the Israeli intervention in Lebanon and the creation of a pro-Israel front in the country's south, which ended in 2000 with the full withdrawal from southern Lebanon and the collapse of the Southern Lebanon Army.

The region has become unpredictable in a way that is almost unprecedented. The relative 'quiet' in some countries conveys the deceptive message that things are 'back to normal.' But those ruling over the region know how deceptive this calm is and how easily it can be broken.

This is the new Middle East Israel finds itself in: all the factors behind the Arab Spring—the marginalization of the youth, lack of economic opportunity, lack of representation—are still there. The only change is the fear it created in the seats of power across the region, a fear only matched by that of the chaos fostered by the Arab Spring. This de facto 'equilibrium of terror' between the people of the Middle East and their rulers isn't new, but it has grown more fragile and unstable.

The region's pro-democracy movements were, and in many ways still are, young and disorganized, but this century started with them, and their aspirations will certainly be its common thread.

2

THE RETURN OF GREAT POWER COMPETITION

In 2019, Iran launched one of the most devastating attacks against an American ally since Iraq's invasion of Kuwait in 1990, targeting two massive Saudi energy facilities in Khurais and Abqaiq, situated in the oil-rich Eastern Province.

A Saudi, US and UN investigation in the months that followed revealed the attack was quite sophisticated—it involved several drones, some possibly armed with precision-guided munitions, others laden with explosives. Alongside those drones, Tehran had also fired a number of ballistic and cruise missiles. The attack resulted in the single-largest day-to-day drop in oil supply not tied to market movements or demand.

This was a bold act of aggression, bypassing multiple regional air defenses, flying above Kuwait and Iraq, to strike at the beating heart of the global economy. Iran did not claim the attack—its Yemen proxy, the Houthis, did. Yet the attack was later proven to have come from the north, namely from the direction of Iran or southern Iraq, possibly from an air base in Ahvaz, in southeast Iran.

The latent rivalry between Saudi Arabia and Iran had taken a very noticeable and stunning turn, with Iran taking aim directly at the Saudi Kingdom and at the heart of the Saudi economy. That Tehran considered and later executed such an unprecedented operation was a game-changer in the Middle East. The Saudi Kingdom was within its rights to expect a solid response from its backers.

But the US response was just as stunning as the attack: Washington did nothing.

Even amid an ongoing debate over Washington's disengagement from the Middle East, this left the Gulf monarchies in a state of deep shock. The bond between Saudi Arabia and the United States—a bond that can be traced back to the very early years of the kingdom—was based on the assumption that Riyadh could count on US protection in times of need. This was such a time. And yet Washington did nothing.

To make matters worse, this purported indifference came from a president whose sympathies for Gulf monarchs and princes were well known. A president whose son-in-law, Jared Kushner, was sending WhatsApp messages to the de facto leaders of the Gulf, including Saudi Crown Prince Mohammed bin Salman (MBS) and the UAE's Mohammed bin Zayed (MBZ).[1] The level of direct contact between the actual decision-makers in the United States and in the Gulf had never been this close. The two crown princes felt they were dealing with people who understood them, were from the same generation and shared their appetite for frank and direct talks and for bypassing a cumbersome US bureaucracy that felt cold and often hostile.

The oil industry brushed off the attack as a one-off, and the Trump administration carried on with its policy of maximum pressure against Iran. Even the decision-makers in the Gulf chose to ignore what they could easily have viewed as a betrayal, all for the sake of maintaining friendly ties with an administration that was still committed to isolating Iran. But they never forgot. In many ways, the 2019 attacks and the ensuing US reaction, or lack thereof, were the last straw for the Gulf and another sign that the United States was disengaging from the region.

President Trump's isolationist policies sent mixed messages on the US commitment to the region's security. Impulsive decisions, such as the killing of Iranian General Qassem Soleimani in January 2020 or the joint strike with France and the UK against Syria following a chemical attack in April 2018, made it difficult to read.

But, to many in the region, the trend was clear, and it was one of shrinking American influence in the region. In that sense, President Trump's 'America First' policy and his pledge to end the 'Forever Wars' were no accident of history. After two decades of engagement, the American public still wasn't convinced of the necessity of the American presence in the region. Trump's isolationist policies were just a symptom.

The 2019 attacks against Saudi Arabia were the closest to actual proof that America's commitment to the Gulf's security had vanished, and that the Gulf needed to fend for itself. President Trump even said as much: in his own simplistic view of the world, he summed up how some segments of the American public felt—keeping American allies safe is a costly and often unrewarding task. Why should America be the one bearing that cost? President Trump was clear: be it NATO or Middle Eastern partners, American allies needed to start paying for Washington's protection or fending for themselves.

But from Riyadh's perspective, this was exactly what the Saudi Kingdom had been doing for years.

The Gulf monarchies had, in fact, made sure to 'pay up' for the American protection in juicy defense contracts worth billions. Saudi Arabia is the largest buyer of US equipment.

The year before the attacks, President Trump himself made a gleeful show of those expensive defense contracts: as he was sitting with one of the Gulf's rising stars, MBS, he showed pictures of the various weapon systems the Saudi Kingdom was buying and their associated price. The young Saudi leader smiled awkwardly next to him, accepting that this slightly humiliating show may be the price of the privileged relationship Riyadh enjoyed with the Trump administration. The American president ended the conversation by jokingly saying that those billions of dollars of contracts were 'peanuts' for the oil-rich kingdom. And in a way, Trump was right: the price Riyadh was paying for what it thought it was buying was 'peanuts.'

Where President Trump was wrong is on what Riyadh thought it was buying. The truth was that, in the mind of the Saudi elite, the purpose of those contracts was not to buy American planes or missiles but to buy America's protection. That part of the transaction was not upheld in 2019.

The attacks were a foundational moment for the Gulf and led to some deep rethinking, some of which gave birth to the Abraham Accords and, paradoxically, to the Iran–Saudi détente. It was one of the visible consequences of something much larger: the much-discussed US disengagement from the region.

This disengagement has been an ongoing topic of discussion for around a decade. From Obama's 'pivot to Asia' to Trump's erratic withdrawal from Syria or Joe Biden's effort to keep some of his bandwidth on Ukraine and China, the Middle East doesn't sit at the top of US priorities anymore.

In 2017, the US National Security Strategy stated that '[g]reat power competition has returned,' pointing directly at China and Russia as America's main rivals. One of the unintended results of this great power competition was that US resources and bandwidth were pulled away from the Middle East. The irony, of course, is that the Middle East is very much part of that new global competition.

The re-emergence of great power competition is, in a sense, one of the least surprising developments affecting the Middle East. After all, the region has been marked by great power competition from the age of the Greek and Roman Empires to the Cold War. The two decades of unimpeded American dominance over the region, which followed the end of the Cold War, were the exception. The historical rule is that a region whose name derives from being 'in the Middle' is bound to find itself entangled in the conflicts of this world. In that sense, the return of great power competition means that the region is 'back to normal.'

The conjunction of those two trends—the supposed 'US disengagement' and the return of great power competition—is of critical importance to the region and to Israel.

However, while those trends won't disappear, they should also be considered carefully. The almost universally accepted concept of an American 'withdrawal' from the region begs further scrutiny. In a 2016 article, Derek Chollet, a former Obama official, called the idea of American disengagement a 'myth.'

The alleged 'American disengagement' contradicts some of the actual trends of American foreign policy. Whether Washington likes it or not, the Middle East does have a way of jumping back up to the top of US foreign policy priorities. Over the 2010s and early 2020s, the US backed a military intervention in Libya, supported the opposition in Syria and fought a multi-front war against ISIS—one it is still waging today. Washington also has more troops and bases than any other foreign power in the region. After Hamas's 7 October 2023 massacre, the United States also sent a massive force consisting of two aircraft carrier groups, several thousand troops and a dozen air defense systems (in addition to the military assets already present in the region). If the story of America's involvement is that of an effort to leave the region, then it certainly has a strange way of going about it. This is a story of persistent frustration, as America always seems to find a way back into the region.

This is even more glaring when comparing US influence with that of other would-be global powers. An outsider's analysis focusing solely on sheer numbers of troops when comparing Washington's and Moscow's respective influence in the region would logically conclude that the United States is the giant and Russia the dwarf—with China's influence being non-existent. And yet, this is far from the perception one may get from the region, and how the US presence is viewed.

Chollet was right: American disengagement is a myth, and the reality behind the 'US disengagement' is certainly more complex than the concept.

But a widely accepted myth can be more powerful than an ignored truth. At least that is the case here: the American 'withdrawal' and the power vacuum it allegedly created are discussed not just as possible theories or models but as solid facts. Regardless of whether this myth is pure fiction or grounded in reality, it is one of the main factors contributing to the creation of this new Middle East in which Israel has and will continue to evolve.

What the concept of American withdrawal truly involves is more difficult to grasp. It is less about American presence than about American action. It is also, at times, less about what America does than what America says it will do and doesn't do.

We've moved away from a nearly decade-long era of American 'overconfidence' in the Middle East, one in which America felt it was doing the right thing—or that there was a 'right thing' to do to begin with. One in which there was an 'axis of evil,' a 'war on terror.' A decade in which Washington had a vision of what a democratic Middle East could look like.

As with many grandiose ideas, including that of 'bringing democracy to the Middle East,' those ideas tended not to survive first contact and even less the second or third.

The next decade has been one of American self-doubt. During the Obama administration, one of the mottos of Washington's foreign policy was 'don't do dumb shit.' This reflected the perception that doing catastrophically 'dumb shit,' like the invasion of Iraq, had become a pattern of US foreign policy.

The Obama administration drew the conclusion that Washington had become trigger-happy, quick to act, slow to think. But instead of reflecting on the failure to think, this motto became an incentive not to act. This pervasive idea that inaction, or soft power, was in most cases a better course of action than other more direct alternatives has become a pattern that still permeates the US administration. It likely won't quickly disappear, and Israel will be powerless to change it.

This shift from an era of American overconfidence to one of self-doubt is perhaps more accurate than the often-used concept of 'US disengagement.' It explains why US allies in the region are still looking to Washington, hoping that the American giant will wake up. Nowadays, Saudi Arabia or the UAE may be dancing with Russia or China, but they are also looking to America in the hope of seeing cracks in what they perceive as US indifference. It also explains why other actors, with less means but perceived as more willing to use them, have been able to chip away at America's prominence in the region. The question is: How much flirting does it take before the flirt becomes an actual partner?

For Israel, this is bound to become a clear issue. To be sure, Israel does not rely on Washington's protection as much as other partners may have. The mere history of the Jewish people, and of the Israeli state, means that at its heart the security doctrine of the country is one of self-reliance. The risk posed by American self-doubt and rising great power competition is perhaps more insidious, though no less dangerous.

Nothing has exemplified such challenges in a more dramatic way than Russia's intervention in Syria. Well before Russia's full-scale invasion of Ukraine in 2022, the Russian intervention in Syria showed how Israel's neighborhood could be drastically transformed, and how Israel's posture in the region would have to evolve as a result.

Russia's intervention in Syria altered Israel's calculus and forced it to build relations with a country it had, so far, considered mostly as a distant foe. Even today, as pressure to support Ukraine is at its height, Israel cannot ignore that Moscow is now sitting along its northern border. As a result, bilateral relations between Israel and Russia grew exponentially—though in an asymmetric manner, as Israeli officials took trips to Moscow with the opposite being far rarer.

Contacts between Vladimir Putin and Benjamin Netanyahu, including phone calls, high-level visits to Moscow and Sochi and exchanges between National Security Advisors, reached levels never seen before. Between 2015 and 2020, Netanyahu met with President Putin fourteen times—nearly three times a year—making the Russian president one of Israel's most frequent interlocutors. Israel secured a de facto Russian agreement that maintained the Jewish state's freedom of maneuver in Syria.

It was clear that Washington was no longer Israel's sole foreign interlocutor. This is a new Middle East for Israel: at times of tensions in Syria, the country was effectively forced not only to speak to its main and historic partner in Washington but also to send teams of diplomats and officials to Moscow.

This trend is unlikely to disappear: both US allies and adversaries understand the deep bond that exists between the two. Helping or undermining Israel may increasingly be viewed as a way to get the attention of a distracted and hesitant United States.

***

The crisis in Ukraine is another clear example of the challenges posed by the accelerating global competition. Having Russia as a de facto 'neighbor' in the north played a central role in Israel's reaction to Moscow's 2022 invasion of Ukraine. It took weeks for Israel to—symbolically—side with the West on Ukraine. Israel initially attempted a mediation effort that garnered mixed reactions from both Ukraine and the West. US and Ukrainian officials quietly criticized Prime Minister Naftali Bennett, suspecting that the mediation effort, which came early on during the conflict, may have been an effort to maintain a line of communication with Putin and to score domestic points. Although Bennett's mediation effort was likely genuine, it was also clear that the Israeli prime minister was trying to maintain a delicate balance between Israel's longstanding alliance with Washington and its interest in keeping a good working relationship with Moscow.

A decade earlier, Israel's neutrality would have been odd, but in 2022 Israel's balancing act was not a surprise. Not that Israel had no reason to empathize or even support Ukraine: relations between Kyiv and Jerusalem had grown significantly over previous years. The Russian invasion was liable to impact the remaining Jewish community in Ukraine, as well as Israel's high-tech sector, which had partly come to rely on Ukrainian employees. Not to mention that Israel's main ally, and historic partner, Washington, was siding with Ukraine and beefing up Europe's defense.

And yet, despite all of those factors, Israel could not ignore the cost attached to a more principled position on Ukraine and possible material support to the Ukrainian military. It took a set of exceptional incidents, including evidence of war crimes in the suburb of Bucha near Kyiv and antisemitic comments by the Russian foreign minister, for Israel to move away from its initially timid position towards Ukraine. And even then, Israel refused Kyiv's repeated calls to provide it with military equipment, including some public calls to transfer the Iron Dome system, as well as a less publicized effort to provide Ukraine with anti-tank missiles made under an Israeli license in Europe.

For Israel, siding with Ukraine came with clear risks. Moscow knew exactly which button to push. Just weeks before the conflict,

Russian GPS jammers from its Syrian air base were directed at Israel, prompting pilots at the Ben Gurion Airport to use a different navigation system to avoid any incident. The Russian air force also made a show of patrolling the skies of Syria, and the border with the Israeli-controlled Golan Heights, alongside the derelict Syrian air force. The message was clear: any Israeli effort to side with Ukraine would run the risk of a Russian reaction in Syria. Russia was effectively waving the threat of limiting Israel's freedom of operation and ability to destroy shipments of weapons to Hezbollah—the same weapons that will most certainly be fired at Israeli cities in a future Lebanon war. The risks were not theoretical: in a future conflict with Hezbollah, more Israelis would die if the Israeli air force was unable to operate above Syria.

In fact, Russia went further and effectively signaled the possibility of shooting down Israeli planes. During a strike in northern Syria, Russian-made S-300 anti-aircraft missiles locked on to a number of Israeli planes. The system was brought by Russia in 2018 and manned by a Syrian crew that would not have been able to fire or lock on to Israeli planes without Russia's greenlight. Although the details of the incident are still blurry, Israel may well have responded in kind, as several Syrian soldiers belonging to an air defense unit were killed during the same night.

In the future, whether it likes it or not, Israel will have to make clearer choices and bear the consequences of these choices in a region where siding with the United States is no longer the no-brainer it once was.

For Washington, this should be a stunning revelation, perhaps aggravated by the fact that Israel wasn't the only historic US partner not to toe the pro-Ukrainian line. Saudi Arabia and the UAE also showed their independence, refusing to help ease the energy crisis the war had triggered. Some in the United States have taken to criticizing those allies for not supporting Washington during an unprecedented and truly transformative crisis. I wrote an article explaining why I felt Israel had much more leeway than it thought to support Ukraine, despite the Russian presence in Syria.

But the bigger lesson is to be learned in Washington rather than in Jerusalem. That US allies did not show up at such a historic time should push the US to rethink its strategy and change course. Whether Washington can truly do that in the future is another topic of discussion but one that will be critical for Israel and other US allies in the region, who may feel that a less-than-confident America is one its allies are also unable to depend upon.

This does herald the return of great power competition, something Israel will not be able to ignore in the future. Beyond the cracks between the United States and its allies, the crisis in Ukraine also showed that the Mediterranean was not only a theater of local power rivalry but also of great power competition. This shouldn't be a surprise: just like the Middle East, for much of its long history the Mediterranean has been a theater of great power competition. But the past thirty years had seen a notable decline in the Mediterranean's global value, with control of the sea being viewed as a regional European problem rather than a global one.

The Ukraine war showed that the Mediterranean Sea and the Middle East had resumed their roles as arenas of complex global and regional competition. During the crisis, Moscow deployed a significant naval force, using the Tartus naval base as a launching pad for large-scale exercises that mobilized an almost unprecedented number of ships. These exercises were not meant just as a show of force but also to hinder possible Western deployments to the region and the nearby Black Sea. Russian forces pulled naval groups from its nearby Black Sea Fleet, based in Crimea, as well as its Northern Fleet, headquartered in Severomorsk, in the Murmansk Oblast close to Finland. This meant that Russian naval assets had crossed into the Mediterranean, entering the sea in Gibraltar to deploy in the Eastern Mediterranean—with some also heading towards Ukraine.

The Russian show of force did not end with these naval exercises. Just as an almost unprecedented number of Russian assets deployed to the sea, the Russian air force also deployed a MiG-31K fighter and a long-range Tu-22M bomber at Moscow's main Syrian airbase, in Hmeymim. The Russian Ministry of Defense made sure to note that both of those aerial assets were carrying the Kinzhal ('Dagger') hypersonic missile—a missile initially meant to be an aircraft-carrier killer but that is also nuclear-capable. As

Russia was threatening to invade Ukraine, this showed how the various elements of Moscow's newfound power had come much closer to Israel than before.

Effectively, Israel is sitting on the sideline of a conflict that may well rearrange the world order, and perhaps put an end to Russia's global ambition, but one that has revealed that the Mediterranean and the Middle East would surely be affected by a revived world competition between traditional and would-be superpowers.

Long-term factors are bound to increase the strategic value of controlling parts of the Mediterranean Sea. The discovery of large gas fields in the Eastern Mediterranean means that some previous energy-poor countries, including Israel, are now bound to become net energy exporters. This has already revived a regional naval arms race and highlights Israel's need to invest in its navy beyond nuclear-capable submarines. Even before the Ukraine war, Europe was already trying to formulate a strategy to reduce its energy dependence on Russia. The gas fields of the Eastern Mediterranean were an unexpected boon in that sense, and the European Union has since engaged in supporting several possible alternatives to build a new energy infrastructure that would reduce its reliance on Russian oil and gas. Putin's invasion of Ukraine made these long-term considerations even more critical. Prior to the conflict, Russia had already sought to build ties with several key actors who could prove critical for the future of this alternative energy source for Europe, including through its presence in Libya and ties with Turkey. If the conflict in Ukraine turns into a long war of attrition, it is also not unthinkable to imagine that, just as Europe looks to accelerate its plans and shift away from Russian oil and gas, Russia may also work to thwart those efforts.

***

The great power competition doesn't stop with Russia. Israel, and indeed the whole region, is also liable to find itself on the fault-line between a shaken American power and rising Chinese appetites. China has long been an invisible power in the region. This was and still is a deliberate strategy: Chinese investments tend not to come with any political preconditions or demands, in line with Beijing's official policy of non-interference in domestic affairs. Yet, Beijing is still upping the ante in the Middle East, gradually moving away from a phase of quiet investment to one of more overt influence.

This was made clear in January 2022, when several Middle Eastern officials visited China. In a matter of days, China received delegations from multiple rival Middle Eastern powers. A high-level delegation from the Gulf Cooperation Council that included officials from Saudi Arabia, Kuwait, Oman and Bahrain visited the country. Beijing has long courted Gulf countries, and the visit was a significant acknowledgment of the ties between the petro-monarchies and the Chinese Communist Party. The delegation dangled the much-discussed possibility of signing a free trade agreement with China and forming a strategic partnership with the Asian power.

Those closely following Chinese influence in the region raised their eyebrows: just a year earlier, China had signed a twenty-five-year deal to invest USD400 billion into the Iranian economy. In fact, just as Beijing was holding talks with the high-level delegation from the Gulf, other Chinese officials were also discussing this very same 'strategic partnership' with Iran, receiving Iran's new hardline foreign minister, Hossein Amir-Abdollahian.

But the flexing of China's diplomatic muscles didn't stop there. In the first two weeks of January, China also received a visit from Turkey's Foreign Minister Mevlüt Çavuşoğlu while also officially locking Syria's participation into China's massive 'Belt and Road Initiative,' a project meant to consolidate Chinese influence through trade deals along a land route stretching from China to Europe.

Even during the Ukraine crisis, Beijing appeared to benefit from the gap between Riyadh and Washington, with the Saudi Kingdom dangling the possibility that part of its oil exports would be paid in yuan. The Saudis knew this would please the Chinese, as Beijing had long sought to challenge the dominance of the greenback in global trade—despite the Saudis' own currency, the riyal, being pegged to the dollar.

The Saudis later signed the 'Beijing Declaration,' an agreement brokered by China, in which Iran and Saudi Arabia pledged to restore ties. Although there are many reasons to doubt that the deal will end years of rivalry, this was the culmination of careful investment in Saudi Arabia, as well as Beijing's growing leverage over Iran. A few months later, Beijing would ride the regional rise in anti-US sentiment that followed the 7 October Hamas massacre, adopting a position that barely mentioned the group's murders of civilians—and that in fact never mentioned Hamas itself. Beijing was happy to position itself as a 'peacemaker' at a time when segments of the Arab public saw Washington as a warmonger.

The message is clear: China is here, it is here to stay, and this is just the beginning. There are mechanical factors attracting China to the region. The first is the country's growing dependence on oil exports from the region. As of 2023, Russia and Saudi Arabia are respectively the first and second sources of oil for China; Iran and Kuwait are not far behind. It is often assumed that Washington's interest in the Middle East is tied to its oil reserves, and this has indeed been true for some time, though not anymore. As the United States is becoming more energy independent, it is China that has grown reliant upon the region's oil deposits.

As a mercantile power, China is also affected by any instability along maritime trade lines. This includes the Bab el-Mandeb Strait between Yemen and the Horn of Africa, as well as the Suez Canal. The Ever Given debacle, in which a large cargo container operated by the company Evergreen Marine got stuck in the Suez Canal, showed just how disruptive a single incident could be: according to data from insurers and maritime intelligence, the stranding of the ship cost up to USD10 billion a week, adding eight hours to the journey of cargos sailing from Asia to Europe.

Paradoxically, despite this greater dependence on the region, China has not had to shoulder the cost of stabilizing the Middle East. What's surprising isn't China's new investment in the region but rather that Beijing hasn't been involved in the Middle East's security landscape. Yet there is a very straightforward reason for that: when it comes to stabilizing the region, both US and Chinese interests are aligned. Beijing is just as interested in avoiding major disruptions in the region as Washington is, at least when it comes to energy and trade. As such, Beijing is effectively piggy-backing on Washington's political efforts.

If Washington does decide to start disengaging, Beijing may have no choice other than to fill some of the void. And even if Washington stays on course, the leadership of the Chinese Communist Party appears to see some benefits from starting to be more assertive on some issues, including maritime security and the importance of securing trade. This may seem unthinkable now, but the unthinkable of today often turns out to be the reality of tomorrow. China has already carried out two long-range operations to rescue its nationals in Libya in 2011 and Yemen in 2015. Beijing's only overseas military base is in Djibouti, just along the Horn of Africa.

For now, China is competing on a different level, letting Washington bear the cost of securing the region while focusing on increasing its economic ties with local governments.

Israel is sure to find itself stuck in the middle and in fact already has. Washington has expressed significant concerns over recent Chinese investments in Israel, including in the Haifa port, where US ships regularly anchor. Possible Chinese involvement in Israel's 5G infrastructure also led to tensions between Washington and Jerusalem. Over previous years, a Chinese attempt to control several key Israeli pension funds was also shot down—this time because of Israel's own concerns over what this may mean regarding Israel's dependence on China and Chinese leverage over the country. Chinese investments in Israel's successful tech companies also raised some concern both in Israel and beyond given Beijing's penchant for copying successful economic models to fuel its own economy. Chinese investments may not come with preconditions attached, but it would be naive to think that Beijing doesn't view them as a way to slowly build influence. Chinese investment may well be the invisible equivalent of the landing of the Russian warplanes at their base in Syria. Both are, overall, relatively limited events, but over time they may shift the calculus of neighboring countries and force them to take Russian and Chinese interests into account—even without any direct involvement from Beijing or Moscow.

***

Those trends end a parenthesis in the history of the Middle East in which the region was viewed as a distraction from the great power competition rather than a theater of global rivalries. Washington may still see the Middle East as a distraction, based upon the simplistic idea that it needs to 'pivot to China.' That is, of course, a very dangerous idea not only for Israel but also for the United States. The irony is that China's and Russia's growing influence in the region does owe a great debt to the 'myth' of US disengagement and its alleged 'pivot' to Asia—itself meant to confront China. The idea that global rivalries are somehow regionally confined is, in essence, contradictory.

For Israel, this is a new and often more complex Middle East. For many actors in the region, Israel is America's local address, something that comes with risks and benefits. This is a side result of Israel's privileged relationship with Washington—the real one and the one fantasized by some. Both real and imagined Israeli influence over the United States means that local and global powers have knocked on Israel's door, with a mind to sliding a letter back to Washington—or as a threat. It would also be deceptive to think that Israel can somehow replace Washington as its main partner. Whereas Israel can imitate some of the regional powers in 'treading the line' and hedging its bets, none of America's rival powers see Israel in the way Washington does, and most view it largely through the prism of its alliance with America. If America's presence is challenged, Israel will face lower benefits but also higher risks.

What's clear is that the return of great power competition and doubts over America's role in the region have and will continue to shape this new Middle East. The Middle East is no longer a region from which issues affecting the world may emerge but growingly one in which the issues of the world may affect the region. And this is not good news.

3

PALESTINIAN FATIGUE?

The signing of the Abraham Accords was a moment of triumph for Israel but one of doubt for many Palestinians. The newly signed agreements raised a difficult question that some had been quietly whispering for years: Does the Arab world still care about the Palestinian question?

For much of its history, the Israeli–Palestinian conflict was viewed as the central conflict in the Middle East. The two have often been conflated, with the idea that solving the Israeli–Palestinian conflict would somehow 'solve the Middle East,' and that the conflict was the source of all evil in the region. Even today, the United Nations Special Envoy in charge of mediating the conflict is called the Special Envoy 'for the Middle East.' The organization consisting of the UN, the European Union, the United States and Russia and aimed at finding a diplomatic solution to the conflict is called the 'Middle East Quartet'—though it solely tackles the Israeli–Palestinian conflict. Some outlets will still refer to tensions in Israel and the Palestinian territories as 'tensions in the Middle East' as if they were one and the same.

This is the legacy of decades of misrepresenting the conflict as a major driver of regional instability. This legacy has lived its last days: it is an idea that has been proven wrong many times, whether by the Arab Spring, the Syrian Civil War, the emergence of ISIS or the crisis surrounding Iranian influence in the region. Still, the question of the conflict's role and importance in the Arab world remains and has been given a sense of added urgency—at least for the Palestinians—with the Abraham Accords. The agreements didn't kick off those discussions, but they did raise their stakes. Some of the decisions and major developments that followed the agreements in the Palestinian arena, from President Mahmoud Abbas's decision to hold elections (which he later postponed), to Hamas's effort to break the divide between Gaza and the West Bank and to better influence the situation in the Temple Mount/Haram al-Sharif, and perhaps even the decision to launch the 7 October massacre, can all be traced to an effort to maintain relevance in a region where the Palestinian question has lost its centrality.

Along with the Israeli–Emirati agreement and the normalization of ties with Bahrain came a new idea to replace the old misconception: people across the region and beyond are 'tired' of the Palestinian cause. More than half a century of conflict has allegedly turned the natural sympathy most people in the Arab world felt for Palestinians into indifference, if not frustration and annoyance.

According to this 'new idea'—or talking point, I would argue—the proverbial 'Arab street' was becoming tired of the Palestinians, or at least 'indifferent.' Arabs were busy with their own issues, exhausted with the use of the Palestinian cause to divert from domestic issues or to build sympathy for regimes they have grown to hate—generally their own.

According to that same line of argument, this 'Palestinian fatigue' is one of the main drivers of the most recent developments in the conflict, from Israel's normalization deals with the UAE, Bahrain and Morocco to the apparent apathy of most of the Arab world when Trump decided to recognize Jerusalem as Israel's capital in December 2017. The UAE's decision to break a decades-long taboo surrounding normalization with Israel is also the birth child of growing 'Palestinian fatigue.' Before the deal, Arab countries were sticking with the Saudi-backed Arab Peace Initiative of 2002, which offered normalization in exchange for a solution to the conflict. But years later, the world had moved on from the

Palestinian cause, the Palestinians have missed their chance and the issue is taking a back seat.

More than anything else, this idea of 'Palestinian fatigue' or Arab fatigue with the Palestinian cause shows how our views often follow the movement of a pendulum, swinging from one extreme to the other.

Yet as with most underlying narratives, this claim does contain some elements of truth. The Israeli–Palestinian conflict has been going on for more than seventy years now (or even longer, considering that the conflict began before the creation of Israel): as with any conflict, 'fatigue' is a normal trend. The lack of a unified Palestinian leadership capable of speaking with one voice and the state of effective paralysis in which the Palestinian leadership finds itself also plays a role in watering down some of the natural sympathies towards Palestinians. So too does the emergence of multiple other conflicts and friction points in the region. Perhaps it would be more accurate to say that the attention paid to the conflict has 'eroded' support for Palestinians, as this represents an almost natural trend in a world where news cycles quickly move from one topic to the next.

There are also signs that at least segments of the populations in the region are frustrated with the use of the Palestinian cause as a rallying cry to divert attention from local grievances. Arab leaders have used the cause to rally support ever since the conflict broke out. During the first forty to fifty years of the conflict, Arab countries effectively vied to become the champion of the Palestinian cause, for this was equivalent to being the champion of the Arab world. In many ways, the Islamic Republic of Iran and its 'Axis of Resistance' (resistance to Israel, that is) functions in much the same way, capitalizing on support for the Palestinian cause to do something else entirely.

In Iran itself, during a wave of protests in response to the deteriorating economic situation, slogans denouncing Iran's involvement in Syria, Gaza and Lebanon were heard, with protesters calling on the Islamic Republic to invest in Iran rather than its various proxies. A Saudi TV show aired during Ramadan also signaled that blanket Arab support for the Palestinian cause may be coming to an end, showing a debate between two characters, with one defending relations with Israel and even accusing Palestinians of being 'ungrateful' towards Saudi Arabia. This led to a divide on social media between the hashtags 'Palestine is not my cause' and 'Palestine is my cause.' Another example was the blatant anti-Palestinian rhetoric spread by the Egyptian government of President al-Sisi in 2014, following a large-scale attack by jihadists. Cairo blamed the attack on Hamas, and the government-controlled media outlets followed suit. Of course, this stemmed from an autocratic regime, but this would have been unthinkable at the start of the twenty-first century.

***

These are only anecdotal signs of fatigue with the Palestinian cause, and the question of Arab support for the Palestinians is more complex. This is a question of public opinion, and a challenging one: most Arab regimes are autocratic, and expressing any kind of public opinion is difficult. Respondents may try to stick to what they feel is the official position of their own government rather than their own. In other circumstances, they may also express token support for the Palestinians, as the normative opinion rather than their own.

This shows that there are two separate questions when it comes to measuring Arab support for the Palestinians and gauging the true extent and reality of 'Palestinian fatigue.' The first is the most straightforward one but perhaps less central: Do people in the region support the Palestinians? Understanding whether segments of the population in the region have grown less supportive of the Palestinians is one way of measuring Arab attitudes towards the Palestinians, though it only gauges major tides rather than deeper trends. The second, and perhaps more important, is: How much do people in the region care about the Israeli–Palestinian conflict? How much of a priority is the Palestinian cause to Arab people in the region, and what kind of reaction can we expect should new normalization agreements be signed?

A review of the polls on this topic shows an interesting divide in responses depending on how the question is phrased. If the question directly references the respondent, responses were far more negative than if they didn't. When the Arab Opinion Index,[1] for instance, asked the question 'Would you support or oppose diplomatic recognition of Israel by your country?,' a whopping 88 percent of respondents said they opposed—ranging from 65 percent in Saudi Arabia to 99 percent in Algeria. This differs significantly from the other questions asked in similar polls. The Washington Institute, for instance, asked whether existing normalization agreements were a positive or negative development. Another poll by Zogby Research in 2019 asked whether it was 'desirable that some Arab states will develop normalized relations with Israel, even without peace between Israel and the Palestinians' and got strikingly positive results in the UAE (84 percent saying it was desirable), Saudi Arabia (79 percent), Egypt (73 percent) and Jordan (72 percent), even prompting the pollsters to go back and re-interview respondents to understand this dramatic shift in opinion.

What they found, then, was that the responses were motivated by some form of resignation, or as the pollsters said, a 'begrudging acceptance' that this is where the region is going and that they do not have the 'power to say no.' The same group asked the same question a year later and found that a lower percentage of respondents said that normalizing without solving the Israeli–Palestinian issue was 'desirable' (from 41 percent in Saudi Arabia and Jordan to 56 percent in the UAE).

This trend that sees the Middle Eastern public internalizing what they view as a regional trend was also clearly apparent in another poll. Pollsters asked whether it was 'likely' that additional Arab states would develop normalized relations with Israel even without a peace deal: once again, the numbers showed that seven out of ten respondents thought it was 'likely' or 'somewhat likely' that some Arab states would normalize relations with Israel.

**

Measuring how important the question of solving the conflict is may be even more complex. Several polls do address it: the 2017–18 Arab Opinion Index poll showed that in eleven Arab countries and territories, an average of 77 percent of respondents felt the Palestinian cause concerned all Arabs rather than the Palestinians alone, while only 15 percent of respondents felt that the Palestinian cause concerned Palestinians alone. Notably, the highest percentage of respondents who felt the Palestinian cause only concerned Palestinians was among Palestinians themselves. This shows that fatigue may cut both ways, and Palestinians may also be wary of attempts by others to guide their own fate. A similar Arab Opinion Index poll a year later found around the same ratio, with 79 percent of the respondents stating that the Palestinian cause concerned all Arabs rather than the Palestinians alone.

These polls show that the Palestinian cause is still important to most in the Arab world, but they fail to measure just how important it is. The natural erosion in public attention is truly difficult to measure, leaving many observers to measure it in silences rather than in words or actions: the absence of protests after the Abraham Accords, the relatively muted response to the Trump 'Deal of the Century'—the proposed agreement the Trump administration put forth to solve the Israeli–Palestinian conflict—are viewed as signs that the Arab world may have moved away from the Palestinian cause.

But silences are hard to understand and easy to misinterpret. Another 2020 poll may hint at one possible element of explanation, beyond natural erosion.[2] While the poll showed that most in the Arab world still attach significant importance to the conflict's resolution, the picture was far less clear when it comes to their overall confidence in the upcoming establishment of a Palestinian state. The only two regions with a clear majority expressing confidence in the future creation of a Palestinian state were Jordan and the Palestinian territories themselves, whereas in countries like the UAE, Saudi Arabia and Egypt, a majority (albeit only slight for Egypt) were not confident.

Incidentally, this almost seems to contradict another poll by the same pollster, in which respondents were asked whether they felt a resolution of the conflict was likely in the next five years. A clear majority of respondents in Egypt, Saudi Arabia and the UAE said they felt it was somewhat likely or very likely that the conflict would be solved. But this begs the question of what they see as a 'resolution of the Israeli–Palestinian conflict.' Do most respondents feel that such a resolution will include the creation of a Palestinian state? Given that those polls came amid debate on the 'Deal of the Century,' one can wonder what this resolution entails.

More broadly, this shows that perhaps one of the reasons for the relative regional 'silence' felt in the wake of the Abraham Accords was the growing pessimism and even despair at the enduring deadlock. It is not that the Arab world no longer cares about Palestinians; it is that the issue feels unsolvable.

This is an important trend in that it gives us some insight into the future of 'normalization.' These polls show that the Arab public is not a monolith and that its opinion changes and is perhaps fickler than the use of the 'Arab street' concept makes it sound.

It also shows that there may be little actual enthusiasm for normalization even among those who are ready to 'begrudgingly' admit that this is where the region is going. This diminishes the prospect of people-to-people ties and could suggest that 'cold peace'—similar to that between Israel and Egypt or Jordan—may be more likely than the relatively warm peace between the UAE and Israel, for instance.

It's enough to speak to those in Israel who are in charge of fostering 'people-to-people' ties between Egyptians and Israelis, for instance, to understand the tremendous task ahead. This is an unrewarding job, with anecdotal successes and real setbacks. No wonder most prefer to avoid it entirely, seeing it for the career killer that it is.

This lack of real enthusiasm doesn't mean that normalization is impossible. The polls do show that there is 'space' for normalization as Arab publics begrudgingly see it as a regional trend. Perhaps it also has to do with the emergence of the notion of the nation-state in the Arab world, as other competing ideologies such as pan-Arabism or the religious 'Ummah' (the Islamic community) are losing ground. As this concept of nation-state takes hold, Arab publics may be prepared to acknowledge that national interests may be different from the desires of a pan-Arab or Islamic majority.

There is enough space for continued normalization. But this 'space' is that of indifference and resignation, rather than acquiescence and support. A taboo was broken with the signing of the four-state normalization agreement, but this doesn't mean there is any kind of enthusiasm for ties. Perhaps this is the best Israel can hope for without a resolution of the Israeli–Palestinian conflict, illustrating how, in some cases, the best is the enemy of good.

***

It is critical to understand that measuring the amount of support for the Palestinian cause may be extremely difficult and will continue to be. Much of the Arab population is young and disenfranchised, living under coercive regimes where speaking freely is impossible and where taking a political stance, even on a foreign issue, is frowned upon. The number of polls in these countries is also limited, making it difficult to see clearer trends in public opinion that would be far more obvious in more transparent countries.

This means that both the region's leaders and commentators or analysts are not provided with the means to accurately measure support for the Palestinian cause but need to decipher what's merely a perception.

This difficulty changes everything.

Perception can be different from reality and is often far more 'erratic' than actual trends: whereas trends tend to be more gradual, perceptions often move like a pendulum from one absolute to its opposite. The normalization agreements and lack of popular Arab response to what was viewed as a major taboo just a few years ago is no exception to this rule. The narrative mentioned earlier thus self-validates: in a world where decision-makers curtail free expression, they measure the opinion of their constituents on the Palestinian issue through the distorted prism of 'anger' and 'protests'—the same unrest they deliberately limit.

This conclusion is also important for Israeli leaders themselves, who are at risk of believing that perception is reality. There is a sense in Israel that the region may have 'moved on,' but this impression is deceptive. The widespread outrage of the Arab and

Muslim world to the Israeli campaign in Gaza following the 7 October attacks, as well as the fact that the Hamas attacks brought the region to the precipice of regional war, showed how far back the pendulum of perceptions can swing. The truth may be more complex: a mix of natural 'erosion,' actual 'fatigue' with the Palestinian issue in general (rather than Palestinians) and this self-validating argument that interprets silences as a sign of decreased support for Palestinians—in a region where speech should not be taken for granted.

But complex trends don't make for eye-catching headlines, nor do they make great arguments to justify political decisions. The rare polls coming out of the region can be used as tools to motivate or influence political actors.

In 2022, during a visit to Washington, Khalid bin Salman, the brother of Saudi Arabia's MBS, came armed with a new poll that showed a clear trend in favor of normalizing ties with Israel. The poll was presented to US officials as a sign that the kingdom was ready to officialize the longstanding but unofficial relations it has maintained with Israel. Khalid bin Salman's visit to Washington had one aim: to convince Washington to turn the page on two years of poor relations since President Biden's inauguration. The American president had promised to make a 'pariah' out of Saudi Arabia and its young crown prince over his involvement in the murder of Saudi journalist Jamal Khashoggi in Istanbul. The real prize for Riyadh was a visit by President Biden to Saudi Arabia and a meeting with MBS. Such a visit would show the world—and the Saudis—that there was no bad blood between the two and was critical when considering that MBS was bound to become king and could not be seen as having poor relations with Riyadh's American ally.

The possible normalization of ties with Israel raised by the Saudis was meant to sweeten the deal, and the polls conveniently said exactly what the Saudis wanted them to say.

This raises the question of whether this narrative of Arab 'fatigue' with the Palestinian cause doesn't, in fact, more accurately describe perceptions among Arab leaders rather than Arab people. While Arab people clearly haven't moved on, Arab leaders may wish they had.

It is an open secret that several Arab leaders have very different views of the Palestinian conflict from those they publicly express. The frustration conveyed by the Saudi TV show regarding Palestinian 'ungratefulness' towards the kingdom may be far closer to the sentiment of the Saudi elite than that of the Saudi population as a whole. Would the average Saudi truly know about such Palestinian 'ungratefulness'?

The normalization agreements emerged just a few years ago, in 2020, but relations between Israel and the Arab world date back decades. The Israeli Mossad has often acted as a parallel diplomatic corps in countries where official diplomatic relations didn't exist. Some Mossad front companies also acted as de facto 'embassies' in countries that have since decided to officialize their ties with Israel.

For Arab elites and decision-makers, the 'natural erosion' in attention towards the Palestinian cause comes with an added sense of urgency. Time spent dealing with the Israeli–Palestinian conflict may take away from other issues Arab leaders view as more pressing.

This is in addition to a trend of 'diminishing returns' of the Palestinian cause for regional and global leaders looking to score points in the international arena. The same trend explains why the various US administrations have been less and less interested in pushing for a resolution of the Israeli–Palestinian conflict: whereas breakthroughs appeared possible decades ago, this is not the case anymore. The current status quo and lack of Palestinian or Israeli leaders that are capable of striking a 'fair' agreement (if it ever emerges) means there's little benefit in engaging with the issue.

The Trump administration's focus on the Israeli–Palestinian conflict, in that sense, was the exception rather than the rule, driven by a president whose ego may have led him to think he could solve this historic conflict with a 'Deal of the Century,' as it has come to be known. This was a form of naivety on the part of the president. Conversely, this shows that more knowledgeable leaders have learned by now not to get too involved and never to put their reputation on the line. This shows that the mere perception that the conflict is unsolvable makes it a self-fulfilling prophecy.

The picture is no different when looking at the broader region. Even countries such as Egypt that have been most invested in finding solutions to key aspects of the conflict have generally only done so to the extent that it has served their own interests. Egypt's policy has been driven by an interest in stabilizing the Gaza Strip for fear that it would be used as a safe haven for jihadists operating in Sinai, and because stability in the two regions is more closely aligned than one could think. By mediating between Israel and Hamas or Hamas and Fatah, Egypt also gains influence in Washington, which is far more critical to its standing than actually solving the conflict. Solving the conflict would require far more pressure and political will, with few clear benefits. Being viewed as an unavoidable mediator when the conflict boils over, on the other hand, means scoring key political points in Washington at very little cost.

Perhaps the only country interested in resolving the conflict is Jordan. For Amman, the Palestinian conflict and the stabilization of the West Bank isn't simply a foreign policy matter but an internal one. With most of Jordan's population composed of Palestinians or people of Palestinian descent, as well as Jordan's special relation to the Haram al-Sharif holy sites—Jordan's royal family has played the role of Custodian of the Holy Sites since before the Second World War, a role Israel recognized when it signed its peace treaty with Amman—the Hashemite Kingdom is directly impacted by any key development in the conflict. Amman, however, has found itself largely isolated after years of notoriously bad relations with Prime Minister Netanyahu and with the Trump administration to the point that it is more than happy with the new US and Israeli administrations and won't press its luck any more than needed.

The Palestinian leadership also shoulders a good deal of the blame for breaking the ties they used to maintain with Arab leaders. Recently, a Fatah leader lamented that whereas in the past 'Arab leaders would lose their sleep' waiting for decisions of the Fatah Central Committee, now they are soundly sleeping as the party deliberates in its own echo chamber. For decades, the Palestinian leadership had a de facto 'veto' on ties between Israel and its neighbors. This veto has gradually vanished.

This attitude certainly didn't play well with some of the region's leaders. President Abbas has been largely isolated on the regional scene: the ailing Palestinian leader rarely embarks on regional tours, nor does he cater to many Arab visitors. When he does, this is mostly to visit the two main countries still invested in the Palestinian question, namely Egypt and Jordan.

The Palestinian president is himself largely unpopular, which begs the question of why anyone in the region would lose sleep over empty statements and rhetoric. This may change in the future when Abbas is replaced. The question of whether he is replaced by a figure of the status quo, who is liable to be just as unpopular as him, or by someone who is more representative of the Palestinians is bound to have an impact on how much attention and weight regional leaders will place on the Israeli–Palestinian conflict.

Abbas isn't the only factor behind the regional leaders' Palestinian fatigue. The internal divisions among Palestinians, particularly since the death of Yasser Arafat in 2004 and Hamas's rise to power in 2007, have also played a role in isolating and dampening Palestinian voices.

Both Hamas and Fatah have proven far more adept at reaching behind-closed-door agreements with Israel than among themselves. And if Fatah can maintain its security cooperation with Israel and continue to meet with Israeli leaders, if Hamas can negotiate ceasefires and 'arrangements' with Israel, then why shouldn't other Arab leaders do the same?

The shift in the strategic thinking of Arab leaders can also be explained by the tectonic changes brought to light by the Arab Spring and the ensuing 'Arab Winter.' There is a domestic aspect to this Palestinian 'fatigue' that also explains why several Arab regimes—the ones Israel calls 'moderate'—are now less inclined to support the Palestinian cause.

The leaders of those 'moderate' Arab countries have increasingly found that their political opponents were the most adamant supporters of the Palestinian cause. Whereas the Palestinian cause served to bolster support for populist regimes, such as that of Egypt's Gamal Abdel Nasser or the Baath party in Syria and Iraq, Arab leaders increasingly found that the Palestinian cause was most vehemently defended by their opponents rather than their allies.

The Muslim Brotherhood is the most well-known example of such trends. The group's anti-Israel rhetoric is at the core of its doctrine, one that is often mixed with antisemitic tropes—at least in Arabic, as the group's communication is often 'sanitized' in English so as not to alienate Western publics, whose sympathy is still needed.

More broadly, political activism in general, even unrelated to local grievances, is also viewed by the region's autocratic leaders with suspicion (at best). Egyptian leaders will surely remember that some of the activists who spearheaded the 2011 revolution started off at pro-Palestinian demonstrations, where they learned to organize, mobilize and stage protests. They learned not to start protests in big squares where their small numbers would deter others from joining and where they would easily be crushed by security forces but to kick off demonstrations in small side-streets and alleyways where they could gain momentum before moving on to main roads and squares. Those skills were used to denounce Israel and to support Palestinians, but they are easily transferable to any other cause they may choose to defend—including demanding the ouster of their own regime, as they did in 2011.

That most pro-Palestinian supporters were found among the Arab regime's opponents made it even easier to sideline and ignore them. They are not the regime's main constituents and are viewed with hostility anyway. Any attempt to amplify the importance of the Palestinian cause would be a self-inflicted wound that could fester.

***

This also explains why normalization started from the top, rather than the bottom. The most realistic track for actual people-to-people ties in the absence of a solution to the Palestinian conflict is that of a top-down approach.

The implicit hope is that peace treaties largely driven by Arab leaders rather than Arab people will, with enough time, lead to the emergence of people-to-people relations. The burgeoning of UAE–Israel trade ties and tourism could be an example of a successful top-down approach. The opening of borders could also see stereotypes on both sides disappear, with educational books being transformed, and anti-Israel rhetoric being toned down, as has been the case in several countries that have made peace with Israel: Egypt, for instance, has worked to remove some of the antisemitic and anti-Israel rhetoric that could previously be found in some of its textbooks.

The process may seem unnatural, but in history, most countries that started off as enemies built peace first and bonds second. One people's hostility towards another tends to take far more time to dissipate, particularly when compared to the ebb and flow of cold and pragmatic state interests.

But when it comes to the specific case of Israel with its neighbor, the situation may be different, as the cause of hostility isn't so much in the bilateral relationship as in the sympathy segments of the population feel towards the Palestinians.

The case of Egypt is the perfect example. Despite being the first country to sign a peace treaty with Israel, sentiments towards Israelis have always been marked by hostility. People-to-people ties, with some very minor and anecdotal exceptions, have generally been non-existent. It was only in 2021, for instance, that Egypt's state-owned carrier made the first official flight between Israel and Egypt. Before that, the route was manned by 'Air Sinai' to avoid having EgyptAir actually fly to and from Israel. In 2022, the first Egyptian trade delegation openly visited Israel. The dozens of representatives who flew to Tel Aviv agreed, for the first time, to have their picture taken.

Although it has certainly increased, trade between the two countries is noticeably limited when compared to the potential market Egypt represents for Israel. Even after a landmark agreement that let Egypt (and Jordan) export products to the United States free of tax on condition that there be an Israeli input, trade with Egypt still represents less than 0.5 percent of Israel's total exports. Most of the trade also largely stems from state-sponsored deals rather than purely private business—which is in no small part due to the weight of the Egyptian military on the country's economy. With the exception of Israeli tourism in

Sinai, there are few people-to-people connections between the two countries, and the two rarely interface.

This is a cold peace, one where people learn to live side by side rather than together.

But the fact that the peace deal did not appear in clear danger also gives us some hope that normalization, at least the kind of normalization that involves government-to-government ties and formal peace, may survive the likely decades of change that are ahead of us in the Middle East, and that ties won't be broken off, and that this will serve as a building block for future relations.

The other form of normalization, however, that between people, is still very much in its infancy and is both more difficult to measure and to secure. This is one of the challenges that explains why some in Israel and outside may feel that the Palestinian issue is secondary, or that there is some form of 'Palestinian fatigue.' It may also explain why the first country to decide to make the jump, the UAE, was one that cared little for its own domestic opinion. After all, as one trip to Dubai will teach anyone, the immense majority of the UAE's residents are expatriates who have no say in domestic politics. Actual Emirati citizens are effectively taught to be neutral and not to engage in politicized discussions or debates.

Overall, this suggests that the current impasse in the Israeli–Palestinian conflict still represents an upper limit to some of the ties. It is not the 'veto' Fatah seemed to think it had in the past. Arab fatigue with the 'Palestinian' cause is a real trend but one that applies far more to Arab leaders than ordinary Arab people.

This may change as more normalization agreements are signed and as some relationships will form, thus deepening the superficial bonds between states. But Israel would be mistaken to see this as a broader sign that the region has 'moved on.' The space for normalization is one that has grown out of indifference and begrudging acceptance, as well as a shift in perceptions that may only partly reflect realities. It shouldn't be taken for granted, particularly as the region is in the midst of profound change. For the danger of mistaking perception with reality is that reality generally has a tendency to be far more obtuse and eventually returns to dispel illusions.

PART 2

BREAKING ISRAEL'S ISOLATION

4

A DEEP DESIRE FOR ENGAGEMENT

On 12 June 2020, the UAE ambassador to Washington, Yousef al-Otaiba, published an opinion piece in the Israeli newspaper *Yedioth Ahronoth*. The article was significant on multiple levels. It was the first-ever opinion piece by an Arab official to be published by a mainstream Israeli newspaper, thus representing one of the few times Israel's public opinion appeared to matter to an Arab official and one of the few times an Arab official has tried to convince the Israeli public in a direct and straightforward manner. Other examples exist, but they are few, including Egyptian President Anwar Sadat's visit to Israel and speech to the Knesset in 1977 and a visit by Jordan's King Hussein in 1997 to express condolences after an attack carried out by Jordanian soldiers.

The Emirati article was translated into Hebrew and appeared in the Friday edition of *Yedioth Ahronoth*, one of the most widely circulated newspapers in the country, as well as in English on the newspaper's website. A poll released later showed 38 percent of Israelis were at least somewhat familiar with the article,[1] a relatively high number.

The content of the article was also groundbreaking. The message was relatively clear: according to the ambassador, Israel needed to decide between two mutually exclusive paths. The first was that of isolation with the annexation of the West Bank, a project supported by Prime Minister Netanyahu at the time. Al-Otaiba warned that annexation would be a 'misguided provocation' that would 'ignite violence and rouse extremists' and 'send shock waves around the region, especially in Jordan whose stability—often taken for granted—benefits the entire region, particularly Israel.' The ambassador also warned that annexation would 'certainly and immediately upend Israeli aspirations for improved security, economic and cultural ties with the Arab world and with UAE.'

The second path was that of engagement with the Arab world. The ambassador offered a vision of the future, a future in which the UAE and Israel would collaborate on several issues, from terrorism to climate change, water and food security, as well as technology.

The article was a straightforward, matter-of-fact attempt at discussing the choice Israel faced, at a time when Israelis may not have felt they had that choice. The ambassador did not make a moral argument but a pragmatic one, based on considerations that were close to the heart of most Israelis. In Hebrew, some could have qualified the article as being 'tachles'—frank, straightforward and devoid of the flourish that often comes with diplomatic language.

Was it a turning point? Evidently not. Some in Israel chose to take offense at the article and denounced what they described as an attempt at 'interfering' in Israeli politics. Others described it as a 'threat' and a repeat of what they saw as the same tired argument that any move away from the status quo would create chaos. The same poll mentioned earlier showed that those aware of the article were almost equally divided between those who viewed it in a positive light and those who didn't.

But more than two months later, opinion polls would show a very different picture. A survey published before the signing of the historic Abraham Accords[2] showed that a clear majority of Israelis preferred normalization with the UAE over the annexation of the West Bank. When asked which option they preferred, more than 75 percent of Israelis said they preferred normalization over annexation, with only 16.5 percent saying they still preferred annexation.

This was a stunning change in public opinion in a country where polls rarely show that amount of support for anything or anyone. The issue of annexation itself had been divisive, but the choice of skipping it entirely for the sake of better ties with an Arab country appeared a no-brainer to most.

This showed a somewhat surprising and deep desire for engagement, in a way that justified a course correction when it came to the Palestinian issue. This is rare and significant enough to be highlighted: in a country that had good reasons to view its neighbors with mistrust, Israelis overwhelmingly approved of a change of course for the sake of establishing relations with one such neighbor.

To be sure, this desire may have been there to begin with, at least in theory. The Israeli declaration of independence does state that Israel seeks to 'extend our hand to all neighboring states and their peoples in an offer of peace and good neighborliness, and appeal to them to establish bonds of cooperation and mutual help with the sovereign Jewish people settled in its own land.'

But there has been a clear gap between words and deeds, at least until now. Even previous peace treaties weren't necessarily embraced in the same way: the Israeli peace treaty with Egypt also divided Israelis. Of course, the peace treaty between Israel and Egypt was far more painful than the Abraham Accords: Israel had to withdraw from Sinai, an area where Israeli blood had been shed and where Israelis were living. The Sinai Peninsula also provided Israel with some 'strategic depth,' something the Jewish state always lacked. Israel made a sacrifice then that was far greater than the decision to halt the annexation process—a process many in Israel thought would not materialize anyway. Yet the parameters of the equation, as different as they may be in scope, are the same in nature: Israelis effectively accepted the idea Ambassador al-Otaiba defended, that engagement with the Arab world would still require moving away from a path of escalation in their conflict with the Palestinians.

This raises the question of whether the coming years will see more of this trend, and whether Arab public opinion will have some form of weight in the public debate in Israel.

The situation today makes this seem like a fantasy. The idea that the Israeli public can somehow be convinced to take its neighbors' sensitivities into consideration is still in the realm of theory rather than reality. The mere prospect that Israel has or will have to cater to the public opinions of its neighbors is taboo. For instance, there is virtually no awareness in Israel of how fragile its eastern neighbor (Jordan) is, or how unrest in Jerusalem's old city directly impacts and damages the Jordanian monarchy. This is despite the tremendous strategic benefit Israel derives from having a stable neighbor that has effectively shielded it from the major turbulence the region experiences in Iraq and Syria, for instance. Imagine if Jordan was unchecked, in the same way that Sinai has been for instance. The consequences in the West Bank would be disastrous. And yet, the 1994 peace treaty with Jordan is taken for granted. There is no effort by Israeli politicians to educate the public about the strategic importance of a stable Jordan.

The very few politicians who dared to place some emphasis on better ties with Jordan or the Palestinian Authority (PA) have opened themselves up to attacks from their adversaries. This was the case with Benny Gantz, who had made it clear in the series of Israeli elections in 2019–20 that he would seek better ties with the Hashemite Kingdom and faced an onslaught of criticism from the right. Some of this criticism was deeply cynical and deliberate misinformation, as Netanyahu did not hesitate to claim that Jordan was tilting towards supporting Iran—an absurd claim given the kingdom's overall defiance of Iran and its ideology. But politically, this was a smart and effective move.

Tensions surrounding Jerusalem have also involved this dilemma between domestic and regional politics. The issue of Jerusalem and particularly the holy sites in the Old City still carries significant emotional value both for Jews and Muslims. Images of Israeli soldiers entering the al-Aqsa Mosque often shock the Arab world and are used and amplified by Israel's adversaries, including Hamas. The Islamist group regularly circulates disinformation about upcoming Jewish religious sacrifices around the holidays. There has also been legitimate criticism of the perceived effort to 'Judaize' Haram al-Sharif (the Noble Sanctuary, the compound that includes al-Aqsa and the Dome of the Rock). This includes efforts to narrow the ability of religious Islamic authorities to operate on site or take care of Islamic monuments and shrines, or increasingly to limit access to the compound. These claims are compounded by broader Israeli efforts to assert demographic and political control over the city, including by favoring Jewish populations over Palestinians. There is little understanding among average Israelis about the damage those tensions still continue to inflict on Israeli–Arab relations—perhaps more than any of the wars in Gaza.

The tensions that erupted over Jerusalem in 2021 and at the beginning of 2022 put many countries who signed the Abraham Accords, and some who were considering it, in a difficult position. Bahrain, the UAE and Morocco issued notable condemnations. The UAE 'strongly condemned' the 'storming of the al-Aqsa Mosque,' while Morocco expressed its 'firm condemnation of the incursion by Israeli occupation forces into the al-Aqsa mosque.' Will those countries break off relations with Israel because of such incidents? Most likely not. The Abraham Accords survived their first test in 2021 with the conflict in Gaza and similar tensions in Jerusalem that preceded the conflict.

But those condemnations should not be ignored: both the UAE and Morocco are aware of the sensitivities surrounding al-Aqsa and the possibility they will be used by their enemies or domestic opponents. Those tensions have the potential to create friction, delays and force at least some temporary distance. There are many reasons why Hamas has increasingly sought to build a presence around al-Aqsa, but one of them is to have a pressure point at its disposal that it can use on a yearly basis around the Muslim and Jewish holidays.

And yet there is no one in Israel willing to raise that issue, beyond its security aspect. Even the short-lived government formed by Prime Minister Bennett and alternate Prime Minister Yair Lapid—a government that showed many times that it was in fact aware of such sensitivities—eventually authorized the yearly nationalist Flag March marking the capture of East Jerusalem and the reunification of Israel's capital following the Six-Day War in 1967. The government was, at the time, beset by internal tensions and facing pressure on its right-wing members that eventually led to its downfall in June 2022. By authorizing the march, and even approving an itinerary through the Damascus Gate (a typical hotspot of tensions) and the Muslim Quarter, the government hoped to avoid being attacked by the then Netanyahu-led opposition for 'caving' in to Palestinian and regional pressure. This is despite Netanyahu himself having refused to authorize the same itinerary the previous year.

The Israeli public's lack of awareness or care for the regional impact of such tensions is a sore point that regularly puts the brakes on deepening engagement. And yet, no one in Israel is able to argue that point. Anyone publicly expressing these concerns in Israel would simply be inaudible.

At the same time, the idea that change from the outside can affect Israel from the inside cannot be ruled out. Less than a year after the signing of the Abraham Accords, Israel saw the emergence of the first coalition to include an Arab party in decades. Can the Abraham Accords explain this development? Most likely not, but they may have contributed to the general perception that allying with Arab parties had now become a more credible option—one that even Netanyahu himself considered as he negotiated with the United Arab List (Ra'am), a party that ended up aligning with his opponents.

Either way, this question will be critical for the future of Israel's relations with its neighbors. Educating the Israeli public about the possible need to cater to some Arab concerns may be taboo in Israeli politics, but it is no less necessary, both to materialize Israel's deep desire for engagement and to avoid the pitfall of isolation.

5

ALIGNING THE STARS

Since the 2020 signing of the agreement between the UAE and Israel, and the following deals with Sudan and Morocco, one question has been on everyone's mind: Which country will be next? The agreements broke a taboo. Until then, Arab–Israeli relations were discussed as an open but mostly shameful secret. Articles have regularly discussed the possibility that Saudi Arabia, or Oman, or other Muslim-majority countries may normalize ties with Israel. But little has been written on the factors that brought the Abraham Accords to light, and whether they can easily be replicated in the future.

The Abraham Accords were the product of a set of very specific circumstances. Replicating them may be akin to aligning the stars.

First, the accords were very much the product of the Trump administration. The Biden administration has been reluctant to pursue that legacy even though it essentially agrees on the need for improved ties between Israel and the Arab world. Biden may be looking for a different way to expand normalization, but Trump set the precedent in both style and content.

In a way, the agreements were an attempt to reconcile the various contradictions in President Trump's foreign policy and his vision of the US role in the world. Trump saw himself both as a dealmaker, capable of solving the most complex of issues, and as the president who put an end to the 'forever wars' and disentangled the United States from a complex network of alliances and treaties that tied it down.

The agreements were thus born from a desire to present the president as a 'deal maker' who could solve even the most unsolvable conflict—and the Israeli–Palestinian conflict certainly matched that criterion. Unsurprisingly, the conflict turned out to be far more complex than a real-estate or commercial dispute, and the plan proposed by President Trump's team came up short. But the president's taste for 'the art of the deal' can still be found in how the Abraham Accords came to be, and how transactional they were.

The accords were also the product of a certain type of diplomacy that may well be an exception rather than a rule. Whether the proposed 'Deal of the Century' was realistic or not, it is clear that the Trump administration did engage in a serious and intense diplomatic effort, the likes of which haven't been seen in years. One may have questioned the credentials of Trump's appointee, his own son-in-law Jared Kushner, as the point man for solving the Israeli–Palestinian conflict. But no one can deny that as part of the president's entourage and family he had a direct line of communication with Trump.

Kushner's way of doing things broke many of the established bureaucratic codes of the American administration. He managed negotiations with Arab states through WhatsApp and by directly engaging with the key decision-makers in the region, bypassing any intermediary. This turned into an asset when dealing with the Gulf monarchies, whose diplomatic style is closer to that of Kushner. No one would find it more natural for a member of the presidential family to be appointed to such a critical post than the heirs and princes of the Gulf petro-monarchies. After all, this is exactly the way monarchies do function, particularly in the Gulf.

The American engagement, at the time, was profound in a way that made participants in the negotiations feel like this was at the top of Washington's foreign policy priorities. This served Washington well, but it was also exceptional and unlikely to be replicated. And yet this is the precedent that was set. It would be foolish to try to predict how America's foreign policy will be dealt with, but it is also clear that in the country's history, this 'Kushner paradigm' has been the exception rather than the rule.

***

Beyond that, the normalization agreements were also deeply tied to the perception that the road to Washington goes through Jerusalem.

This is evident simply from the various demands that were made by the Arab countries that did decide to join the Abraham Accords: none of them made any significant demands on Israel. Looking at the preconditions for signing the normalization agreements, you would be excused for thinking that the agreements were between the United States and the UAE, or the United States and Morocco. Barely any of the conditions related to Israel, and all of the deal's key parameters were directed at Washington.

The UAE famously requested the sale of US-made F-35 fighter jets. Morocco secured Washington's support for its occupation of Western Sahara. Sudan was crossed off the US list of 'state sponsors of terrorism.' Even the article published by the UAE's Ambassador al-Otaiba was aimed at American Jews as much, if not more, than at Israelis: there is a reason why it was written by the UAE's ambassador to Washington rather than another official. Al-Otaiba has long maintained quiet ties with the Jewish community in the United States, and Abu Dhabi launched a charm offensive targeting the American Jewish community months before the signing of the agreement. Al-Otaiba himself said he took advice from Haim Saban, an Israeli American businessman, on writing the opinion piece. The UAE's effort to portray itself as the epitome of religious tolerance also aims to pander to the powerful pro-Israel lobby in Washington.

This is not a coincidence, nor is it new. The potential candidates to expand the Abraham Accords and regional players looking for better ties with Israel have all effectively viewed the Jewish state as a conduit rather than as the prize. In 2002, for instance, Saudi Arabia encouraged the Arab League to offer Israel a deal known as the 'Arab Peace Initiative.' The deal was unprecedented at the time: it proposed full normalization with the Arab world if Israel agreed to withdraw from all the territories Arab countries viewed as occupied and if a 'fair settlement' of the Israeli–Palestinian conflict could be reached.

This currently seems like quite the stretch, given that Israel has effectively been able to formalize its ties with part of the Arab world without making any such concessions or solving the conflict. But at the time, it was viewed as a welcome formalization of a possible 'end game' to solve the Israeli–Arab conflict. Many commentators refer to the Arab Peace Initiative as the previous roadmap for normalization before the Abraham Accords, which served to decouple the Israeli–Arab conflict from the Israeli–Palestinian one. But we also tend to forget the unspoken context of the deal, and one of the key reasons why Riyadh pushed for such a groundbreaking initiative: it came a few months after 9/11, at a time when the image of Saudi Arabia had been damaged significantly by the participation of several Saudi citizens in the attacks. Although the offer was clearly on the table, for Saudi Arabia the Arab Peace Initiative was also a way to mend ties with part of the American establishment and improve its tarnished image as an exporter of radicalism and terror.

The same can be said of Egypt's involvement in the Israeli–Palestinian conflict. Egypt has been mechanically involved in the Palestinian question as one of the countries most affected by it. The situation in Gaza, in particular, has affected the nearby Sinai Peninsula, be it as a result of the widening of the smuggling trade using tunnels, which the Egyptian army curtailed in 2013–14, or the use of Gaza as a rear base for a jihadist group. But there is also a political component to the Egyptian interest in the conflict that has to do with Washington more than any of the two parties to the conflict. President al-Sisi's efforts to improve ties with Israel are largely aimed at preserving the bond between Cairo and Washington and Egypt's efforts to brush concerns over human rights in the country under the rug.

The same can be said of President Recep Tayyip Erdoğan's sudden change of heart and decision to mend ties with Israel after years of diplomatic crisis: the Turkish president had Washington on his mind when he met with Israel's President Isaac Herzog in

March 2022. Even the son of Libyan warlord Khalifa Haftar offered to normalize ties between Libya and Israel in the hope of securing Washington's backing for his father.

The realization that Israel's improved ties with its neighbors owe much to Washington should, once again, temper the idea that Washington has somehow disappeared from the region. It also shows just how fragile the normalization effort may be: once again, Trump will have imposed its style and set the precedent for an agreement. Future candidates for normalization will know that they can expect not only a boost in standing in Washington but also some material perks. They'd be naive not to make any demands, be it new weapons or Washington's support on a specific issue.

This is the clear paradox that is at the heart of the normalization effort in that the Abraham Accords also emerged as a way to reduce US involvement in the region. President Trump wanted the region to start overseeing its own security. Washington's goal was to try to reduce the Arab states' dependence on the United States for their defensive needs. The administration was certainly more than pleased to sell weapons to the wealthy petro-monarchies of the Gulf, but US weapons did not necessarily mean US protection—at least not in the minds of policymakers in Washington. The Abraham Accords are, in that sense, in line with a failed effort to create the equivalent of an 'Arab NATO': it was Washington's way of making sure US partners in the region could fend for themselves. The accords were part of a larger effort to break barriers and foster cooperation among allies. Facilitating relations and building security partnerships on top of an existing history of cooperation was a step in that direction.

This idea is not only Trump's. It is part of a broader principle in the West towards what's been dubbed 'regionalization,' the idea that regional issues should be dealt with regionally, giving global powers more time to deal with global conflicts and issues. In the Middle East, this means that outside powers, like the United States and Europe, should ideally only play a minimal and supporting role when dealing with conflicts that only affect the region rather than the world (the Israeli–Palestinian conflict for instance, as opposed to the fight against ISIS). But ironically, while the goal is to reduce the need for US involvement in the region, building such a partnership requires even more bandwidth from Washington than before. This unavoidable paradox won't be easily solved and may be at the heart of the ebbs and flows of normalization that impact the deepening of the Abraham Accords. Some US administrations may follow Trump's example and seek to invest time in building and improving regional alliances, but others may prefer to continue to 'manage' the issue reactively.

A less committed US administration means less incentive for Arab countries to formalize their relations with Israel. One only has to look at the difference between the dynamic during Trump's presidency compared to the slower pace of normalization under the Biden administration. The pace of the normalization agreements slowed significantly after President Biden's inauguration. Despite Biden's commitment to pursue the legacy of the Abraham Accords, it is clear this was not at the top of the new administration's foreign policy priorities. The COVID-19 crisis already left very little bandwidth to tackle foreign policy issues. The new administration's main priority in the Middle East was to deconflict. As such, it focused on rejoining the Iran nuclear deal and on solving the long-lasting Yemen conflict, which broke out in the wake of the Arab Spring and specifically after the Houthis (a Shia Islamist group and political movement also known as Ansar Allah) captured the Yemeni capital of Sana'a. The crisis in Ukraine further diverted the United States' already divided attention.

The realization that the United States is central to the normalization process also undermines the idea that Israel's strategic partnership with the United States has lost some of its importance and that Israel's security can be hedged by developing ties with other major powers like China or Russia, or that such a relationship can even be abandoned altogether. In fact, the US–Israeli relationship is at the heart of the normalization process, and public damage to the relationship may well slow down the normalization engine.

Israeli ties with its neighbors are still very much dependent on Israel's own ties with Washington. This is not to say that Arab partners see no benefit in opening formal relations with Israel.

They do. The defense agreement signed between Morocco and Israel during Defense Minister Gantz's visit to the country, or the emerging partnership between Israel and the UAE on topics like missile defense and cyber-security, are notable side benefits.

But they do not explain why those countries decided to take the jump and normalize ties with Israel. Israel is, in fact, still untested on that topic: the value of the defense relations with Israel has yet to be truly gauged.

This is another important 'star' that was aligned in 2020 and may need realigning in the future: the agreements owe much to Iran. Although this component is often exaggerated, and wrongfully described as the main driver behind the agreement, it is also true that Iran's aggressiveness and influence in the region did push Arab countries towards Israel. Iran's expansionism and use of proxies to spread its influence and ideology has made it one of Israel's best 'salesmen' in the Gulf.

In 2020, tensions with Iran were at their height following the killing of Iranian General Soleimani and Abu Mahdi al-Muhandis, one of Iran's point men in Iraq. Soleimani was a rising star with unprecedented influence, acting far beyond his role as the head of the IRGC's external arms, and his killing resonated in the region—a sign that perhaps the United States was more willing to engage Iran but also as a warning that tensions had risen to boiling point. President Trump was also still engaged in a policy of 'maximum pressure,' piling up sanctions on Iran in a way that also increased the regional temperature far above what had previously been the case, which incentivized more in-depth security ties between Israel and the petro-monarchies of the Gulf.

But one year later, Iran had also learned from this mistake. In 2021, the conservative Ebrahim Raisi was elected president (or more accurately 'selected,' as his most serious contenders were all disqualified). Raisi's political platform contained one interesting aspect: the conservative cleric sought to re-engage with Iran's neighbors and pledged to improve ties with regional powers. And he did: despite being part of Iran's hardliner faction, under Raisi Tehran engaged in a series of talks with Saudi Arabia to try to normalize relations, eventually leading to the China-backed agreement that restored relations between the two archrivals. The powerful Emirati national security advisor Sheikh Tahnoun bin Zayed Al Nahyan also traveled to Tehran and held talks with Iranian officials on how to improve relations.

Part of the logic behind this effort to create a 'diplomatic reset' with longtime adversaries likely stemmed from the Abraham Accords. The Iranian leadership may have realized that Iran's expansionism without any kind of diplomatic outreach had effectively pushed Arab countries into the arms of Israel.

It is open to question whether Raisi's charm offensive will ultimately work: the same year, the Yemen-based, Iranian-supported Houthis also launched a series of missiles and drone attacks against Abu Dhabi. Decades of hostility won't disappear overnight, and Iran remains committed to its strategy of regional expansion. But this raises a broader point about the correlation between an aggressive Iran and the deepening and expansion of the Abraham Accords. Should Iran successfully reset ties with the Gulf, or should the threat stemming from Iran recede, Israel–Arab ties may well be affected. Though the connection to Washington may in fact have played a greater role in the Abraham dynamic than the threat from Iran, this still shows that some of the factors behind the normalization may well disappear, or ease, particularly if ties between the United States and Israel grow weaker.

Even if Iran was to fail in its effort to reset ties with its neighbors, which is likely, or remain a significant threat to the region's stability, there are still challenges to be overcome. Whereas the Abraham Accords may have been built partly on the idea that a partnership with Israel will deter Iran, the benefits of the deal on that specific issue have yet to materialize.

Before the Abraham Accords, Gulf–Israeli relations were largely based on shared concerns over an increasingly assertive and ambitious Iran. Those concerns were crudely revealed by the leak of thousands of diplomatic cables by WikiLeaks in 2010, showing how Arab leaders viewed Iran, with former Saudi Ambassador Adel al-Jubeir expressing the Saudi king's demand to have Washington 'cut off the head of the snake' in reference to Iran. Riyadh was even rumored to have agreed to indirectly assist Israel in attacking Iran's nuclear installations, including by letting Israeli planes into Saudi airspace and even offering to refuel Israeli aircraft participating in the strike.

Even before the agreements, Mossad officials often traveled to Saudi Arabia and the UAE and operated there. This was revealed to the greater public in 2010 with the assassination of Mahmoud al-Mabhouh, a Hamas official in Dubai, by a team of Mossad assassins carrying European passports. The debacle, which saw tapes of Mossad agents waiting by the luxury hotel where al-Mabhouh was staying, showed that Israel felt relatively confident operating in the Gulf—though the public revelation did strain the unofficial bilateral relationship. Israel also operated a de facto embassy in Bahrain before the normalization agreement.

The Second Lebanon War (2006) also showed how Israeli and Gulf interests may be aligning—though Gulf states felt that the harsh Israeli response to the kidnapping of two Israeli soldiers and the civilian death toll limited their ability to side with Israel. In the wake of the war, Israeli Prime Minister Ehud Olmert met with the Saudi national security advisor Prince Bandar bin Sultan. Rumors also circulated about a meeting in Jordan's southern port of Aqaba between bin Sultan, then Mossad chief Meir Dagan and the head of Jordan's General Intelligence Directorate to discuss the perceived threat from Iran's growing expansion in the region. In 2007, Olmert again met with Prince Bandar bin Sultan in a follow-up summit. None of those meetings were acknowledged, and they likely represent only a small and known portion of a much broader set of secret bilateral ties.

This was already a stunning level of cooperation and relatively in-depth relations for states that, technically, had no diplomatic relations. And we shouldn't forget that this stunning cooperation was already possible and in fact existed before the Abraham Accords. The question is not whether Israel can cooperate with Arab states on curtailing Iran's influence but whether this cooperation will significantly improve following the signing of the accords and the development of formal ties.

At the time of writing in late 2023, only a couple of years have passed since the signing of the Abraham Accords, and it is too early to gauge how the normalization agreements will truly reshape the region beyond state-to-state relations. Yet a quick inspection of what motivated the accords shows that they owe much to a set of very specific circumstances. These include a highly involved US administration with a business-like mentality that appealed to the Gulf as well as growing concerns over a US withdrawal in the context of a rising Iran. Those stars may be more difficult to align in the future. In the coming years, prospective candidates for potential relations with Israel will also be able to gauge whether those already part of the Abraham dynamic have managed to reap the expected benefits, as well as the limitations and drawbacks of normalization.

6

SECURITY TIES

Before the 2020 Abraham Accords, little was known about security ties between Israel and the Arab world. It is not that they did not exist—they very much did—but they were shrouded in secrecy. Much of the Israeli–Arab security relationship was handled by intelligence services on both sides. The Mossad acted as Israel's main conduit to the Arab world and mostly interfaced with its Arab equivalent. This is typical of unofficial relations: when the need arises, spy agencies act as the cold and pragmatic hand that can reach the farthest—far beyond what's politically accepted or acceptable.

Today's security ties are still defined by this heavy and far-reaching past that extends almost to Israel's formation. In the same way that Arab–Israeli ties aren't people-to-people ties, security relations were largely constricted by the same taboo and confined to closed-door meetings between senior officers within intelligence agencies. These were not military-to-military ties for instance, even with countries like Jordan or Egypt, which have long been signatories to a peace agreement with Israel. Instead, security ties were, and to a large extent still are, very much driven by personal ties built during the years that preceded the Abraham Accords.

This is unlikely to change in the short term. Intelligence agencies are still viewed as the safer vector of interface between the Arab world and Israel when it comes to security and will continue to be one of the key drivers in this field. Intelligence agencies also played a key role in facilitating the Abraham Accords themselves. One key operative, for instance, was a man known by his codename 'Maoz,' who has had a long career in Israel's intelligence apparatus and has been credited with being central to the building of ties with the Gulf states as well as Egypt and Sudan. His name, Ronan Levy, was finally revealed in 2023 when he was appointed as the director general of the Israeli Ministry of Foreign Affairs—showing once again that this not-so-distant past still puts the intelligence agency at the center of bilateral ties between Israel and the Arab world.

Not to mention that intelligence agencies in most of the Arab world are, by nature, often positioned close to decision-making centers and thus are by design good conduits for access to the highest echelon of regional (and often authoritarian) governments.

***

Still, with the Abraham Accords, some of the components of Israeli–Arab cooperation have now been brought to light, and others have expanded. In just a few years since the agreements were signed, Israel has managed to sign several other agreements and open several previously shut doors.

At the strategic level, Israel has been able to formalize a security partnership with its neighbors and build ad-hoc partnerships that had previously been impossible when Israel's 'hush-hush' relations with its neighbors largely confined it to one-on-one relationships.

One of the possible benefits of the accords is Israel's integration into the regional security landscape and the possibility of creating broader partnerships either on specific topics or to tackle specific threats.

Nothing embodied that change more than Washington's decision in 2021 to integrate Israel into the US military Central Command (or CENTCOM), the military command in charge of the Middle East and parts of Central Asia. Until 2021, while CENTCOM was in charge of ties with the Middle East, Israel was the exception. Instead of being included in CENTCOM, Israel was officially part of EUCOM, US Europe Command. This inclusion was a political decision tied to the historic hostility between several countries under CENTCOM's responsibility and Israel. This is not the only example in which Israeli–Arab tensions have led to Israel's isolation in regional organizations—it is not part of the World Health Organization's regional office in the Middle East, for example—but this was certainly one that took on a particular importance.

As a result of this decision, the Israeli army had been training mostly with European countries and US forces based in Europe, which have a very different focus. Despite the peace treaties signed between Israel and Egypt, as well as Jordan, in 1979 and 1994, up until 2021 Israel had not made it to CENTCOM: the Abraham Accords and the normalization agreements with Morocco and Bahrain—where the US Fifth Fleet is headquartered—served as the tipping point.

Within weeks of the Abraham Accords being signed in 2020, Israeli F-35 fighters and American fighters based in the UAE's al-Dhafra air base were training together and participating in joint maneuvers during the third edition of the 'Enduring Lightning' exercise. In the months that followed, the US military officially announced that CENTCOM would take charge of military relations and training with the Israel Defense Forces (IDF). A naval drill dubbed 'Noble Waters' took place as part of an effort to pave the way for Israeli integration into CENTCOM. This was the beginning of a major shift in Israel–Arab military relations under the umbrella of Washington.

CENTCOM units could of course always carry out training with IDF units even before Israel's integration into CENTCOM. But this meant that relations were still more limited and often took the form of higher-echelon exchanges. Those exchanges, while valuable, do not provide the level of cooperation and interoperability one would expect from close allies. In other words, Israel's absence from CENTCOM had an impact not only on non-existent Israeli–Arab military ties but also on US–Israeli military relations and the ability of the two armed forces to act together efficiently.

Beyond that, the real change was that the IDF would now also be participating in drills that included Arab partners. In November

2021, Israel held the 'Blue Flag,' a large-scale aerial exercise planned every two years with participation by the United States and several European countries. Coming just two months after Israel's formal integration into CENTCOM, the 2021 edition expanded upon previous iterations of the exercise and showed how political overtures were already having an effect on military-to-military ties.

During the 2021 edition, the UAE's air force chief Vice Marshal Ibrahim Nasser Mohammed al-Alawi visited Israel and met with senior Israeli commanders and his Israeli counterpart at Palmachim—one of Israel's most extensive air bases. This was the first time such a high-ranking military official from an Arab country had visited Israel and showed just how serious the Emiratis were when it came to building bridges with Israel's security apparatus.

The visit was also of note because of the nature of the exercise and the scenarios the various allies rehearsed. The Blue Flag exercise was based on days of aerial fighting, dealing with surface-to-air threats and aimed at enhancing coordination between the fifth generation of aircraft fighters, particularly the F-35 stealth fighters, and fourth-generation fighters. The goal was to 'mop up' aerial threats and defenses to pave the way for a series of air-to-ground strikes. This scenario is close to what a strike on Iran's nuclear facilities would look like. The UAE chief must have appreciated his visit—the Israelis certainly did.

In an even clearer message to Iran, dozens of nations also coalesced in an unprecedented maritime exercise in the Gulf and the Red Sea. During the first two months of 2022, the United States spearheaded a massive naval exercise dubbed 'International Maritime Exercise/Cutlass Express' or IMX alongside more than sixty partners. The exercise saw the participation of several Middle Eastern countries: countries Israel had ties with, such as Egypt, Jordan, Morocco, Turkey and the UAE, but also countries with whom it had no official diplomatic relations, such as Saudi Arabia, Oman and even Pakistan.

The nature and scope of the exercise was also quite striking, as the drill involved fifty ships and 9,000 personnel as well as eighty unmanned systems—aerial surface and underwater drones—making it the largest use of naval drones in history.

As per the US Fifth Fleet, the exercise simulated the use of naval and aerial drones and other ships in surveillance and maritime security operations. Participants also practiced 'mine countermeasures' in the Red Sea and in the Gulf as well as the Horn of Africa.

Reading between the lines and beyond the military jargon, the message was clear: the various partners involved in IMX effectively aimed to counter Iran.

Iran's coasts sit near one of the world's busiest energy routes, with oil and gas fields off the Gulf just a few kilometers away. Iran has used this position as part of its defensive doctrine by effectively threatening to close the Gulf should it be attacked. At times, it has also carried out limited attacks against shipping in a bid to raise the specter of a broader disruption of maritime traffic in this critical region. These attacks were only a taste of what Iran would do should any foreign power attack its nuclear installations.

In that sense, despite its relatively innocuous description as a purely defensive exercise, IMX was not just another maritime safety exercise aimed at having multiple forces working together or tackling 'pirates,' as had previous similar missions. Combating pirates clearly doesn't require sixty partners and dozens of ships. The military maneuvers were designed with the goal of tackling the growing asymmetric naval threat posed by Iran and its proxies and mitigating the threat to close the Gulf—a threat that's essential to Iran's defensive doctrine. It was also the first expression of what a regional alliance could achieve: a regional effort to pool resources and find common ground and goals—maritime safety—as a basis for a future joint military initiative.

The exercise also included a new element: the idea of using unmanned vessels (so far mostly used by Iranian proxies for offensive purposes) to counter Iran's 'swarm' tactics. Iran has made a point of frequently harassing ships using a fleet of small fast ships that are difficult to monitor in an already densely packed environment. More conventional navies, like those of outside powers like the United States or the UK, tend to rely on a smaller number of heavier vessels. In this context, the idea of using drones was also important in limiting the potential for friction between Iranian ships and those of the countries participating in the exercise while expanding the ability of this de facto 'coalition' to more thoroughly monitor maritime traffic.

The drill was accompanied by another message: a surprise visit by Israeli Defense Minister Gantz to the island of Bahrain, in which he signed Israel's first memorandum of understanding on security and military ties with a Gulf country—and the second with an Arab country following an agreement reached with Morocco in November 2021. The agreement, the first of its kind since the Abraham Accords, was another clear message to Iran, which lies only a few kilometers away on the other side of the Persian Gulf.

It was also clear that Bahrain was not the only instigator of the agreement. The country is effectively a vassal of its bigger brother: the Kingdom of Saudi Arabia. Gantz's visit and the memorandum of understanding signaled that the idea of building closer security ties between the Gulf and Israel was still very much alive. To make it even clearer, the Israeli delegation flew a military plane above Saudi Arabia for the first time. Tehran likely took note, perhaps remembering that, in 2010, Riyadh had effectively given Israeli warplanes a 'green light' to cross its airspace provided they were on their way to strike Iran's nuclear program.

**

The burgeoning of formal multilateral security ties between Israel and its neighbors is unprecedented. This new era has only just begun, merely a few years after the signing of the Abraham Accords. It's only natural to wonder what these new ties may look like a decade or two from now, to look at the dynamic witnessed between 2020 and 2023 and extrapolate a similar rate of expansion in the coming years, to think about grand projects, including the formation of a 'regional security alliance' or defensive pact, drawing parallels with NATO. After all, the region is in the midst of its own mini-cold war, threatened by an enemy, the Islamic Republic of Iran, that has proven capable of projecting power and exporting its ideology.

Comparisons, however, rarely make for convincing arguments or pass the test of time. While the potential for cooperation is visible, the limits are also fairly clear. Attempts to create a solid defensive partnership have already proven difficult even without Israel's involvement.

The idea of establishing some form of defensive alliance between like-minded neighbors is not new. In 2015, the Arab League sought to create a 40,000-strong force financed by the Gulf states. It never materialized. In December of the same year, Saudi Arabia unveiled a new Islamic alliance of more than thirty countries. This alliance has since been forgotten.

During his administration, President Trump floated the idea of the 'Middle East Strategic Alliance' (MESA), or what some came to refer as an 'Arab NATO.' It was planned that the alliance would include Saudi Arabia, the UAE, Kuwait, Bahrain, Oman and Qatar (most of the Gulf with the exception of Yemen) as well as Egypt and Jordan, with Israel as a silent partner. But years later, the alliance is little more than a series of words.

Even without taking Israel into consideration, forming a military or defensive alliance in the region is a daunting task, to say the least. Forming such an alliance requires overcoming a set of significant obstacles. The first is finding a working set of goals: Is the purpose to enhance deterrence by signing a defensive treaty, or to simply act as a platform for military cooperation in case this is needed? If the goal is to form a defensive alliance, the question then becomes: Are Egyptians, for instance, ready to die defending Saudi Arabia? Are Jordanians ready to fight to defend Kuwait's borders? In a region where most regimes view their people as a threat, the possibility of one state agreeing to defend another country seems highly remote.

The second obstacle is the lack of military balance between the various possible partners: Egypt is a giant when compared to most of the possible members of this 'Arab NATO.' Cairo would have to front much of the cost of regional security, despite being far less affected by some of the threats that other countries in the Gulf face—mostly tied to Iran. Though the same can be said of NATO, with the US military budget representing an overwhelming share of the added budgets of the alliance, Washington accepted this disproportionate cost for fear of the alternative—a divided Europe whose members were at risk of being picked off one by one by a much greater foe. Decades later, President Trump also took aim at NATO for this very reason—just as France's President Emmanuel Macron called the alliance 'brain dead.'

Most of the region's militaries are not comparable in size, which reflects their different anticipated functions. Several of the region's militaries are meant to protect their own regime from domestic threats rather than outside invaders—the exception being Egypt, as the Egyptian army *is* the Egyptian regime. Building a strong and independent army, beyond the purpose of an internal security force, runs contrary to the idea of preserving power in the hands of the region's rulers, and military commanders are viewed as a possible internal threat. Although largely supported by the Gulf, the Egyptian coup in 2013, which later led to the rise of al-Sisi, served to underscore those concerns.

The region's militaries also rarely interact. The members of 'MESA' have yet to truly engage in meaningful efforts to build this alliance through joint training. An Arab NATO would have to include a meaningful defensive agreement to protect each other in case of aggression as well as having actual joint capabilities. Short of those components, adversaries are likely to dismiss the pact as mere words—and they would be correct.

Building what's often called 'interoperability,' the ability to operate efficiently together, takes time. Two or more partners need to establish trust, standardize communication and even military production/material and train again, and again, and again. Interoperability is the opposite of riding a bike: when not practiced, it is swiftly forgotten. One look at NATO's regular exercises should give an idea of just how much work is needed to build a truly capable defensive pact.

Although there have been joint exercises between some of the members of this 'Arab NATO,' most of them have been very limited in scope and in the number of participants. Members of MESA have generally been far keener to work with other Western nations, including the United States, France and the UK, than among themselves.

And when such exercises do take place, they are rarely held in a broad format: they tend to involve two or three countries and a limited number of units. The members of the alliance have little experience of training together without their US partner and even less in an actual conflict. The conflict in Yemen, for instance, theoretically involves most of MESA's members yet has mostly been a Saudi and UAE affair.

These issues raise questions about whether even an entirely Arab-focused alliance may work beyond symbolic measures and limited cooperation. The threat posed by Iran has motivated Arab countries to take steps beyond their comfort zones. But that doesn't mean that all of the possible members of an alliance have the same perception of the Iranian threat. In fact, Tehran has been able to play a policy of 'carrot and stick' to try to convince its neighbors that (1) Washington was no longer the guarantor of their security, and (2) that allying with Israel would carry with it its own set of risks.

The 2019 attacks against Abqaiq and Khurais were consistent with an effort to achieve the first goal, but these were followed by a far more complex Iranian strategy combining diplomatic incentives and military coercion. The 2022 surprise visit of Israel's Defense Minister Gantz to Bahrain, for instance, came days after the Iranian-backed Houthi rebels in Yemen had fired a number of ballistic missiles at Abu Dhabi. The Houthi rebels, a Yemeni minority that gradually aligned with Iran and took over the capital of Sana'a, triggering a Saudi intervention, have been carrying out increasingly bold air attacks against Gulf countries. Their know-how came from Iran, which provided it with increasingly sophisticated and relatively cheap missiles and drones.

One of these attacks was carried out during the visit of Israeli President Herzog. Yahya Sarea, the Houthi spokesperson, claimed that the group fired several ballistic missiles at Abu Dhabi and drones at Dubai. No attacks were reported in Dubai, and, contrary to a previous attack, the projectiles did not result in any casualties, but Iran had made its point: it was willing to exact a price for the UAE–Israel rapprochement. Tehran would not hesitate to shatter the UAE's image as a safe haven in the region—an image the

Emiratis had painfully built over the years despite its very active foreign policy.

Days later, in a call after the Herzog visit, Iran sent a message to the Emirati foreign minister that almost read as a quote from *The Godfather*. Iran warned its neighbors they should refrain from letting 'crisis-creating elements' (i.e. Israel) gain a foothold in the region. Tehran typically tries to maintain a distance from its proxies to lend them the appearance of legitimacy. This time, Iran disregarded that rule to address a message to Abu Dhabi.

The message Iran was trying to convey was that the deepening of the security partnership between part of the Gulf and Israel was going to have a 'cost,' particularly if some countries allowed more offensive capabilities to be installed in their territories. This strategy shouldn't be brushed aside: the UAE is a mercantile nation that strives to present the image of a commercial and touristic hub. This image is not a simple byproduct of the Emirates' vision of its own future; it is a core aspect of the Emirati vision. Iran knew exactly where to press to make sure the Emiratis listened.

This message was received. Countries in the Gulf have generally acted carefully since the unprecedented attack against two key energy facilities in Saudi Arabia in 2019. Indeed, in the wake of those attacks the Emiratis reached out to Iran to try to ease tensions, leading a notable UAE effort to restore ties with Iran that led to the visit of Sheikh Tahnoun I mentioned in the previous chapter. Intimidation, alongside diplomatic overtures, sometimes works.

Riyadh, which generally moves second after Abu Dhabi, also engaged in a similar effort to ease tensions with Iran in 2020–1. The bilateral talks were held in Iraq through the mediation of (then) Prime Minister Mustafa al-Kadhimi. At the time of writing, they have led nowhere. A set of factors, including the replacement of the relatively neutral Kadhimi by an Iranian pawn in Iraq, as well as the significant wave of protests in Iran since 2018, have effectively tempered both sides' appetite for talks. But this diplomatic opening—piled upon the trauma of previous attacks—does explain much of the kingdom's hesitation when it comes to military cooperation with Israel.

This was also made clear ahead of the 2022 visit of President Biden to Saudi Arabia. Weeks before the historic 'fist-bump' between President Biden and MBS, rumors swirled regarding a possible 'Middle Eastern Air Defense Alliance' that would see Israel join its neighbors in an effort to counter Iranian drones and missiles. During a session of the Senate Armed Services Committee in February 2022, a Pentagon official confirmed that this was being discussed, calling the idea of an 'integrated air and missile defense' between Israel and some of its Arab neighbors an area with 'some of the greatest opportunity.' The official highlighted that these kinds of opportunities would not have emerged without Israel's integration into CENTCOM.

The *Wall Street Journal* leaked news of a regional meeting that took place in March, months before Biden's visit, in the Egyptian city of Sharm el-Sheikh. According to the American newspaper, the meeting saw the participation of military officials from Israel, Saudi Arabia, Qatar, Jordan, Egypt, the UAE and Bahrain.

But weeks later, Saudi and Emirati officials would dash hopes of a grand 'alliance.' Anwar Gargash, a former Emirati minister of state for foreign affairs, dampened speculations that the UAE would join an anti-Iran alliance and in fact revealed that Abu Dhabi was looking to send its ambassador back to Tehran. Saudi officials also stated that no such alliance was discussed during the meeting. Saudi Foreign Minister Faisal bin Farhan also made sure to highlight that Riyadh had no plans to participate in an 'anti-Iran' alliance.

These statements were not made to alienate President Biden or Israel. They don't even preclude cooperation between various countries on air defenses. They were first and foremost a message to Iran that there would be a limit to the depth of their cooperation with Israel. They also showed that both the Saudis and Emiratis were looking to strike a balance between initiatives that would deter Iranian attacks or mitigate their impact and those that would cross a line and trigger an Iranian response.

Iran's intimidation tactics only work to a point. In the wake of the series of Houthi attacks that shook Abu Dhabi in 2022—despite ongoing talks to reduce tensions with Iran—Israel offered to assist the UAE with its air defenses. Israel laid out a proposal to sell new radars and early warning systems that would help spot ballistic threats, with some even speculating that Israel could sell its state-of-the-art Iron Dome missile defense system. A few months later, Israeli radars did arrive in the Emirates, through direct flights from Israel to the UAE. Satellite imagery also showed that Israeli air defenses, in the form of Barak-8 anti-aircraft batteries, had been deployed to the UAE. While Israel never acknowledged it, the Jewish state also likely provided Emirati airplanes with the coordinates of one of the ballistic missile launchers that was used by the Yemeni rebels to target Abu Dhabi, marking a further deepening in military relations.

Iran has been Israel's best salesman in the region. Each of the security initiatives mentioned earlier owe a great debt to Iranian appetites in the region. But the flip side is that Arab–Israeli security ties are also prisoners of this anti-Iran dynamic. The recent Iranian charm offensive didn't last very long, nor was it very convincing. But it was enough to make some potential and actual Israeli partners pause and ponder the risk/benefit ratio of their decision.

This in turn raises the broader question of what regional cooperation would look like without Iran. This is both a theoretical and a practical question. The theoretical question relates to the other pillars of Israel's military and defense cooperation with its neighbors, to gauge whether those are sustainable. This can be viewed as just an exercise of the mind, but it is not: the actual chance that the Iran that we know will, in the medium term, change drastically, isn't negligible. As of writing, brave and mostly young Iranian men and women are protesting under the slogan 'Jin, Jîyan, Azadî'—'Woman, Life, Freedom.' Iran's foundations have been shaken, and while it may take time for the edifice to collapse, damaged pillars never carry their weight very long. I will discuss this further in the chapter on Iran, but this means the following theoretical exercise may soon become a practical one. To be sure, other enemies may come along to replace Iran. In a way, although these tensions have eased, the antagonism between Turkey and some of the region's main powers, as well as the broader opposition between conservative regimes and political Islam, mean there may be no shortage of divides in the near future even without Iran.

Still, the question stands, as there needs to be something beyond shared enemies to build long-lasting partnerships.

***

So could Arab–Israeli ties grow, excluding those that relate more directly to the threat of Iran? The answer is relatively simple and has to do with Israel's defense industry. Several Gulf countries had been buying Israeli defense products even before the Abraham Accords. In the wake of the agreements, Israeli exports to the Abraham Accords countries made up 7 percent of the total value in 2021, according to a report released by the Israeli Defense Ministry. This is still a small fraction of Israel's total exports but is still notable when considering that this was just a year after the accords had been signed.

There is clear potential for synergies and cooperation. Several Israeli companies have already moved to work in the UAE. The Israeli defense electronics company Elbit established a subsidiary in the UAE in November 2021. Rafael, which is most famous for jointly developing the Iron Dome, also set up a joint venture with the Emirati company Group 42 focusing on artificial intelligence (AI). The two companies had already signed a memorandum of understanding before the Abraham Accords, in July 2020, to invest in research and development to combat COVID-19 in a deal that was seen as a prelude to the normalization agreement. Israel Aerospace Industries also partnered with the Emirati defense giant Edge group to develop counter-drone technology as well as unmanned surface vessels. Israeli companies have been eager to participate in defense shows in the UAE, including the Dubai Airshow, viewing the country as a new and promising market.

And this is not a one-way street. Emiratis have also been very interested in collaborating with Israel, with a specific focus on cyber-security. The Gulf has long been a target for hackers, and Abu Dhabi's appetite for 'future technology' also means that the future of cyber-security is of critical interest.

The Emiratis have been quite comfortable investing in the sector. As with much of the other dynamic, the relationship largely predates the signing of the Abraham Accords by years, if not decades. In fact, some countries that currently have no ties with Israel, including Saudi Arabia, the other tech-hungry monarchy of the Gulf, have been investing and building bridges with Israel, regardless of the official political situation. It's not uncommon for employees of Israel's cyber-security firms to hold meetings with residents of countries that have no official ties with Israel. The Abraham Accords have simply fostered a more public and straightforward effort by neighboring countries to invest in Israel's world-famous 'start-up nation'—with a specific focus on several key tools of control.

The UAE's cyber-security chief, Mohammed al-Kuwaiti, for instance, has made several visits to Tel Aviv for meetings with his Israeli counterpart, Yigal Unna, the then director of the Israeli National Cyber Directorate who has also visited Dubai on several occasions. Al-Kuwaiti has explicitly and publicly called for joint cyber-exercises to be held between Israel and the UAE and attended the Cybertech Global Expo in Tel Aviv in 2023.

Behind him is a much more powerful Emirati figure who is at the crossroads of the Emiratis' security, geopolitical and technological vision: Sheikh Tahnoun bin Zayed al-Nahyan. Sheikh Tahnoun is a discreet and efficient man who holds much power in the Emirates. He is a full brother of MBZ, who was the de facto ruler of the UAE for years until he became the UAE's president in 2022. In a country where blood is power, Sheikh Tahnoun is part of the influential 'Bani Fatima Six'—the sons and daughters of Bani Fatima, one of the wives of the UAE's founder. Those include MBZ but also Sheikh Mansour, the Emirati billionaire and deputy prime minister most famous for owning Manchester City football club, as well as Sheikh Abdullah, the UAE foreign minister.

Sheikh Tahnoun, whose signature look includes a traditional red and white headscarf and aviator sunglasses, has been entrusted by his brother with responsibility for a number of key issues. On the geopolitical front, Tahnoun is often at the tip of the UAE's spear. In December 2021, Tahnoun visited Iran to launch a diplomatic reset between the two countries in a significant U-turn for the country's diplomacy. Tahnoun also visited Turkey to pave the way for a similar rapprochement between two previously sworn enemies.

He is said to have been behind the UAE's decision to start reducing its involvement in the conflict in Yemen and focus on securing the southernmost part of the country rather than continuing a failed effort to kick the Iran-backed Houthis out of Sana'a. He is viewed as a pragmatic leader whose influence is second only to that of his brother, MBZ.

One of his other functions has been to invest in technologies that are seen as being at the crossroads between future security and economic issues. Sheikh Tahnoun is said to be a firm believer in cyber and AI and has made sure to position himself in those sectors. It is no surprise that Group 42, the Emirati company that self-describes as an 'artificial intelligence and cloud computing company' and has signed several partnerships with Israeli companies, is chaired by none other than Sheikh Tahnoun.

The company was one of the first Emirati companies to set up a subsidiary in Tel Aviv. This came just a few weeks after Tahnoun had met with then Mossad chief Yossi Cohen, who had traveled to Abu Dhabi. The two met just a week after the UAE announced it would normalize ties with Israel. The Emirati national security advisor was quite comfortable with the Israeli Mossad head, for this was not his first interaction with the Israeli security apparatus—just the first to be made public.

But for all the purportedly happy embrace between Israeli and Emirati companies, validated at the very top of each countries' political echelons, the partnership is not without controversies or limits. To no one's surprise, Tahnoun's interest in information technologies isn't without ulterior motives: in 2019, the *New York Times* quoted a secret American intelligence assessment that raised concerns over an Emirati video call and chatting app called ToTok that was likely designed to spy on its users.

The app was officially developed by the UAE-based 'Breej Holding,' which was chaired by Hassan al-Rumaithi. Al-Rumaithi is a former Emirati mixed-martial arts fighter who turns out to be the adopted son of Sheikh Tahnoun. Sheikh Tahnoun has a passion for martial arts and adopted a number of local Emirati youths who showed promise in their respective disciplines. It's unclear whether al-Rumaithi did take any active role in the app or in the holding—which was really a front for Group 42—and another holding headed by Sheikh Tahnoun.

Despite an aggressive campaign to defend the app, the intelligence report revealed by the *New York Times* led to the app's removal from the Google and Apple Stores. At the time, statistics showed that the app had already been installed 5 million times, initially being promoted in a series of articles in Emirati media outlets.

This was not Sheikh Tahnoun's first attempt to spy on Emiratis and foreigners. In 2012, Tahnoun's name had already surfaced in a case that involved the hacking of a UAE activist, Ahmed Mansoor. Citizen Lab, a Canadian-based organization focused on communication technologies and human rights, revealed that documents initially sent to Mansoor were briefly pinged back to Tahnoun's office.[1]

The same Canadian-based organization would, a decade later, investigate a series of hacks using Israeli-made software best known as 'Pegasus.'[2] These included a number of hacks targeting Arab opponents, including in Bahrain and Jordan, and the phones of Palestinian activists and that of Ben Hubbard, the *New York Times* correspondent to the Middle East who reported from Saudi Arabia and wrote a book about MBS. It is no longer a secret: multiple Arab regimes have become quite interested in Israeli-made spyware that enables tighter control of opponents, journalists and activists. The Pegasus controversy has made waves, but it may be only one in a number of Israeli companies that have sold spyware to governments in and outside of the region.

***

The reasons behind the UAE's investment in Israel's cyber-security industry, as well as the Saudi interest in Israeli-made spyware, are not hard to fathom. Both Gulf states are interested in technologies that may help them spy on their population, as well as opponents from within and—most likely—from without.

We're entering a future where a major problem faced by dictators and autocrats alike may soon be solved. The disproportionate cost of surveillance, control over large swathes, if not all, of the population has generally given an edge to people against their leaders. This is about to change: the widespread use of smartphones, the rise of AI, machine learning, natural language processing, face identification, as well as the massive internet footprint most of us leave, mean a digital police state will be far stronger than its predecessors. And in the never-ending race between encryption and decryption, the Israeli-made Pegasus software was one of the first to reliably give an edge to decryption in a world where encryption software made it far more difficult for authorities to hack smartphones.

Israel, as a 'start-up nation' that has heavily invested in the digital world, has and will continue to be a prime destination for the dictators of the region and of the world. The 'Pegasus' affair was the first and most covered such scandal, but it is unlikely to be the last. Countries like the UAE and Saudi will feel like small-timers when China knocks on Israel's door, asking for the next generation of spying and surveillance devices.

But even without considering this bigger future challenge, Israel will face a choice over whether to continue providing regional autocrats with the tools to spy on their own population. As most Arab populations are still hostile to Israel, supporting regimes that have been more prone to engage with the Jewish state may seem like a logical, if cynical, decision.

But this may only be a short-term approach. If the Arab Spring is the beginning of a longer struggle for freedom in the region, then siding against it also comes with a future price that shouldn't be brushed aside.

In the Middle East, the concept of security rarely perfectly matches that of 'public safety,' for the 'public' is rarely the one truly being protected. Selling security systems, and cyber-weapons such as the Pegasus program, isn't neutral and aims to protect some people against others, rather than the people of a specific country. What may feel like a theoretical and moral debate may soon become a practical dilemma, should new pro-democracy movements emerge in the region.

In 2022, the then Israeli National Security Advisor Eyal Hulata traveled to Bahrain to attend the Manama Dialogue held by the International Institute for Strategic Studies. Hulata spoke during a panel called 'New Security Partnerships in the Middle East.' This was the second time the Israeli security advisor had attended the conference, and, after thanking his Bahrain hosts (the king and crown prince), he highlighted Israel's successes in building security ties with regional powers. While he hit the anticipated note on the threat from Iran, his statements were optimistic, reflecting several Israeli achievements and what he felt was a 'visible Israeli contribution to the region's stability.' The 'sky is the limit,' he said.

He certainly had reasons to be optimistic, even though his own government would soon be replaced by a new Netanyahu-led cabinet. But there are, unfortunately, clear limits to the security partnership Israel can build with its neighbors. The Abraham Accords have paved the way for better integration, and regional partnership, but the format of this cooperation may be more limited than what the high pace of cooperation of those past years has led us to believe. Israel will also have to manage the political nature of its security relationship with the Arab world. In a region that's going through an unfinished identity crisis, the allies of today are not necessarily those of tomorrow, and the cost of defending autocrats today may only be made clear decades from now.

7

THE CROWN JEWEL

The quick conclusion of the normalization agreement with the UAE, followed by the agreements with Bahrain and Morocco as well as Sudan, gave the impression that the 'Abraham' dynamic (as the normalization dynamic is sometimes called) would lead to new agreements being reached at a rapid pace.

But since the unprecedented breakthrough in Arab–Israeli ties, the pace of normalization agreements has slowed. In fact, since Morocco joined in 2020, and as of this writing in 2023, no new countries have joined the normalization process. Some countries may be waiting for the right moment to normalize ties, while others may consider such a step more carefully, as they ponder the risks and benefits of such a move.

Keeping the dynamic alive has now become an objective of any Israeli government: in the three years that followed the Abraham Accords, rival governments have come to power with different ideological make-ups, but all of them have been committed to the expansion of the normalization process—an incredibly rare common cause in an increasingly divided Israeli political scene. This appetite for new ties won't disappear and is fueled by the relative consensus in Israel surrounding engagement with the region.

This 'consensus' isn't a monolith. The exact motivations for each camp's support for normalization are different: some see the economic benefits of integrating Israel into the region (discussed in the next chapter), others see it as a sign that Israel is being accepted as a legitimate regional actor, while others view each agreement as another swing of the shovel, further burying the Palestinian cause. As a result, each side may disagree on the price Israel should be willing to pay to secure the next step in the normalization process. But they certainly all agree that if normalization involves no significant cost, or a cost paid by someone else (the United States, for instance), it should definitely be pursued.

Whether this dynamic continues or not also shapes the narrative, either depicting the Abraham Accords as a mere 'accident'—the alignment of the stars described in Chapter 5—or as being destined to happen regardless of whether or not Israel makes compromises on the Palestinian issue. As always, the truth likely lies between the real historic opportunities that have opened and the existing challenges that mean nothing is ever bound to happen if nobody is here to make it happen.

But this means the question of 'who is next?'—and whether someone is next—is critical for Israel's future. And when considering which country may more definitely show that the 'normalization dynamic' is the unstoppable force most in Israel want it to be, the answer is clear: Saudi Arabia.

***

The normalization agreements with both the UAE and Bahrain have indeed paved the way for what could be an even bigger prize for Israel: Saudi Arabia.

Officializing the existing ties with the Saudi Kingdom would represent a clear victory for Israel. Not only is Saudi Arabia an energy giant but the Saudi king is also the custodian of Islam's Two Holy Mosques of Mecca and Medina. As such, Saudi Arabia is also a religious power: the two mosques have a central place in Islam but also concretely in the life of millions of Muslim pilgrims from across the world who regularly visit the sites.

Riyadh's religious power goes beyond that: the kingdom has cultivated its own religious network in and far outside of the region. Saudi religious schools and teachings reach far beyond the kingdom's borders. Views expressed by religious scholars in Saudi Arabia have the potential to affect the attitudes of millions of Muslims, perhaps not always in dramatic ways but in more subtle ones that should not be discounted. If the goal of the normalization process is to change the attitude of millions of Muslims towards Israel, no country is better positioned to do so than Saudi Arabia. Riyadh could push for a more inclusive Islamic narrative, going against some of the teachings that have been spread by radical clerics that were actively paid by Saudi-based entities.

In the fight against antisemitism in the Arab and Muslim world, getting Saudi Arabia to effectively greenlight and proactively push for a change in tone by simply vetoing radical antisemitic discourse—something the kingdom has already started to do on its own—would be a significant victory.

This has been on both Israel's and Washington's mind: in 2022, just ahead of President Biden, the US administration sent its newly named Special Envoy to Monitor and Combat Antisemitism, Deborah Lipstadt, to Riyadh. This visit was meant to acknowledge a clear change in Riyadh and was a sign that the kingdom was taking the issue seriously. The Saudi monarchy may be following the example of the UAE, which has increasingly sought to cement its image as a tolerant and multi-confessional country. The UAE often takes the lead and is willing to run risks its more powerful, and by definition more careful, Saudi neighbor can't, such as building a set of non-Islamic religious sites, including a synagogue. From a cynical perspective, this narrative of religious tolerance is more marketing than substance—a narrative largely aimed to appeal to Americans and American Jews in particular. This may well be right. But even marketing can turn into reality in the long run.

Saudi Arabia is also a potential market for a number of Israeli technologies. Saudis are already buying security-related products and services, but the potential for Saudi–Israeli economic ties goes far beyond this. 'Vision 2030,' the pet project of MBS that aims to transform Saudi Arabia into a modern and attractive non-oil economy, includes a grandiose project to turn the kingdom into a technological powerhouse. The city of NEOM, which is being built on the Red Sea just south of the Israeli port of Eilat, embodies the crown prince's vision—both its ambition and its pitfalls. The city's name is a mix of the Greek prefix for 'new' (*neo*) and *mustaqbal*, the Arabic word for 'future.' The project is built around smart tech and a new vision for future cities, including a 'line' city that makes some of the writings of sci-fi authors appear quite tame in comparison.

In the Middle East and outside of it, such pharaonic projects tend never to see the light of day, or at least rarely match their original intent. But if any country has the means to bring such an ambitious project to light, it is Saudi Arabia. It is also clear that there are synergies between this project, the broader vision behind it and Israel's own identity as a 'start-up nation.'

These economic, political and religious factors all underscore how important Riyadh is to the normalization dynamic: the kingdom is its crown jewel and perhaps its most central element. However, the Saudis are very much aware of this and understand the leverage they have over Israel but also, as is always the case when it comes to the Abraham dynamic, over Washington too. A crown jewel never comes cheap.

***

Although Saudi Arabia is perhaps the most significant and obvious 'next candidate' to normalize relations with Israel, the process of normalization is far from straightforward. An episode in the months following the signing of the Abraham Accords showed how Israel could easily misunderstand the friendly signal the kingdom had sent through its de facto vassal, Bahrain, and how Israel wasn't immune to shooting itself in the foot.

In the immediate aftermath of the Abraham Accords, pressure on Saudi Arabia to agree to a normalization agreement was at its height. Amid speculation that the Saudi Kingdom could be persuaded to normalize relations with Israel, Israeli Prime Minister Netanyahu flew to the kingdom's Red Sea coast in a private jet often used for 'below-the-radar' diplomatic missions. There, he met with the de facto ruler of Saudi Arabia: Crown Prince Mohammed bin Salman.

The prince had a long discussion with Netanyahu. Among all of the royal family, MBS was perhaps the figure most supportive of a deal with Israel. On the opposing end of the spectrum was the Saudi old guard, including his own father, King Salman.

King Salman is a long-time supporter of the Palestinian cause. The Saudi king has been involved in previous Saudi efforts to support Palestinians and was far more cautious than his son. Though King Salman's health meant that the king was and still is far less involved in the day-to-day affairs of the kingdom, a monumental shift such as normalizing ties with Israel would still require the official support of the Saudi monarch.

Perhaps more importantly, as long as the king hadn't officially expressed his support for normalization with Israel, opponents to a deal—as well as opponents to MBS himself—could still argue against it. The king's implicit opposition gave the deal's opponents enough space to express their own opposition.

And there were many opponents, perhaps not only to a deal with Israel but also to MBS himself. The ambitious son of King Salman came to power in what can best be described as a palace coup. By appointing his son as crown prince, King Salman effectively broke with Saudi tradition, which aimed to maintain a balance between the various branches of the vast royal family. Mohammed bin Nayef, the previous crown prince, was forced to relinquish his position after a palace coup that saw him being invited to the king's palace in Mecca and forced by armed guards to resign as crown prince—before being placed under house arrest. MBS's rise was also marked by sweeping anti-corruption probes that famously saw several Saudi billionaires and members of the elite being detained at the Ritz-Carlton in Riyadh, with some describing a 'night of beatings.' Most of them were released after effectively being forced to relinquish money they had made using state funds—a practice that was the rule rather than the exception.

In other words, although he seemed and indeed is quite powerful, the young Saudi crown prince and future king has made some powerful enemies who would love nothing more than to see him fail.

Meeting with the right-wing Israeli prime minister was, in that sense, certainly a risk, exposing MBS to criticism from the royal family and conservative circles who rejected the idea of normalization. Still, the crown prince agreed to meet, in a notable sign that he was open to the idea of building ties with Israel. He may have been acting out of sheer self-interest, ahead of the change in the White House that would see a very Saudi-friendly president, Donald Trump, be replaced by one that had promised to shun MBS over his suspected involvement in the murder of the Saudi journalist and *Washington Post* columnist Jamal Khashoggi in Istanbul.

Whatever the motivation behind the meeting, it was a critical one that could shape the future of the Israel–Saudi relationship for the decades to come, as MBS is the kingdom's youngest crown prince: whereas other kings rose to the throne at an already advanced age, MBS could theoretically be ruling Saudi Arabia for decades. The meeting was an extraordinary opportunity to cement and build upon the dynamic that was put forth by the Abraham Accords but also to foster a personal relationship with the man who is set to be king for decades to come.

But the meeting did more harm than good.

Hours after the meeting had concluded, Netanyahu's entourage—possibly at Netanyahu's behest—leaked the news to the Israeli press. On the same day the two had sat down in Saudi Arabia to discuss a possible path to normalization, Israeli media outlets broke the story of the meeting, turning what should have been a discreet breakthrough into an embarrassment for the Saudis and a very personal one for MBS.

This 'mistake' may have been made for electoral purposes. Netanyahu was facing the prospect of yet another election and was looking for any opportunity to boost his standing. Leaking the news of such a key meeting would certainly play in his favor. For Netanyahu, who was fighting for his future (and to stay out of jail), the possible domestic boost he would gain from leaking the meeting may have outweighed the likely cost Israel would have to suffer and the negative impact on the prospect of Saudi normalization.

Whatever the reason, the incident gave a significant boost to those among the royal family and the Saudi elite who felt it was still far too early and risky to normalize ties with Israel. It was also a personal affront for MBS, who was taking a chance despite opposition from the old guard.

***

The Saudi old guard's argument was simple: Riyadh had already offered a formula for normalization, namely the Arab Peace Initiative, and should stick to it. This initiative dates back to 2002, spearheaded among others by then Crown Prince Abdullah, who later became king. The deal was straightforward: in exchange for withdrawing from all land acquired after the 1967 conflict and reaching a 'fair' solution to the Israeli–Palestinian conflict that would include the creation of a Palestinian state, all Arab states would normalize ties with Israel.

Israel rejected the deal. It fell on deaf ears as, on the same day the proposal was formalized, thirty Israelis were killed in one of the deadliest attacks of the Second Intifada, during the Jewish holiday of Passover in the Israeli city of Netanya. Some Israelis viewed the initiative as nothing new, being merely the expression of a previous unofficial policy conditioning normalization on a solution to the conflict with the Palestinians.

Others saw it for what it may indeed have been: an attempt by Riyadh to improve its image in Washington, one badly damaged by the 9/11 attacks and the fact that most of the attackers were Saudi citizens. Eighteen years before the Abraham Accords, Israel was already being used as a way to build positive relations with Washington.

But the truth is, for the Saudis at the time, it was in fact a breakthrough—whatever the reason behind it. While Israelis were focusing on the preconditions, the Saudis felt that the important part was that they were explicitly mentioning the possibility of normalizing ties with Israel. This, in itself, was quite remarkable at the time. The initiative was launched eighteen years before the Abraham Accords, just eight years after the signing of a peace treaty between Israel and Jordan and in the middle of the Second Intifada that had shaken Arab public opinion and would continue to do so over the years that followed.

As Netanyahu flew to the kingdom's Red Sea coast, eighteen years later, the old guard was still arguing that Riyadh should stick to this framework, viewing it as the breakthrough it was at the time.

King Salman, MBS's father, is very much part of that old guard, having been put in charge of a fund that raised money for Palestinians shortly after the Six-Day War of 1967. In the opinion of the king and his entourage, Riyadh could have its cake and eat it too: the kingdom could easily make the most of the relations it already had with Israel but take none of the risks associated with normalizing ties with a country that a significant segment of the population still viewed negatively.

The leak comforted the old guard in their views that normalization would have to go slow—much slower than had been the case with the UAE. Despite being a rising star and the de facto ruler of Saudi Arabia, MBS's position remained fragile. King Salman's poor health meant that much of the kingdom's affairs were handled by his son, but as long as MBS was not the king, he could still encounter resistance.

The gruesome murder of Saudi journalist Khashoggi had also done much damage to MBS's international standing, and the stain meant his position as future king may not have been as assured as his title of crown prince may make it sound. After all, MBS's rise was itself made possible by his ability to sideline the previous crown prince, bin Nayef, once a rising star in the kingdom—and one who had a much deeper connection to Washington.

MBS likely understood the risks that normalization would entail. The balance sheet was not in Israel's favor, and the leaks made an already risky deal with the Netanyahu-led government even less attractive.

MBS and his entourage may also have sensed that the 'normalization card' may be far more valuable in the future. While Riyadh and MBS in particular had enjoyed very close relations with the White House, through Kushner (among others), a new president would soon replace Trump. President Biden made no effort to hide his disdain for the prince, publicly calling for the Saudis to be turned into pariahs. In private, he also made it clear he had very little respect for the prince, whom he viewed as solely responsible for the death of *Washington Post* columnist Khashoggi.

If MBS was to use the 'normalization card' in the future, now was not the time. The election of a president who was determined to isolate the prince made that card more valuable. The prospect of having a king that would be in direct conflict with Riyadh's main ally clearly hurt MBS's prospects and may have bolstered those who silently resented the prince's meteoric rise.

Once again, Israel's effort to break its isolation would be tied to Washington's own relations with key powers in the Arab world. Normalization would still be viewed as a trump card that could easily be used to sway the White House. But the meeting between MBS and Netanyahu, just months after the Abraham Accords were signed, also showed how normalization would be a prisoner of Israel's own domestic dynamics.

***

Two years later, MBS's gamble that Washington would eventually come to terms with realities and turn the page on the Khashoggi affair effectively paid off. It took the Russian invasion of Ukraine and a global energy crisis to make that a reality, but in 2022, the West was ready to move on.

President Biden's visit to the Saudi Kingdom in 2022 was also surrounded by persistent rumors of an upcoming breakthrough in ties between Riyadh and Jerusalem. Ahead of the visit, news broke regarding ongoing negotiations between the two countries over Tiran and Sanafir, two Egyptian islands in the Red Sea.

Six years earlier, Egyptian President al-Sisi ceded the two islands, situated between the Saudi Red Sea coast and the southern part of Egypt's Sinai Peninsula, to Saudi Arabia. The Egyptian president was returning the many favors he owed to Riyadh, a constant backer of al-Sisi's regime and the fragile Egyptian economy.

Riyadh had grand plans for the islands, hoping they would become part of a regional trade and tourism hub situated between Africa, Europe and Asia. But the Saudi Kingdom also needed Israel's approval: the islands, which were invaded twice by Israel before being transferred back to Egypt, were part of the Camp

David Peace Accords between Egypt and Israel. As a result, and to guarantee freedom of navigation, a multinational force had been deployed to Tiran and Sanafir and could only be removed with Israel's explicit approval.

During the months that preceded President Biden's visit to Israel and Saudi Arabia, Washington acted as a mediator between the two countries with the goal of encouraging a limited breakthrough in ties. Israel's approval would act as a notable gesture of goodwill on Jerusalem's part, a sign of trust that would foster better relations and help overcome the reluctance of the Saudi old guard around King Salman.

The issue was of more than symbolic importance. While US media outlets put far more emphasis on the controversial handshake—which turned out to be a first bump—between Biden and MBS, and on whether Biden would be able to persuade the prince to increase oil production and help mitigate the global energy crisis, Israel's eventual approval of the transfer was no small victory for US diplomacy. In 1950, the Egyptian military occupied the islands as part of an effort to limit Israel's ability to use the Red Sea port of Eilat. In 1967, Egyptian President Gamal Abdel Nasser used the islands to shut down the Strait of Tiran, thus blocking the port and leading to the Six-Day War.

Years later, the idea of conventional conflict between Israel and one of its Arab neighbors seemed unlikely. Riyadh was not interested in a direct confrontation with Israel even when other Arab countries banded together to destroy the nascent Jewish state.

But the decade that preceded the visit also witnessed some of the most drastic political transformations in the Arab world since the 1950s and '60s. Regimes that were deemed stable collapsed in a matter of weeks. Israeli officials certainly avoided the subject with their Saudi counterpart, but behind Israel's reluctance was the question of whether the friendly Saudi monarchy could, one day, be replaced by a much more bellicose regime. The revolution in Iran and more recently in Egypt had shown just how quickly things in the region can change—rarely for the better, from Israel's point of view.

As such, Israeli approval of the Tiran and Sanafir transfer was not just a 'goodwill gesture' but a real leap of faith. Israel agreed to have Saudi forces replace neutral observers on islands that had been used to threaten a key sea route in the past.

But this 'leap of faith' was not met by a Saudi equivalent. Riyadh agreed to open its airspace to 'all flights,' including Israeli airliners flying to and from Asia, framing it as being in line with the Chicago Convention on International Civil Aviation. But these steps took time, and Riyadh made sure to highlight that this was in no way a prelude to normalization—though it was clear to everyone that it was a step in that direction, the unease that followed such a limited step—which was part of a quid pro quo—showed that the pace of normalization between Riyadh and Jerusalem would be quite different from that of the 2020 Abraham Accords.

The agreement with Bahrain and the UAE fostered this deceptive sense that normalization with other Gulf countries, particularly Saudi Arabia, is destined to happen (which may be true), and that there is little difference between the UAE and Saudi Arabia in that regard (which isn't). But there is a world of difference and a significant gap in the risks a Saudi–Israeli rapprochement entails for Riyadh when compared to the same step for Abu Dhabi.

These risks aren't small. The very reasons that make Riyadh a valuable target for normalization efforts also make it far more dangerous for the Saudi monarchy to sign its own version of the Abraham Accords.

As one of the region's main political, religious and economic powers, and as Iran's main rival in the region, Riyadh can expect a much harsher Iranian reaction.

In that sense, there is no minimizing the impact of the 2019 attacks on the threat perception in the kingdom. As mentioned in previous chapters, in 2019 Iran carried out one of its boldest attacks against its archenemy, striking at two key energy facilities in Khurais and Abqaiq in the heart of the oil-rich eastern region of Saudi Arabia. While the Saudis expected a US response to the attack, it never came—and the Saudis never got over it.

This has created a sense in the kingdom that one of the pillars of its security, and perhaps the only one, was far more fragile than previously imagined. It also made the Iranian threat to the kingdom far more serious, raising questions over whether Washington would respect the unwritten contract signed decades ago between Ibn Saud and Franklin Roosevelt: oil in exchange for American protection.

The risks Riyadh would face should it push forth with normalizing ties with Israel grew overnight, as Washington failed to live up to its pledge. Should Saudi Arabia move to formalize its ties with Israel, there is a chance that it will become a 'return address' in case of a flare up in violence between Iran and Israel. The move would cement Iran's 'Axis of Resistance' narrative and Tehran's incentive to further undermine the Saudi monarchy and depict it as an illegitimate occupier of Islam's most sacred shrines.

And this latter argument wouldn't only come from Iran but also from another of Riyadh's adversaries: jihadists. Saudi Arabia has also been the target of ISIS attacks, with the group issuing a series of threats against the kingdom in the wake of the signing of the Abraham Accords. The jihadist group accused Riyadh of being behind the move to normalize ties with Israel and threatened new attacks against the kingdom, deeming it to be the true 'return address' of any move to further entrench the 'Zionist entity' into the region. This argument largely fits with ISIS's and al-Qaeda's depiction of a partnership between local Arab regimes, chief of which is the Saudi monarch they deem illegitimate, and what they've often referred to as the 'Zionist–Crusader' alliance (the alliance between the United States and Israel).

These may seem to be empty threats given that the kingdom has been relatively successful in quelling the threat posed by jihadist groups, but they are not. Hundreds of Saudis have traveled to Syria and Iraq to fill ISIS ranks, showing that at least some, even within Saudi Arabia, still feel the pull of the jihadist ideology. At its peak in 2015–16, ISIS was also able to operate on Saudi soil, carrying out a series of attacks against Shiite minorities in the country as well as government forces. A normalization agreement would almost certainly lead ISIS and other groups to place Riyadh higher on their list of targets.

Any attack would also prove to be an embarrassment for the kingdom, and particularly for MBS, who aims to make Saudi Arabia a global economic and touristic hub, rivaling Dubai.

***

Any public rapprochement with Israel would fuel both the Iranian and jihadist threat. Domestically, it would also challenge Riyadh's traditional role as a conservative religious power, one that still remains despite MBS's effort to redefine the kingdom's relationship with its religious elites.

These risks cannot be ignored by the Saudi leadership, be it King Salman, or his son who is set to succeed him. The common assessment is that MBS may be keener to build a relationship with Israel than his father—and this is indeed the case. MBS has made several statements highlighting how he saw Israel as much more of an ally than an enemy. In private, he also surprised American Jewish leaders in 2018 by criticizing the Palestinian leadership and claiming that it had missed several opportunities to resolve the conflict.

But the expectation that the crown prince will rush to normalize ties with Israel as soon as he becomes king is misleading. Though MBS has shown himself to be much more pragmatic and less ideological than the kings that preceded him and has made few efforts to hide his indifference towards the Palestinian issue, the prince also knows that, as a reformer—or at least someone who views himself as such—he must pick his battles. As a new king, and one that will have a history of breaking taboos and moving away from tradition, MBS may in fact be tempted to first reassure the religious elites and secure his position. He will send clear messages guaranteeing that he will not challenge the religious authorities more than is needed to ensure the kingdom's interests. MBS views his 'Vision 2030' as a cornerstone of his future reign, and this plan already implicitly entails significant changes, as it seeks to transition the Saudi economy away from oil and towards the high-tech and tourism sector. This requires a change in perception from the outside, but also actual changes within the kingdom.

And in that sense, the new king will have to tread lightly. Openings will come at a cost, as was the case for one of MBS's most ambitious domestic reforms: the decision to let women drive. This decision broke with a long tradition of guardianship that makes Saudi women dependent on their male guardians (be it their father, brother or husband). It contributed to MBS's popularity among the youth and to his image as a reformer. But the crown prince was also careful not to give the impression that women activists who had actually fought for this right for years would take credit for the reform. In the lead up to the lifting of the ban, from May to June 2018, the government arrested several women activists who had long campaigned for the right to drive. The message was clear: the kingdom's reform should not be taken as a sign that activism works. It also showed how any ruler would always have to balance reform with tradition.

The new king will have to prioritize: some reforms will be viewed as both critical and risk-free; others will be deemed less urgent, while still being risky. Swiftly normalizing ties with Israel may not be at the better end of that spectrum. MBS may have kept the 'normalization card' as a way to gain favor in Washington, but Biden's visit has shown that the kingdom also has other cards that may trump the need to upgrade ties with Israel.

Perhaps the reason why MBS is more 'optimistic' or open to normalizing ties with Israel is as simple as this: time. The young crown prince has shown an appetite for long-term projects, the kind of which he can undertake as the kingdom's future king for the coming decades (if all goes well for him). Peace with Israel may be one of those 'long-term' projects that only come at the end of a road paved with small incremental gestures and a slow change in mentalities in Saudi Arabia. Several polls, including a series of polls conducted by the Washington Institute, the latest from September 2023,[1] have shown that while the Saudi population may be more open to cultural or economic ties with Israel, support for an Abraham Accord-type deal remains limited.

***

As important is the compensation Riyadh expects for taking the risks mentioned above. This 'risk premium' isn't small. A set of reports by the Israeli i24 channel and later the *Wall Street Journal* indicated two major Saudi demands as preconditions for a full-fledged normalization agreement. The first was to make Saudi Arabia a major non-NATO ally, similar to Israel, Qatar or Jordan. This status would give clearer security guarantees to Saudi Arabia, sending a signal to the region (i.e. Iran) that the United States is still committed to the kingdom's security. It would also give Riyadh easier access to US weapons, turning the page on years of US flip-flopping and limiting weapons sales due to the war in Yemen and suspicions that they were being used against civilians.

The second condition is no less daunting: the Saudis want US support for the development of a civilian nuclear program. Nuclear for peace. The narrative is that the Saudis want to shift away from their dependence on oil and develop their own civilian nuclear plants. The Saudis have plans to develop a nuclear power plant by 2032 and kicked off the formal process of building a four-core nuclear reactor in 2023. In January 2023, Saudi Energy Minister Prince Abdulaziz bin Salman also announced the kingdom's intention to use newly found domestic uranium deposits as part of its nuclear development plan, suggesting the kingdom would develop its own independent enrichment industry.

Everybody had a sense of *déjà vu*: Saudi Arabia isn't exactly the first state in the region to make the not-very-convincing claim that its nuclear program would be peaceful.

There are many reasons to doubt that Riyadh will keep its pledge or that its purpose in developing nuclear energy is purely to edge itself out of dependence on other sources. There are questions about the economic viability of such a program when compared to other sources like solar energy that would make more sense in the kingdom. The Saudi refusal to adopt new protocols pushed by the UN nuclear watchdog that would allow more transparency is another reason to doubt the Saudis' intentions, and so are the regular, if unsubstantiated, rumors of secret Saudi nuclear facilities or cooperation with key nuclear ally Pakistan. Perhaps more importantly, Saudi officials themselves have made it clear that if Iran were to acquire the bomb, 'all bets are off': they would look to develop a military-focused nuclear program.

The details of the Saudi demands also raise questions. Washington has in fact already agreed to help support a Saudi civilian nuclear program—the real problem stems from the small print of any US support. Washington has asked Saudi Arabia to commit to international scrutiny, to guarantee that the kingdom does not move closer to producing a bomb. Riyadh has so far refused. In other words, what the Saudis are really asking isn't just for US support but more flexible conditions, ones that would make it clear that they will retain a pathway to the bomb. What the Saudis want is US support without the strings and limitations attached.

These conditions give pause for a number of reasons. The first is whether this would, in fact, be in Israel's interest. Given the possibility that Saudi Arabia would use a civilian nuclear program as a jumping pad for a military one, the 'risks of peace' certainly have to be pondered. What happens if the next Saudi king, in a frenzy of reform and pharaonic projects, loses touch with his conservative base, fails to bring about real economic change for those who believed in him and ultimately destabilizes the monarchy itself? A similar situation has unfolded in the past: it was called the Islamic Revolution in Iran. Decades later, the region is still dealing with its fall-out, compounded by Iran's nuclear ambition. Remember the Israeli 'leap of faith' I mentioned earlier, regarding the transfer of the two Red Sea islands. This would be nothing in comparison to greenlighting a nuclear path for Saudi Arabia.

The second element that should give Israelis pause is the relative absence of any condition related to the Palestinian conflict. To be sure, other reports have suggested that the kingdom did in fact make several demands. But those are mostly akin to maintaining the status quo and not inflaming the situation rather than actually breaking the current impasse. In other words, Palestinian fatigue is certainly real in Saudi palaces.

The only condition remotely tied to advancing the peace process came not from Riyadh but from Washington. Although the fist-bumping Biden administration hasn't accepted the Saudi conditions, it made it clear to Israel that any normalization with Saudi Arabia would have to entail some gestures towards the Palestinians, possibly in the form of resuming the long-dead peace negotiations with the PA. Were the Saudis happy about this American precondition? They weren't unhappy. Did they care? Not enough to make it *their* precondition.

This may have changed since the 7 October Hamas attacks. Riyadh has found itself in an awkward position in the aftermath of the Simchat Torah massacre carried out by Hamas.[2] The attacks have shown that the region had not moved on from the Israeli–Palestinian conflict and that Saudi Arabia could easily be affected by it. As the Israel–Hamas war escalated regionally, the Iran-backed Houthi rebels in Yemen fired missiles into Israel, some of which flew above Saudi Arabia. Some members of the group even called on Saudi Arabia to 'let them in' and allow Houthi fighters (who were fighting Saudi Arabia and its allies in Yemen) to cross into the kingdom and fight Israel. The kingdom also understood very quickly that Iran was exploiting the crisis to torpedo the normalization efforts between Saudi Arabia and Israel.

The crisis that followed the 7 October massacre was one where Riyadh likely came to reflect on several policy changes it had made. The first was its efforts to hedge its traditional alliance with the United States through its ties with China. After all, it was not China that came to the rescue of the kingdom, deploying significant assets in the region and in Saudi Arabia itself as Houthi missiles were flying above: it was Washington. For all the dancing with Beijing, Washington remains critical to Saudi Arabia's security. Second, any illusions Riyadh may have had about the nature of its engagement with Iran were quickly dispelled. Sure, the Iran–Saudi deal likely acted to dampen the appetite of Iran and its proxies for attacks against Riyadh. But this is more akin to a restaurant paying a tax to the mafia for 'protection' than the basis for prosperous and friendly relations.

Finally, and more importantly, whether Riyadh truly does care or not, Saudi Arabia will have to package a deal with Israel alongside a more comprehensive breakthrough in Israeli–Palestinian peace. The good news is that those who understand that the 7 October massacre will require an effort to resume peace talks are also inclined to deliver that 'win' to Saudi Arabia. Riyadh has also taken steps to restore its relationship with the PA. It has managed to tread carefully in its coverage of the Gaza War: Saudi officials have released multiple statements condemning Israeli strikes that led to significant Palestinian casualties. But several Saudi television channels have also challenged Hamas's narrative, highlighting the barbarity of the attacks. An al-Arabiya interview with Hamas's Khaled Meshaal even turned confrontational when the interviewer relentlessly challenged him,[3] highlighting Hamas's barbarity in killing civilians and its disregard for civilian life in Gaza itself—a rare sight in Arabic media.

Even amid the escalation, several Saudi officials have said that normalization efforts were 'paused' but not suspended. But while Saudi Arabia has seen the benefits other countries have derived from their ties with Israel (and bolstered ties with the United States), Riyadh is also now more than ever aware of the risks—and the deal that was discussed before 7 October may not be the one that will be discussed after.

8

BUILDING ROADS, HOPING PEOPLE WILL USE THEM

In his 1994 book *The New Middle East*, former Israeli President Shimon Peres wrote that '[r]egional common markets reflect the new Zeitgeist ... Ultimately, the Middle East will unite in a common market—after we achieve peace. And the very existence of this common market will foster vital interests in maintaining the peace over the long term.' These words were already visionary at the time. Some may have thought them naive, overly optimistic or dismissed them as the thoughts of an idealist. And indeed they were, but men of vision often sound like fools before being viewed as prophets. The book was also written at a time of optimism tied to the historic Oslo Accords that offered a way out of the Israeli–Palestinian conflict. It was a time of idealism, though it was not one that lasted for long— the assassination of Yitzhak Rabin in 1995 and a series of deadly bombings by Hamas the following year would kill that momentum.

The vision Peres offers in his book is consistent with his long-held support for economic measures as a vehicle for peace. It is also in line with the overall philosophy of part of the Zionist left wing, which has often thought of economic prosperity as the be all and end all of peaceful cohabitation.

Peres's book is inspired by the history of Europe after the Second World War and the creation of a common market between longtime foes such as Germany and France. The Oslo Accords did pave the way for growing integration, and Peres was not the only leader to quietly encourage economic initiatives. The then Jordanian crown prince, Prince Hassan, also called for the creation of a free-trade zone in the Middle East, calling it the 'ultimate goal' of peace efforts. In Peres's vision and that of the Jordanian crown prince, formal peace between neighbors would be cemented by economic integration and prosperity, which would in turn ease previous rivalries and deep-seated hatred between the people of the region. Prosperity would, in Peres's mind, be the factor that would turn peace between countries into peace between people.

***

As of writing this book in 2023, this vision has failed to materialize. But it is also evident that Peres's vision is not necessarily an impossibility. Peres was envisioning an integrated Middle East, and while he may have been ahead of his time, the past three years have shown that this is in fact possible. Israeli tourists have flown in droves to Dubai. Israeli banks have created ties with their UAE and Bahrain counterparts. Just a few days before a key visit by US President Biden to Saudi Arabia in 2022, several Israeli businessmen also quietly traveled to the kingdom to explore avenues for cooperation—and there are many, from the high-tech, energy and medical to agricultural sectors.

Peres's vision also offered a rare view of what the Middle East could be, as well as the possible benefits of peace. Visionaries typically start with the ideal and walk back the steps needed to get there.

For Israel, the benefits of an integrated Middle East are immense. Israel's economy is often viewed through the angle of its booming high-tech and start-up scene. To outsiders, the 'start-up nation,' as it is often depicted, is a land of entrepreneurs and innovators that has brought some of the biggest corporations to one of the region's smallest countries. Access to the world is seemingly infinite.

But there is another side of the coin, a 'darker' or perhaps more mundane side to the Israeli economy that partly stems from Israel's de facto isolation in a region that is still very much hostile. This reality is experienced by anyone who has actually lived in Israel, gone grocery shopping in one of the country's supermarkets or paid rent for a decrepit apartment in Tel Aviv.

Israel is no entry point to the region but rather a last stop, a destination in itself—surviving by nothing else but its own merit, to be sure, but also failing to benefit from its geographic position. If one was to ignore the actual history of the country and region, it would be a surprise to discover just how isolated the country's economy is from the rest of the region, and one would wonder why a country that sits between three continents, at the crossroads between Europe and Asia, close to some of the main global arteries of the world, can't figure out how to reduce the price of cottage cheese (a staple of Israeli daily cuisine, so central that price hikes led to social protests in 2011).

While it may have attracted some major corporations looking to benefit from the country's spirit of innovation, Israeli consumers and the Israeli market itself do not have the same commercial appeal. Amazon may have set up one of its largest Middle East offices in the country, but rumors that the giant would soon start regular operations and offer quick deliveries by setting up warehouses in Israel have yet to materialize. The main obstacle preventing Israel from being more economically attractive is fairly straightforward: with fewer than 10 million Israelis, the incentive to actually invest in a market that's still heavily protected is low, to say the least. Israel is no giant, like its neighbor Egypt, for instance, with its 102 million inhabitants.

To be sure, the populations of many other Middle Eastern countries are comparable or even smaller than that of Israel. The UAE has turned itself into a global economic hub with a comparable population. The difference is that the UAE is a door to the rest of the Arab world, whereas Israel is, still today, nothing else but its own space.

This partly explains one of the key features of the Israeli economy: a quasi-monopolistic market with little space for real competition. This is particularly true in several specific sectors such as the agri-food market, where five giants hold half of the market, with the other half spread across more than 1,000 small companies. As a result, the average Israeli shopping basket typically ranks as one of the highest-priced in the world.

Lesser known but as important is the tight monopoly on imports, with only a handful of companies importing some of the major brands used by Israelis in their daily lives. This means that toothpaste, baby products and deodorant, for instance, are far more expensive than in other countries where imports are more fluid. Israelis are generally not even aware of companies like Diplomat or Schestowitz, mediators between Israel and the world who import well-known foreign brands far more recognizable than they ever will be. Not to mention they generally tend to keep a low profile, given that they are in effect rentiers, profiting from Israel's unique isolation and their own position as quasi-monopolies.

In a country where people hate to be called 'freiers' ('suckers'), that's quite the paradox. To be sure, Israelis are aware of the issue and how it affects their daily lives. In 2015, for instance, Moshe Kahlon managed to secure ten out of the 120 seats at the Knesset, mostly by promising to deliver the 'coup de grâce' to monopolies after managing to cut the average phone bill of Israelis by 70 percent. He did show that state intervention could help, though this didn't last. Years later, Kahlon has retired from politics, and monopolies are still very much part of Israelis' daily lives, adding a premium for living on the Israeli island.

The Israelis' aspiration for a better and more just economy has often clashed with the country's security needs. In a country that faced a war from day one of its existence, any issues other than life-threatening ones can seem mundane. Whether real or not, this opposition has generally shaped Israeli politics, with an enduring perception since its creation that Israel has been living on the edge, threatened from all sides, and couldn't really deal with problems such as the price of groceries. To a significant extent, this perception has changed today as multiple political parties have made reforming the economy a significant part of their platforms, and Israeli voting patterns are increasingly shaped by economic concerns. Still, the conflict between those two priorities continues to weigh on the public debate in Israel. In a 2022 poll for the Madad Institute, for instance, economic and security issues stood as the two main concerns of the Israeli respondents. The Israeli center-left bloc has tried to position itself as the one most concerned about the economy, while Netanyahu's Likud has mostly focused on security issues. While the high cost of living has often topped the list of concerns expressed by Israelis, Netanyahu's focus on security issues and infantilizing his opponents as not being serious enough to tackle the country's immense geopolitical challenges has also often been successful.

This may feel like an eternal dilemma, but there are in fact topics that may be considered wins on both sides: normalization agreements with Arab neighbors are one of them. And to an extent, this is already at play—though the average Israeli has yet to feel it. The Abraham Accords opened the way for global companies heavily invested in the Arab world to also start investing in Israel. One of the main examples is the US company Chevron, which bought Noble Energy—the main foreign operator of Israel's gas fields—just a few weeks before the official announcement of the Abraham Accords in 2020. Before the Abraham Accords, such an investment in Israel by a major US oil corporation had never been considered by such companies, who prioritized their relationship with the Arab world.

But the issue goes beyond the limited scope of Israel's newfound natural riches. In 2023, a conference of French businesses involved in the region also took place in Israel, with representatives working in countries with no official ties with the country, such as Saudi Arabia and Qatar. Those brands have hinted that the Abraham Accords paved the way for the conference and may have opened the door for additional companies to enter Israel. This includes for instance the grocery brand Carrefour, which has an extensive network in the Arab world, including Egypt, Turkey and the UAE, the sport brand Decathlon, and the solar and hydrogen company ENGIE, which is heavily invested in Egypt and Saudi Arabia.

***

To be clear, the factors behind Israel's monopolistic economy go beyond its regional isolation. Yet it does play a role, by lessening the appeal of the Israeli market for foreign companies who could consider setting up regional headquarters, or warehouses, if Israel was an entry point to the region.

Connecting the Israeli economy to the region could have a significant impact not only on the broader parameters of the economy but also on the daily lives of Israelis, whose main economic hub (Tel Aviv) often tops global rankings in terms of cost-of-living.

But how realistic are those projects?

Since the signing of the Abraham Accords, efforts to foster Israeli–Arab economic integration have focused on major government-sponsored projects and treaties, with broader trade between the private sector trailing behind.

In November 2022, for instance, Israel signed a landmark 'water-for-energy' deal dubbed 'Project Prosperity,' in the framework of which Jordan would provide 600 megawatts of solar power, through facilities built by Emirati firms, while Israel would provide Jordan 200 million cubic meters of desalinated water through desalination facilities. This 'blue-for-green' deal fits with regional efforts to integrate regional economies and should be welcomed as a climate-friendly and peace-conducive project. For both sides, it is a clear win-win, as water-starved Jordan receives additional quantities of water while Israel receives clean solar energy to start reducing its dependence on fossil fuels. But it wasn't saluted as such. Although the deal objectively serves Jordan's interest, the agreement was denounced by members of Jordan's parliament. Hundreds of protesters also gathered in the Jordanian capital to protest the agreement. This wasn't the first time a deal with Israel would cause controversy in Jordan, as Jordanians have regularly denounced a gas deal with its neighbor that brings Israeli-produced gas to the Hashemite Kingdom.

These protests didn't prevent the gas deal from being signed, nor did they force the Jordanian king to reconsider the water-for-energy agreement. But they do indicate that private sector trade is lagging far behind: private sector exchanges are the closest to 'people-to-people' ties and perhaps the most difficult milestone to achieve.

They also put a 'political risk' premium on any major infrastructure project, forcing companies involved in any such project to consider how stable the governments they are interacting with may be. Consider one of the most grandiose megaprojects to be considered, namely the creation of a railway between the Gulf and Israel. The project was born more than two decades ago in the Gulf and traces its origins back to the partially completed Ottoman-built Hejaz line between Damascus and Medinah.

In 2019, Israel's Foreign Affairs Minister Israel Katz presented an even grander project to link the UAE, Saudi Arabia and Israel, using the al-Marj train, between the port city of Haifa and the city of Beit Shean, only 10 kilometers from the border with Jordan. The project had already been unveiled in 2017 under the title 'Railway for Peace' but took on a new impetus after the signing of the Abraham Accords. The route would be extended up to the Jordanian border, which could pave the way for a link between Israel and Saudi Arabia, bypassing Jordan by linking with the existing North–South Railway in Saudi Arabia.

Building and later exploiting such a project would require significant capital—even though some of the infrastructure is already there. The project has clear economic prospects considering how such train lines could be an alternative to costly sea routes. Politically, Gulf countries also have an incentive to try to bypass two chokepoints, namely the Bab el-Mandeb and Hormuz Straits, both increasingly under threat from Iran and its proxies.

The initiative was brought up again in another form in 2022, ahead of President Biden's visit to the region. The Finance Ministry then sought to present an even more ambitious plan that would create 'corridors for Economic Integration.' The plan was to create a regional transportation network that would link Israel with Jordan, Saudi Arabia and the rest of the world, using the Middle East's geographic position between East and West.

But to materialize the benefits of such an investment, any company would require clear skies and clear assurances that the bilateral and international ties that would be a precondition to the project are solid. Any company operating such a line, or putting in the initial investment to build it, would be exposed to long-term geopolitical and political risks: the risk that one of the regimes involved in the project will fall, the risk that friendly countries become enemies. The 1979 Revolution in Iran, which turned the Iranian regime into one of Israel's main enemies, or perhaps more recently the 2011 Egyptian Revolution and rise of the Muslim Brotherhood, show that these prospects shouldn't be ignored. A company that fronts the cost of such a massive project would have to take these enormous and highly unpredictable risks into consideration, for their investment would only be made economically viable through decades of exploitation.

It would be easier if the private sector was not involved—in fact, the private sector may not be interested in the project to begin with. There is a reason why railway construction and infrastructure-building have historically been government-backed projects. The 'dynamic' geopolitical situation in the region only serves to reinforce those reasons.

What is true for the railway line from Israel to the Gulf may also be true for any other major infrastructure project linking Israel to its neighbors. Any such project would be subject to significant political and geopolitical risk and primarily government-driven—which in turn also compounds the political and geopolitical risk as they would instantly disappear with any change of the political landscape.

Building a road or a railway implicitly suggests there is an expectation that people will use them. Measuring the impact of, say, linking Jordan to Israel may be quite difficult and tied to a set of economic factors, as well as regional perceptions, security conditions and the ebb and flow of regional politics. The Jordanian Kingdom may be aware of how fast outside connections can shut down in the Middle East: over the 2010s, it found itself partially isolated by both the Syrian Civil War and later the emergence of ISIS in Iraq. This also led to an uptick in ties with Israel but more broadly underscores the idea of a 'political and geopolitical' premium added to any infrastructure project that would tie countries in the region together.

***

This doesn't necessarily discount this approach or a more general strategy that envisions governments as the 'trailblazers' opening new avenues of commerce that would later be exploited by private businesses. In many ways, 'building new roads in hopes that someday people may use them' encapsulates this broader economic integration effort: an immensely costly leap of faith.

There may indeed be a virtuous-cycle effect, with government deals and projects fostering trade. The Abraham Accords did lead to a significant boost in trade. According to the Israeli Central Bureau of Statistics, Israeli exports to the UAE grew from USD11.2 million in 2019 to USD74 million in 2020 when the Abraham Accords were signed and USD383 million in 2021. Israeli imports of UAE products went in the same direction, from zero in 2019 to USD114.9 million in 2020 to USD771 million in 2021.

Perhaps just as interesting is the fact that countries like Egypt, which signed a peace treaty with Israel in 1978/9, have seen the volume of trade increase noticeably in the wake of the Abraham Accords. Israeli exports to Egypt grew by almost 60 percent between 2020 and 2021, as opposed to 6 percent in 2019–20 and 10 percent the year before. The same cannot be said for Jordan, with Israeli exports fluctuating rather than growing steadily. This may reflect the different nature of the Egyptian and Jordanian economies, given the heavy weight of the state (and specifically the military) in Egypt, while also likely being the result of far more significant hostility towards Israel among average Jordanians when compared to their Egyptian counterparts.

A similar effort to 'build roads' also comes from the signing of trade agreements. Those agreements are aimed at facilitating trade, opening 'economic corridors' not only through actual roads but also by lifting some of the invisible barriers to trade. In 2022, Israel and the UAE signed a free trade agreement, the aim of which is to raise bilateral trade to USD10 billion annually by 2027.

***

The numbers mentioned in the deal did raise some eyebrows: if Israel and the UAE were to actually reach the target of USD10 billion in trade, this would make the UAE one of Israel's largest trading partners. But it may also reflect a long-term ambition, which is not only to boost bilateral trade but also to provide a blueprint for future economic integration. The pattern of growth also supports this ambition (whether the two countries do hit that target or not). According to Thani Al Zeyoudi, the UAE's minister of state for foreign trade, '[n]on-oil trade between UAE and Israel hit $2 billion in the first nine months of 2022, up 114 percent from the same period in 2021.' The UAE–Israel partnership is viewed by Israel as the locomotive driving potentially wider regional economic integration.

After all, the two countries have much in common and may be some of the most compatible economies in the region. Both the UAE and Israel have put a lot of focus on developing their tech sector. The UAE views itself as a potential global hub for new technologies, smart cities and cyber, which certainly speaks to the 'start-up nation.' Abu Dhabi also views these sectors as essential to its critical transition away from an energy-focused economy and towards a knowledge-based one. This points to the fact that the economic aspects of the deal weren't just the 'cherry on top' for the UAE but very much a portion of the cake itself—one that shouldn't be underestimated.

More broadly, the deal aims to develop a vision of the future, betting that synergies can be found not only in sectors that are currently a driver of growth but also those that will be in the coming decades. These synergies have to do with specific sectors that are viewed as having significant growth potential. The deal provides for customs exemption immediately or gradually on 96 percent of trade between the countries: food, agriculture, cosmetics, medical equipment, medication and more. This gives an insight into where the two countries are putting their focus: agri-tech and med-tech are two of the domains that are believed to be growth sectors and critical for the future of the region. The Ukrainian crisis has shown how easily supply chains providing basic food products can be disrupted, and as the world's population continues to increase, these disruptions may become more likely—and more consequential.

This adds on to another geographic component of the partnership: both countries are looking to build their partnership as a 'corridor' to Asia. The UAE–Israel partnership is completed by a focus on India in particular: both the UAE and Israel have already built significant ties with the Asian giant. The synergies here are great, given the UAE's experience as a logistical hub and Israel's own expertise in smart agri-tech, clean energy and water, all of which will be needed to fuel sustainable Indian growth. The partnership is focused mostly on economic issues but has attracted Washington's interest given the ongoing US effort to build up India as a bulwark against China in the region—though this is something that is of far less interest to Abu Dhabi and Israel.

More broadly, Israel hopes that it can use the UAE as a trading hub, a door to other markets. This includes countries in Asia but also closer partners like Saudi Arabia. These hopes may have been tamed by the reaction of the Saudi Kingdom, which revised its tariffs with other members of the Gulf to specifically sideline Israeli-made products in July 2021, but the principle still stands.

The potential for a significant deepening of economic ties is there, but so are the obstacles. For all the embrace of the agreements on both sides, and the existence of previous relations that predate the deal, suspicions remain. In 2021, the Israeli Central Bank sent a letter to the leadership of all of Israel's banks highlighting the need for high supervision standards to be applied for money transfers between the UAE and Israel. Although barriers were being brought down, the bank's letter revealed Israel's particular concerns over money laundering and terrorist financing when it comes to trading with the UAE. The letter directly mentions a previous report by the international organization in charge of setting the standards for combating both money laundering and terrorist financing, which pointed to significant deficiencies in the UAE's banking sector. This may seem like a remote concern, but several Israeli businessmen have pointed to the extremely invasive process required to make simple money transfers to the UAE from Israel as one of the key obstacles to trade between the two countries. Israel is aware of the issue and is seeking to tackle it, but so far no solution has been found.

Another obstacle stems from Israel's reluctance to let Abu Dhabi invest in some of the critical sectors of the Israeli economy. The agreement certainly surprised the Israelis who were expecting most of the trade to flow in the UAE's direction, fantasizing about Israeli products being sent in their droves to the Gulf. But one key aspect of the trade relationship has been the UAE's own appetite for investing in Israeli companies. Although those investments are mostly welcome, some of them have caused concern.

The security sector immediately comes to mind, but other Israeli companies have also been affected, including a bid by ADQ, the Abu Dhabi Developmental Holding Company, to acquire 25 percent of the shares of the Israeli Phoenix Insurance Company from two US funds. Phoenix offers a range of services to Israelis, from life and medical insurance to pensions, making it a key actor in Israel's economic life. The investment by ADQ, which is controlled by none other than Sheikh Tahnoun bin Zayed, mentioned earlier, made some commentators and officials uneasy: it would make the Emirati fund the biggest stakeholder in Phoenix. ADQ, a government-controlled sovereign wealth fund, would effectively control a significant part of the savings and pensions of hundreds of thousands of Israelis.

Investments in Israel's pension funds have always been of particular importance, given how much they affect the daily lives of Israelis and the kind of leverage a foreign government would have should it secure a significant share of the few companies investing the money Israelis are putting away for retirement. A similar Chinese bid to acquire controlling stakes of Phoenix, and an earlier one by an Israeli group to sell its share of the Clal Insurance company, had both been rejected a few years earlier.

But this time, it came not from Beijing—a country at odds with Israel's main ally, the United States—but its newfound regional ally, which, as mentioned, Israel viewed as a critical partner in showing how economic integration with the region could work. And yet several Israeli economic commentators vehemently opposed the move, asking what would happen if the funds of thousands of Israelis were invested in failed projects? Corrupt deals? Or worse, what if details about the savings and pensions of a non-negligible segment of the Israeli population was to be sold to a foreign government? Or used as leverage against Israel?

Those may be extreme scenarios, but they also show that, for all the deep-rooted cooperation between Israel and the UAE, trust is something that still may elude the partnership and will take time to build. Such scenarios also point to another limit of the 'top-down' and 'government-first' approach: that ADQ is so close to the circle of power in the UAE worked against the bid rather than for it. Israeli commentators may not have reacted in the same way if ADQ was a fully private fund and if the economic culture in the UAE—and in much of the Gulf for that matter—wasn't one in which government control permeates much of the economy. As of writing, the story of ADQ's bid to buy a significant share of Phoenix isn't over. The Netanyahu government may still decide to take the jump and pray for the best. But the unease the deal prompted on Israel's side shows that, while much of the Arab world may not be ready to accept Israeli products with open arms, in some cases the same can also be said of Israel.

This highlights the last obstacle to future economic cooperation between Israel and the UAE and the rest of the Arab world. Most of the trade between the UAE and Israel remains confined to major companies in the UAE. Small and medium-sized companies have shown little appetite to invest in the relationship.

This perhaps serves as a broader lesson about this 'top-down' approach to normalization—that it is, by essence, fragile. It is also the perpetual dilemma encountered by Peres and any other of the advocates of the 'dividends of peace' or 'peace through prosperity': while it may be true that economic prosperity favors peace, it is not the sole factor behind it. And on the other hand, true and lasting prosperity absolutely does require peace.

PART 3

MANAGING DESPAIR IN THE ISRAELI–PALESTINIAN ARENA

9

TRADING PEACE FOR QUIET

In 2005, Israel unilaterally withdrew from Gaza, a decision taken by then Prime Minister Ariel Sharon. The disengagement divided Israeli society in a way that can't be understated. The divide was visible to anyone walking the streets of major Israeli cities: Israelis who supported the move wore blue bracelets, while those who rejected it wore orange. The country split along those 'colors' in an almost physical way.

As the withdrawal took place, images of Israeli soldiers and police officers forcefully removing Israeli settlers from the Gaza Strip were painful to watch for some, and so were the images of Palestinians later entering and destroying those settlements, including the most notorious of them—Gush Katif. Some of those who inhabited Gush Katif had previously resided in the Sinai until it was given back to Egypt as part of the Camp David Accords. For supporters of the withdrawal, this was worth it: the disengagement would bring new impetus to a faltering peace process and with it the prospect of ending the endless cycle of violence. For those opposing it, it was a risky gamble that traded a concrete Israeli presence for vague promises of peace. Years later, after Hamas's 7 October 2023 Simchat Torah massacre, some would recall Gush Katif's residents' warnings that leaving Gaza would lead to a spike in terror.

The Gaza disengagement is one of these moments that most people outside of Israel barely remember yet one that still shapes the Israeli psyche. The withdrawal and ensuing rise of Hamas is part of a long series of domestic turning points that explain the situation we are in today, namely the weakness of the peace camp in Israel and Israel's growing disillusion with the very idea of peace itself.

The significance of the Israeli withdrawal from Gaza can be compared to the series of bombings that followed the signing of the Oslo Accords in the 1990s and the assassination of Yitzhak Rabin by a Jewish extremist in front of the Tel Aviv city hall just as he was exiting a rally celebrating peace. These moments delegitimized the idea of peace and killed hope. To many Israelis, they showed that striving for peace could be just as perilous as aiming for war, if not more.

Looking at the conflict in an objective way requires a good understanding of these moments. For many in Israel, the rise of Hamas after the Gaza disengagement is absolute proof that a policy of separation is flawed. Israelis fear that the minute Israel does the same in the West Bank, it will find itself fighting two-pronged wars both in Gaza and the West Bank. For some within Israel, each rocket from Gaza is a reminder of the price Israelis paid for seeking peace, and the same also applies to the 7 October attacks, which even led to a spike in calls to 're-occupy' Gaza—including by rebuilding settlements like Gush Katif. Israeli soldiers entering Gaza posted pictures and videos showing Israeli flags flying above Gaza as if they were 'righting a wrong'—making up for what they saw as Israel's fatal mistake in 2005.

Reality is of course different from perception. The disengagement was a cold and calculated move driven mostly by Gaza's demographics and by the need to fend off international pressure. The Israeli government would not have considered disengaging from Gaza if the number of Israelis living in Gaza was higher. The demographic balance was so clear and the resources needed to protect Israelis so high that the Israeli government felt there was no point in staying. It was less of an ideological choice than a pragmatic one. There were fewer than 10,000 Israeli settlers in Gaza as opposed to the 1.5 million Palestinians then living in the Gaza Strip.

Disengaging was viewed as a shrewd and rational move by then Prime Minister Sharon. It did carry with it the opportunity of a renewed push for peace, but this opportunity was never seized— be it by Israelis or Palestinians. Israel pulled out unilaterally and did not make any effort to engage with the PA. A few months after the Israeli disengagement, Sharon had a stroke and remained in a coma until his death in 2014.

Some believe Sharon was also planning a series of unilateral withdrawals from the West Bank. Sharon would not be the first 'hawk' to turn into a 'dove': Rabin, the man most known outside of Israel for signing the Oslo Accords, was in many ways a hawk who quelled the First Intifada before shifting gears and recognizing the Palestinians' aspiration to a state.

But the idea that Sharon was preparing a broader disengagement is unlikely to be true. Given how difficult and controversial the withdrawal of the 10,000 Israeli settlers from Gaza was in Israel, it is unlikely that Sharon intended to pull out from the West Bank or that he could have done so. Indeed, multiple officials and reports have suggested that the goal was to expand settlements in the West Bank rather than limit them. Sharon did not engage with the PA, which would have been needed if the goal was peace. But the goal was not peace; it was separation.

The stroke that ultimately killed Sharon years later means we will never know for sure. What we do know, however, is that members of the new party he founded ('Kadima' or 'Forward') did clearly pursue peace. The Israeli prime minister and vice prime minister from Kadima, namely Ehud Olmert and Tzipi Livni, both sought engagement with the PA and offered unprecedented terms to the Palestinian leadership. In doing so, they rectified what they may have seen as a flaw in Sharon's plans—though the lack of engagement with the PA was likely deliberate.

We also know that regardless of the factors behind Gaza's disengagement, those who supported Sharon believed he was acting for peace. While Sharon's calculus was likely more cold-hearted, many Israelis genuinely believed disengaging from Gaza would lead to peace. Yet years later, Hamas—a group defined by its insistence on not making peace with Israel—rose to power, and the first rockets would rain from Gaza. In a complex conflict such as the Israeli–Palestinian one, perception matters just as much as realities.

***

Ever since, the notion of peace has faded. Peace has gradually been replaced by a far less ambitious objective: 'quiet.'

Israel often says its main goal when dealing with flare-ups in Gaza is not peace but the return of 'quiet.' Israel's political leaders never utter the word 'peace,' so we're left with this uneasy notion of 'quiet.' The same can be said of the other side. Hamas often uses the word quiet: a ceasefire is often marked by Hamas's pledge to answer 'quiet' with 'quiet.' At best, the group utters the word 'hudnah,' a concept that refers to a long-term truce.

But quiet is not peace. A truce is not peace. By essence, both carry with them the idea of conflict. Both refer to the interlude between wars. The wide acceptance that the idea of peace needs to be traded for a less-ambitious goal of 'quiet' is one of the many symptoms of a broader loss of hope. It is a sign that solutions are no longer thought to be realistic; that the conflict needs to be 'managed' and cannot be solved. It is the internalization that this conflict may know quiet but will not know peace. Quiet is the silence between destruction—of which we've seen plenty.

The mere notion of 'quiet' shows that neither side believes those ceasefires will ever turn into more than a temporary pause. Some on both sides may applaud this concept, believing that destroying the other side is the only solution. More than seventy years since the conflict began, and thirty years since the Oslo Accords, polls continue to show that a significant proportion of Israelis and Palestinians still believe the conflict can effectively be 'won' or that it can be decided through violence. According to a poll released in January 2023 and jointly conducted by the Ramallah-based Palestinian Center for Policy and Survey Research and the International Program in Conflict Resolution and Mediation at Tel Aviv University,[1] 40 percent of Palestinians would prefer to 'wage an armed struggle against the Israeli occupation.' The same poll found that 26 percent of Israelis would seek 'a definitive war with the Palestinians.' Both of those numbers have grown when compared to a similar poll conducted by the same two organizations the year before.

In other conflicts similar to the one pitting the Israelis against the Palestinians, the very basis for peace generally emerged from the realization that the enemy cannot be destroyed or that the cost of war is too high to bear. In a bitter war, we cannot count on the humanization of the other to make way for peace, because wars by essence de-humanize the enemy. It is the realization that a war cannot be won and of the need to find alternatives that generally leads to peace.

Yet these polls and many others show that this premise is far from widely accepted. Both sides view themselves as the victim of the other, with Israelis the victims of Palestinian terrorism and Palestinians the victim of Israeli occupation and military operations. This victimhood narrative leads both sides to ignore the other and conduct themselves in a way that prioritizes survival and survival alone. Neither side has truly moved from striving to survive to striving to live together.

But what's unique about the Israeli–Palestinian conflict is that this realization that the cost of conflict is too high to bear and calls for an alternative did in fact take place. It's not that the Israeli–Palestinian conflict never reached a phase where it had 'matured' enough for peace. It's that it reached this phase of 'maturation' and, for several reasons, rolled back downhill from it.

The equation has effectively been flipped on its head. While the premise for peace was that the cost of winning was too high, the premise of the current phase of the Israeli–Palestinian conflict is that it is in fact the cost of peace that's too high to bear.

This leaves both sides with the choice to either embrace the fight—which a sizeable minority does on both sides—or to sue for 'quiet' instead of peace. The thirst for 'quiet' is the terrible symptom of this 'post-peace' era: it is the deep desire by most to try to ignore the conflict, to live their lives despite it or view it as a mere annoyance. This may explain why flare-ups in violence, over the 2010s and early 2020s at least, have never really led to a renewed desire for peace.

***

The equation has also been flipped when it comes to the complexity of the answer to the conflict. The Israeli–Palestinian conflict had come to be seen as the 'epitome' of a complex problem, requiring complex solutions. However, a growing segment of the population on both sides is going for 'simple,' that is, extreme, answers.

This is particularly true of the youth. New generations of Palestinians and Israelis have now grown up in a post-Oslo world in which peace is a faint and naive concept. They may have heard echoes of 'peace talks' but have not experienced what hope truly feels like. Even on the Israeli side, all the perceived 'victories' that Israel may have achieved, from the transfer of the US embassy to Jerusalem to the Abraham Accords, were met with little fanfare. No one came out onto the streets to celebrate. This is the generation that will determine the future, and in many ways is already doing so, as radical attitudes have grown among Israel's youth just as much as among the Palestinian youth, a post- or even 'past' peace generation that has increasingly embraced a one-sided view of the conflict, wherein they are the victim of the other, justifying violence that makes for the foundation of the other's victimhood narrative wherein the conflict can be won but not solved.

10

THE PALESTINIAN 'AUTHORITY'

In January 2021, Mahmoud Abbas, the president of the PA, surprised everyone by announcing that the PA would hold both legislative and presidential elections. In his more than fifteen years in power, the Palestinian president had always refrained from any promises to hold presidential elections. The last legislative elections, held in 2006, had cost him control of the Gaza Strip after his main opponent, Hamas, managed to secure a majority of seats at the closest equivalent to a Palestinian parliament. Holding elections could insufflate new blood in a stagnating leadership in need of a new vision.

But this was of course far from being the point. No one can claim to know the motivations behind the ailing Palestinian president's decision, but the timing suggested it was an act of desperation rather than one of renewal. The past years had shook the already fragile PA to its core. To be sure, Abbas had never been popular, contrary to his predecessor, Yasser Arafat. He is a man of apparatus who would always walk in the shadow of his predecessor, considered a Palestinian national hero. A man stuck between his unwillingness to embrace violence, which should be saluted, and his inability to make peace. He also oversaw a period of slow decay in the peace process that raised questions over the nature and purpose of the PA.

The PA had been created as part of the Oslo Accords and was viewed by the Palestinians as a transitory government meant to pave the way for the creation of an actual Palestinian state. This goal, and the perspective of an eventual peace agreement that would see Israel live alongside a Palestinian state, is the *raison d'être* of the PA. Yet, decades after the Oslo Accords were signed, this *raison d'être* has entirely disappeared: the peace process is at a standstill, Palestinians are divided between Gaza and the West Bank, and those in Israel who still support a two-state solution have been marginalized. Israeli settlements are expanding, and depending on the government, Israel is flip-flopping between maintaining an untenable status quo and creeping annexation and settlement expansion. The PA is stuck in its initial form as a proto-state, unable to achieve full or even limited sovereignty and faced with the reality of its declining ability to administer even the limited swathe of territory it still controls.

***

Upon these inherent and dramatic weaknesses would pile a set of events that shook the remaining pillars of the PA.

The first is the Abraham Accords themselves. The Palestinian leadership had long thought the equation proposed by the Arab Peace Initiative inalterable. The Palestinian ability to prevent Israel's presence in the region from being normalized was at least a source of leverage and a sign that while the Palestinian cause may have been eclipsed by other regional conflicts, Arab solidarity and support for their brethren remained.

In that sense, the 2020 agreement showed that the Palestinians—chief among them President Abbas—may have misjudged the status of the conflict. It suggested that the conflict was not at an impasse and that time may not be on the Palestinian side. Abbas was the embodiment of paralysis, but up until then, his inability to move things forward may have been portrayed as innocuous, as the broader parameters of the conflict did not change. The 2020 agreement shattered the idea that the conflict was 'frozen.' By sitting there as a placeholder for someone with an actual vision or the means to achieve it, Abbas was killing the Palestinian cause. This alone required a change of course.

***

The Abraham Accords were not the only development that showed time was not on the Palestinians' side. Months before the UAE chose to normalize ties with Israel, Prime Minister Netanyahu launched an unprecedented project to annex the West Bank. The timing of Netanyahu's project may have been driven by political considerations aimed at appealing to voters on the right and far right of the political spectrum. It emerged as Netanyahu faced tough elections. But it was also a reflection of the situation in the White House. With the Trump administration in the driving seat, Israel found not just an ally but one of the most fervent supporters of settling the conflict in a way that gave Israel the upper hand. The Trump administration was not pro-Israel in the 'traditional' sense of the term: it was deeply aligned with Israel's right and far-right movement and even with the settlers' movement.

One of the results of this unprecedented political set-up in Washington was President Trump's 'Peace to Prosperity' plan— or, as it is more commonly known, the 'Deal of the Century.'

President Trump's so-called 'Deal of the Century' effectively sent the message that Washington was moving away from what the PA viewed as a 'fair' solution. President Trump took a simplistic view of the conflict but one that isn't fully disconnected from reality: in his view, decades after the Oslo Accords, the Palestinian leadership had effectively 'lost.'

The deal President Trump offered proceeded from this simplistic conclusion and offered less than what the Palestinian leadership had come to expect from a peace agreement: a diminished and demilitarized Palestinian state comprising a set of loosely tied together enclaves, having to renounce around 30 percent of the West Bank and with limited sovereignty. The Palestinians dubbed the plan the 'slap of the century,' a very apt name: beyond the justified indignation it provoked, it was also a wake-up call.

The message was also received in Gaza: Yahya Sinwar, the newly elected Hamas chief in the Palestinian enclave, responded by launching a series of border riots (the 'March of Return') meant to put pressure on Israel. Years later, after those marches failed, and another round of war led him nowhere, Sinwar would move to a more sinister plan to make what he saw as a necessary 'course correction' in the conflict. This would lead to the 7 October massacre.

Adding insult to injury, the United States and Israel did not wait for any sort of Palestinian approval of the plan—which would have never come. In the eyes of the American and Israeli administrations, the plan justified immediate action, including Israel's annexation of parts of the West Bank, and ultimately led to the transfer of the US embassy to Jerusalem.

In other words, the growing perception that the Palestinians had 'lost' wasn't just theoretical: it was actively shaping the situation and threatening to create new 'facts on the ground' that would turn this perceived 'loss' into a self-fulfilling prophecy.

Abbas's election announcement was an attempt to seize the initiative while also appealing to a new US administration led by President Biden, who was committed to a more typical American position on the conflict. But the elections were also an act of desperation, a risky bet by a man and an entity that had both been losing ground.

The election announcement represented a change of course that seemed and eventually proved far too radical to believe. President Abbas was extremely unpopular, as he has been almost consistently since his rise to power and was predicted to lose against all of the possible contenders. Any victory would have to be secured by backroom deals and a fair amount of electoral manipulation.

Beyond this known state-of-play, one that has defined Palestinian politics for years, the elections also revealed deep fractures within Abbas's own party, Fatah. Abbas would not only be challenged by outside contenders but, perhaps more importantly, by internal rivals. Fifteen years of impasse had not only fostered the rise of outside challengers, such as Hamas, but had also broken Fatah from within.

As he announced his candidacy, Mohammed Dahlan, one of Abbas's longtime opponents within Fatah, began to set up his own list for the elections. Dahlan, the former Fatah head in Gaza who now lives in exile in the UAE after being booted out by Abbas, had long been looking for a chance to make a comeback. He had sought to maintain good relations with elements within Fatah as well as with other Palestinian groups.

The announcement of another candidacy would give the elections the final *coup de grâce*. Despite a desperate and last-ditch effort to negotiate a closed-door arrangement, Marwan Barghouti, a Palestinian leader detained in Israel, also positioned himself to challenge Abbas both in the parliamentary and the presidential elections.

By all counts, Barghouti, who is serving a life sentence in Israel for fomenting attacks against Israelis and foreigners, is the most popular of all Palestinian candidates. Multiple polls, including one conducted in 2022, showed that he would defeat all possible contenders, including Abbas, as well as the head of Hamas, Ismail Haniyeh.[1] Many Palestinians view him as a national hero. His imprisonment largely preserved him from the natural political decay other Fatah leaders suffered and drew comparisons to Nelson Mandela.

What's more, despite being imprisoned in Israel, Barghouti managed to maintain his network of support among the officially defunct armed wing of the Fatah party and the youth. Barghouti played a role in the First Intifada that he cemented during the second, as the head of the 'Tanzim,' a popular-movement-turned-armed-group tied to Fatah. After being arrested in 2002, he kept his image as the leader of a popular and violent uprising. More than twenty years later, after two decades of impasse and disillusionment with the peace process, this idea of 'popular resistance' is gaining ground among most Palestinians, boosting Barghouti's popularity.

This is why Barghouti's initial decision to run in the parliamentary elections raised alarm bells in Ramallah. Barghouti decided to ally with Arafat's nephew, Nasser al-Kidwa, whose longtime opposition to Abbas escalated as he formed a separate parliamentary list for the upcoming elections. Barghouti could not be a candidate himself, but his support was clearly expressed by the inclusion of his wife as the number 2 on al-Kidwa's list.

Barghouti's de facto participation in the legislative elections sent shockwaves through Ramallah. But what truly worried Abbas was that Barghouti himself would later make a bid for the presidency in the elections that were due to be held in the summer. Abbas sent one of his closest advisors, Hussein al-Sheikh, to Barghouti's prison to negotiate a deal that would preclude Barghouti from running in the July elections. Abbas was ready to offer significant concessions to Barghouti, including seats in the Palestinian parliament and the position of vice-president of the PA, which would be created for Barghouti.

But the negotiations quickly turned sour. It was clear that Barghouti had no intention of making any kind of deal with the unpopular PA president. Allying with Abbas offered short-term benefits, including the possibility of pressuring Israel to free the prisoner-turned vice-president. But in the longer term, it was equivalent to a political suicide. Barghouti's popularity came not only from his status but also from his lack of ties to the Palestinian president. Abbas was poison, and it didn't take long for the detained Palestinian leader to realize it.

Barghouti was still viewed as the representative of the Fatah of the old days, before the corruption and the compromises. He would eventually make his choice clear by announcing his intention to run against Abbas in the July presidential elections in a direct challenge to the ailing leader.

Days later, the elections were 'postponed.' The PA claimed it had backtracked from the decision to hold elections due to an Israeli refusal to let Palestinians living in East Jerusalem participate in the vote. But this was just an excuse. The truth is that the Palestinian president backtracked because he found himself faced with an uncompromising adversary that was sure to win if fair elections were held.

What's most notable about this episode is that this challenger did not emerge from outside Fatah or the PA. It wasn't Hamas that derailed the elections. For all the talk about the—very real— Fatah/Hamas divide, the Islamist group ruling Gaza had in fact gone out of its way to encourage elections to be held. Hamas had accepted a set of rules that could play in Fatah's favor. There were also rumors that Fatah and Hamas had effectively agreed to 'divide the pie': Hamas candidates in the legislative elections would be pre-approved by the PA, so that the make-up of the future Palestinian Legislative Council (PLC—the closest equivalent to a Palestinian parliament) would reflect a deal between Hamas and Fatah rather than being a reflection of each party's actual local support. It was also rumored that Hamas had agreed not to put forward any candidates for the July presidential elections.

To be clear, this purported flexibility, on the part of one of Fatah's deadliest enemies, was not a gesture of goodwill. The group understood that if it presented a direct challenge to President Abbas, the elections would not be held. The group had adopted a more 'patient' strategy and saw the elections as an opportunity to rebuild a political presence in the West Bank while also seeking the political legitimacy such elections would give the movement. Hamas's goal was still to overthrow Fatah and become the only representative of the Palestinian people, but it was ready to take the long route.

And yet the elections were indefinitely postponed, not because of Fatah's archenemy but because of a challenge from within. Barghouti's candidacy, alongside that of Arafat's nephew, al-Kidwa, also reflected the growing unease within the Fatah movement that spilled over in the lead up to the elections. Abbas's rule had become increasingly autocratic. Not that his predecessor had necessarily ruled through democratic means, but Arafat still allowed some dissenting voices to be heard. Abbas's first years, particularly during the mandate of Prime Minister Salam Fayyad, raised hopes that he would reform the PA to be more inclusive, transparent and less corrupt. But as the legitimacy crisis the PA and Abbas himself faced grew stronger, Abbas increasingly ruled by decree and sidelined the few existing entities that were supposed to act as checks on his power.

Abbas was counting on a shrinking circle of close advisors picked for their loyalty to the president rather than their competence or appeal to the Palestinian public. The official list drafted by Fatah would reflect this trend, sidelining local and respected figures, including from Fatah, and benefiting those closest to the president. This triggered an internal upheaval and partly explains why al-Kidwa was able to enlist so many local figures.

It was not external rivals like Hamas or outside powers uninterested in change like Israel or the United States that torpedoed Abbas's attempt to seize back the initiative. It was Abbas's own party.

And the fracture that appeared ahead of the elections was just the tip of the iceberg.

***

The PA was suffering from a set of compounding crises, including a crisis of legitimacy, a financial crisis and a popular crisis. But even more concretely, its ability to actually control the 'islands' of Palestinian territories theoretically under its authority was shrinking.

The PA's ability to exercise one of the primary functions of a state—its monopoly on the legal use of violence—has also been challenged.

This isn't completely new. Since its inception, the PA and its security forces have faced difficulties operating in certain areas, with that vacuum being exploited by its opponents.

Some areas are out of reach 'per design' due to the Oslo Accords, which divide the West Bank between areas A, B and C, with the PA having security control only over area A—mostly formed by the main Palestinian cities including Ramallah, Nablus, Hebron, Jericho and Jenin, among others. Israel has security control over areas B and C and civilian control over area C. The last two areas represent most of the West Bank's territory. Per design, the PA has only a limited ability to access those areas.

Another limit stems from the more specific situation in East Jerusalem, as the status of the city has yet to be solved and was not part of the Oslo Accords. Israel views Jerusalem as its indivisible capital, a principle that has resulted in a proactive Israeli effort to suppress any PA activities in East Jerusalem.

This does mean that security duties fall under the purview of the Israeli police. While the Israeli police and border police are indeed deployed and regularly operate in East Jerusalem, there are areas where their presence is far more limited. Most notably, that is the case in areas of East Jerusalem that, while not under the PA's control, are also east of the separation wall built in areas of Jerusalem.

This situation has created what some have called 'twilight zones' where neither the Israeli authority nor Palestinian rule effectively apply. One of the most infamous such 'twilight zones' is Shuafat, a refugee camp situated in northern Jerusalem and separated by a wall. For all intents and purposes, Shuafat is its own independent entity, ruled by a refugee council of elders rather than any other governmental entity. It should be no surprise that a significant proportion of the Palestinian assailants who carried out attacks against Israelis have come from this largely unchecked area. The camp has also been a recruitment ground for groups like Hamas.

But Shuafat and the 'twilight zones' more broadly aren't the only areas where control—whether Israeli or Palestinian—is fragile. Even in area A, where the PA and its security forces, the Palestinian Preventive Security Force, are supposed to be active, there are de facto limits to the PA's rule.

This is particularly true in refugee camps in the main cities across the West Bank. The Jenin refugee camp, for instance, has historically been a stronghold for the Palestinian Islamic Jihad. Security forces affiliated with the main power in the West Bank (Fatah) have found it difficult to operate in the Jenin refugee camp to the point that Abbas decided to fire all of the security officials in Jenin in 2021 for failing to wrest control of this part of the city. Two years later, in 2023, Israel would launch a significant operation in Jenin, as the PA's inability to rule had allowed other groups, like Hamas and particularly Palestinian Islamic Jihad, to build a stronghold within the camp. The Jenin refugee camp is just one example: the dense Balata camp in Nablus has also been largely outside of the control of the PA, and to a lesser extent so has the al-Amari camp near Ramallah.

This isn't a temporary setback but the result of a trend that will deepen should the current status quo remain. The PA has failed in many ways in its ability to act as a quasi-state because its *raison d'être*—the peace process—has vanished, as well as failures of its own making, efforts by Israel to marginalize it and the mere nature of the authority itself. This failure is visible to every Palestinian living in the West Bank. Palestinian courts, for instance, are clogged and dysfunctional to the point that most Palestinians have to seek justice elsewhere—either by taking action themselves or by lobbying powerful clans, families or gangs. The rampant circulation of illegal weapons has been an issue for years, as Palestinians feel they need to protect themselves, not necessarily against Israel but against the growing sense of present and future chaos.

Another key example of the PA's failure is the Palestinian Preventive Security Force. Although Western supporters have poured significant resources into building a professional force, Palestinian forces lack a key structural element: legitimacy. Security forces, in any given country, are by essence defined by their role: to ensure public safety and order. To protect their own people. But the Palestinian Preventive Security Force cannot defend Palestinians against what most Palestinians see as the main threat they face, namely Israel and more specifically Israeli settlers. They are a police force aimed solely at policing Palestinians, not defending them.

Even when it comes to defending itself, the PA cannot legitimize its own actions. The arrests of Hamas cells for instance, or cells preparing terror attacks, are largely 'outsourced' to Israeli security forces. The reason is simple: for all the bad blood between Hamas and Fatah, the Palestinian security forces cannot be seen to be arresting a Palestinian 'resisting' Israel. A stronger PA could justify such actions, legitimizing them as a way to avoid a flare-up in violence in the West Bank that never leads to anything and to allow peace talks to continue. This is a position that President Abbas likely believes in. Contrary to his predecessor whose role in the Second Intifada is ambiguous to say the least (Israel has accused Arafat of supporting or even instigating the Second Intifada), Abbas has never supported calls for violence. But this position is untenable unless it is backed by a credible political solution. And so the Palestinian security forces are left playing an important but uneasy role when it comes to stabilizing the West Bank and no role at all when it comes to defending Palestinians.

***

This isn't the only limit to the Fatah-controlled PA. Ramallah has been losing its operational space, but it has also been hemorrhaging a far more critical 'currency': its own people.

There are signs that Fatah is losing control of members of groups that are theoretically working under it or closely affiliated to the party. This includes the al-Aqsa Martyrs' Brigades, a network of militants that emerged during the Second Intifada in the 2000s. Initially centered on the Balata refugee camp in Nablus, the movement expanded to the northern West Bank and gradually to the whole West Bank. The group was never recognized as a Fatah affiliate but had clear ties to the party at a time when Arafat sought to gain leverage by using violence to break the status quo. The United States quickly designated the al-Aqsa Martyrs' Brigades a terror group in 2002 after the group started targeting civilians—despite its initial pledge only to target soldiers—including by carrying out a deadly suicide-bombing attack in Jerusalem during a bar-mitzvah celebration, killing eleven.

Whatever ties the group had with the Palestinian leadership initially were gradually lost when President Abbas took office, after Arafat's death. In the years following the Second Intifada, the PA gradually reined the group in, with some elements being reintegrated as part of the Palestinian security forces and others vowing to renounce violence in a final agreement in 2010 that removed a few militants from Israel's wanted list.

This points to a broader issue that has regularly popped up in the short history of the PA: as the PA grew into a state-like entity, the same people who carried out attacks against Israelis (civilians or military) and were involved in the armed struggle against Israel had to choose to either be part of the security apparatus, which meant collaborating with Israel, or to break away from the main line of the party. This has led to the creation of multiple breakaway factions, some taking on the name of the al-Aqsa Martyrs'

Brigades, while others have simply maintained varying degrees of loyalty to the group.

This also means that although the group is theoretically defunct, it continues to exist as a separate entity—and one that quickly became a thorn in the PA's side. In March 2016, armed clashes broke out in the Old City of Nablus between Palestinian security forces and members of the al-Aqsa Martyrs' Brigades as the security forces affiliated with the PA were trying to arrest a former member of the al-Aqsa Martyrs' Brigades on suspicion of murder. Thirteen people were wounded in the ensuing clashes. A few weeks later, President Abbas dismissed the local Fatah governor, General Akram Rajoub, who responded by publicly criticizing Abbas.

There may have been several reasons for Rajoub's dismissal. The governor had a history of criticizing Abbas for giving too much leeway to Fatah loyalists in Nablus, who often acted independently of the Palestinian leadership and faced few consequences for doing so. Because of the PA's lack of control over Nablus's sprawling Balata camp in particular, the camp also became home to several disgruntled officials who directed criticism at the PA from the camp. Balata effectively turned into a haven for disenfranchised Fatah dissidents, who formed alternative movements that still exist to this day.

The March 2016 incident was only one in a series, often pitting Palestinian security forces against members of the al-Aqsa Martyrs' Brigades or the Tanzim, another group that also emerged during the Intifada. A few months later, the PA arrested Ahmad Izzat Halawa, a fifty-year old leader of the al-Aqsa Martyrs' Brigades, for the murder of two PA security officers. Halawa was beaten to death while in detention, prompting a slew of resignations among Fatah officials and a series of protests.

Similar incidents have continued to take place ever since. In January 2022, for instance, shots were fired at the headquarters of the PA security forces in Jenin just days after the Palestinian forces had arrested and beaten a former commander of the al-Aqsa Martyrs' Brigades in the Jenin refugee camp.

As relations between part of the al-Aqsa Martyrs' Brigades and Abbas loyalists further deteriorated, the brigades also increasingly started to work with some of Abbas's staunchest opponents, be it Hamas or the Palestinian Islamic Jihad. This was nothing new: during the Second Intifada, the group had already built working ties with both groups. This was supposed to be a parenthesis in the growing hostility between Fatah and other prominent Palestinian groups like Hamas and the Islamic Jihad. Yet as Abbas quickly lost control of the group, the al-Aqsa Martyrs' Brigades resumed coordination with Abbas's rivals. This is still the case today.

The 2022–3 escalation in Palestinian attacks in the northern West Bank was led by cells from the al-Aqsa Martyrs' Brigades who were working with members of Hamas and the Palestinian Islamic Jihad. In fact, during this time, the mere meaning of the historic factions that had divided the Palestinian scene for decades began to disappear. The younger, post-Oslo generation who grew up after 1993 were no longer interested in any ideological affiliation. Groups like the 'Lions' Den,' which carried out a series of attacks against Israelis in the northern West Bank, began to emerge. Their members had loose affiliations with rival 'mainstream' Palestinian groups and received help from Hamas and the Palestinian Islamic Jihad, but it appears to be very much a grassroots movement, blurring the lines between historic factions. This trend is very much here to stay, as much of the Palestinian youth agrees on the way forward: violent struggle against Israel.

***

Compounding this very concrete loss of control is a latent collapse of the Palestinian security forces themselves. This is perhaps the most acute sign of the internal crisis the PA is facing. Losing control over your own security forces is generally a sign that latent failures have reached a 'terminal' stage. The Palestinian security forces have been built with extensive US backing and funds. While the results are far from negative, there are signs of a crisis within the force that could become critical in the future. One of these signs is that thousands of Palestinian security officers fail to report on any given day, mostly because they have to take second jobs—sometimes in Israel or Israeli settlements—to make a living. Salaries are not necessarily competitive and rarely paid on time.

The PA has been facing a significant financial crisis, made worse by donor fatigue and the COVID-19 crisis, as well as Israel's on-and-off decision to subtract some of the tax it collects on behalf of the PA—in response to the PA's own policy of paying families of 'martyrs' who participated in attacks against Israel.

This financial crisis is its own problem: the PA is a large bureaucratic organization that buys loyalty through salaries, cronyism and corruption. As such, an economic crisis is never just that. It is always a political one, if not an existential one.

***

In the months following the postponement of the elections, the PA found itself mired in further crises. Perhaps the most significant of these was the wave of protests that followed the death of Nizar Banat, a well-known Palestinian activist from Hebron. Banat was a critic of the PA just as much as Israel, leading to his arrest in June by the Palestinian Preventive Security Force. Banat was beaten to death while in detention. His death led to days of protests in several of the main Palestinian cities in the West Bank, including Ramallah, where Palestinian security forces confronted protesters. Al-Manarah Square was effectively put into lockdown, with security forces being deployed and counter-protests being held by supporters of Abbas.

This was reminiscent of similar protest movements in neighboring countries. In Egypt, for instance, police brutality triggered some of the most significant demonstrations of recent years. Abbas was reacting in the same way as other Arab autocrats, aware that the quiet that preceded Banat's death was largely deceptive.

This movement did not turn into a revolution, but it certainly could have done. A combination of political and economic crisis, as well as an isolated and out-of-touch leadership viewed as no better than Israel, forms the perfect conditions for a revolutionary conflagration to spread throughout the PA.

All the factors behind a possible revolution are there and will continue to be in the near future. Each tactical incident is liable to turn into a bigger and more transformative event.

These are just one of the many signs that Abbas's control over the West Bank, Fatah and the Palestinian institutions is extremely limited. This legitimacy crisis won't disappear and is liable to further worsen in the coming years. At this point, the current PA leadership is simply incapable of changing course without breaking. It is stuck vying for a status quo that becomes less and less sustainable every day. The PA's lack of popularity means that even if Ramallah was presented with a 'fair deal'—which is unlikely at this stage—it simply wouldn't be able to implement the necessary concessions such a deal would entail (the same can be said of Israel, as I will discuss later). Though Abbas can be praised for maintaining stability in a region that has descended into chaos while avoiding the pitfalls of returning to violence, peace, which has been the PA's strategic goal, has become impossible under the current leadership. A new leadership, one with a vision of revitalizing the PA, would be needed to get out of the impasse—provided of course that the political equation also changes in Israel.

But this moment, which may well also offer opportunities for hope, also carries with it tremendous risks. The cracks in the PA have been widening for years, with the looming struggle over Abbas's succession serving as the *coup de grâce*.

11

CHAOS IN THE POST-ABBAS ERA

The question of Abbas's succession and how it may affect the Israeli–Palestinian conflict is far from front page news in Israel. The relative status quo in the PA, Abbas's marginalization and the impression that he keeps on repeating the same old tirades have diminished the interest of the broader public in the PA's future. Or perhaps, more accurately, the Israeli public isn't aware of the potential risks Abbas's succession involves.

The ailing Palestinian president lives in a bubble. During his tenure as the head of the PA, very little has changed, with the hope of the Oslo Accords and the possible creation of a Palestinian state disappearing. Abbas is unpopular: the Palestinian president has not won an election since he was first elected in 2006 and is the product of a Palestinian bureaucracy rather than the Palestinian people. Polls have consistently shown that Abbas would lose any elections against any opponent. In September 2021, a poll by one of the very few (relatively) trustworthy Palestinian pollsters found that nearly 80 percent of Palestinians wanted Abbas to resign.[1]

The current Palestinian leadership's lack of legitimacy has real implications for Israel. Without a legitimate leader capable of convincing Palestinians of the need for compromises, even a 'fair' solution to the Palestinian conflict will never see the light of day. The current status quo and the impression that Abbas is 'all talk' are in no small part tied to the same trend. For Abbas, any change from the status quo in one direction or the other is risky and may have him quickly ousted from the Mukataa, his presidential palace in Ramallah.

This should be viewed as a problem for Israel, but that has not always been the case. Abbas's weakness has emboldened his rivals, particularly Hamas, to the point that a takeover of the West Bank by the Gaza-based group is a not-so-distant possibility.

But to some in Israel, the PA's marginalization is viewed as an asset: a weak PA means limited pressure on Israel to make any concessions to the Palestinians or engage in serious peace talks. For those skeptical of the Oslo Accords and the peace talks in general, the enduring Palestinian divide is Israel's greatest strategic asset. When pressed to resume peace talks, Israel can always argue (as it has in the past) that 'there is no partner'—no one to talk to, no one that legitimately represents the Palestinian people while also being willing to talk.

This situation is akin to a ticking time bomb. Neither Abbas nor the current uneasy status quo will last. The Palestinian president is in his late eighties and suffers from poor health. Should he be incapacitated or die, what may follow will be critical and may include a phase of chaos or even civil war that will have a dramatic effect on Israel.

The Palestinian president is so paranoid and isolated that he is increasingly relying on a clique of 'yes men' who are just as out of touch as he is. These men are bound to pave the way for his successor, who may be among them, yet most of them are just as unpopular as Abbas. Abbas's inherent weakness also means that he has so far been reluctant to indicate who may be his successor in case of his death or incapacitation for fear that this 'heir apparent' would quickly push him out the door.

A number of viable candidates have jockeyed for power, from Abbas's head of intelligence Majed Faraj, Fatah's Vice President Mohammed al-Aloul, Fatah leader and head of the Palestinian Football Association Jibril Rajoub, to his close confidant and newly appointed Secretary General of the Palestine Liberation Organization's (PLO) Executive Committee Hussein al-Sheikh.

Some of those candidates, particularly the last, point to a situation in which Abbas repeats the same scenario that saw him succeed the PA's first president, Arafat. Al-Sheikh has risen very quickly to a position of power in the PA yet remains virtually unknown to the Palestinian public. Since 2007, he has headed the PA's General Authority of Civil Affairs. In that capacity, he has developed relatively close ties to Israel, as the authority handles a number of civilian issues that tend to involve Israeli authority, particularly the Coordination of Government Activities in the Territories, which works under the Israeli Ministry of Defense. Al-Sheikh is one of the few Palestinian officials who speak Hebrew, having learned the language during his time in prison in the 1970s and '80s. Although al-Sheikh has long been an insider, being a member of the Central Committee of Abbas's Fatah party and even participating in negotiations on the reconstruction of Gaza in 2014, his name only started popping up in the media in 2020 after President Abbas announced he would be holding elections.

Al-Sheikh was said to be opposed to the decision due to how weak and divided Fatah was—an opinion that proved prescient. He was particularly concerned about Barghouti, whose candidacy would wreck Abbas's plans to pave himself a route to winning the presidential elections. Al-Sheikh became more widely known when he was picked to handle the negotiations with Barghouti, offering him the hollow position of 'vice president' of the PA and some seats in the Palestinian parliament in exchange for his support and guarantees that he would not challenge Abbas.

The negotiations failed, and the 'elections' were suspended, as discussed previously. Barghouti announced his intention to run, and Abbas used Israel's lack of commitment on allowing Palestinians from East Jerusalem to vote as an excuse to postpone the elections indefinitely.

This was technically a failure for al-Sheikh, but he was on the 'right' side of history, having warned Abbas that his bid to hold elections would end up weakening Fatah, as opposed to figures like Rajoub, who supported an agreement with Hamas to divide power among the two archrivals. As a result, al-Sheikh's star continued shining, at least in the Mukataa. His status as one of Abbas's leading advisors was confirmed when, in February 2022, he was appointed to replace Saeb Erekat, the lead Palestinian negotiator who had died in 2020, as the secretary general of the PLO's Executive Committee.

The rise of al-Sheikh perhaps best embodies the growing sclerosis within the PA tied to the weakness and isolation of its president. Al-Sheikh may be viewed positively in the Mukataa, but he is at best unknown or hated by most of the Palestinian public, who view him as the embodiment of a 'collaborator' with a history of cooperation with Israel. Al-Sheikh is also said to lack charisma, with some diplomats wondering whether he was picked for that very reason: he is far from a threat to Abbas.

If al-Sheikh were to be picked, he would have almost no legitimacy. His support within Fatah would be limited, which would in turn open his succession bid to challenges. The chances of an armed confrontation would be high.

He is the second closest confidant of President Abbas after Major General Majed Faraj, the powerful head of the General Intelligence Service (GIS), the Palestinian intelligence service. Despite his lack of popular support, Faraj is seen as another possible successor to Abbas. The head of the GIS since 2009, Faraj also learned Hebrew in Israeli prison and has been key to maintaining the relative quiet in the West Bank. In 2016, he even boasted in an interview with the Israeli newspaper *Haaretz* that the service he is heading had foiled 200 attacks against Israelis and prevented ISIS from establishing a base in the West Bank.

This also put a target on his back. In 2018, Faraj along with the then Palestinian Prime Minister Rami Hamdallah were the target of an assassination attempt. As their convoy was making its way along Salah al-Din Road, the main thoroughfare in Gaza, a roadside bomb exploded. The bomb didn't wound or kill either of the two Palestinian officials, but it certainly killed the efforts ongoing at the time to reconcile Fatah with Hamas. It was also viewed as a sign of pride for Faraj, who had grown to be more than just Abbas's 'éminence grise'—he was a target himself.

Although Faraj's claim in *Haaretz* may be an exaggeration, his successes in security terms are real. But so are the abuses the GIS is regularly accused of and the fact that Faraj is largely unpopular. Regardless, his pragmatic views—despite his time in Israeli prison and the death of his father in an Israeli raid in 2002—and the fact that he is a known quantity, contrary to others, make him a candidate that's acceptable to both the United States and Israel. Faraj also controls an armed force that is said to have around 3,200 members, all relatively loyal to him, with a long track record of quelling dissent and rounding up opponents—including those tied to Hamas. Still, picking a security official with such a track record would be a risky gamble, further showing just how little the PA relies on popular support. What's certain is that Faraj will play a key role in the succession and possibly in consolidating the power of Abbas's replacement.

There are other contenders including al-Aloul, whose appointment as vice president of Fatah's Central Committee in 2017 led to a flurry of articles speculating this could be a move to designate him as Abbas's successor. Al-Aloul was also the head of the Abbas-backed Fatah list ahead of the legislative elections, underscoring his position as one of Abbas's trusted loyalists—a list that has grown shorter and shorter with time. He has been in charge of the group's recruitment effort and local branches, making him perhaps less cut off from reality than others. Contrary to the two others, al-Aloul has been more willing to advocate popular resistance and even at times armed attacks. In 2022, for instance, al-Aloul went to the funeral of three members of the al-Aqsa Martyrs' Brigades who had been killed in a raid by Israeli forces in Nablus and were suspected of being behind a series of shooting attacks, praising them for their actions and adding that Israel was not 'leaving us any other choices.'

Just like Faraj, he is likely to play a key role in Abbas's succession. In March 2018, the Fatah Revolutionary Council, Fatah's legislative body, passed a resolution that stated that, should President Abbas be incapacitated, the vice president of Fatah would take over for a period of sixty days to prepare for elections. The appointment and later resolution were seen as a possible sign that Abbas was finally ready to make a choice regarding his successor. Journalists investigated the profile of al-Aloul, another relatively unknown figure at the time.

The truth is perhaps different: technically, according to the Palestinian Basic Law, should Abbas be incapacitated, resign or die, temporary leadership of the PA would then be transferred to the head of the equivalent of the Palestinian parliament, the PLC. As of 2018, this was none other than Aziz Dweik, a Hamas member who had been elected in 2006 as the head of the Hamas-led 'Change and Reform' list. The victory of the 'Change and Reform' list in 2006 had led to clashes in Gaza, when Hamas took control of the strip and expelled Fatah. In other words, should Fatah not find a work-around, at a time when Abbas's health continued to decline, Hamas would simply have to wait to see one of its members assume the presidency.

The intention behind al-Aloul's appointment was made clear when, after appointing al-Aloul as vice president of Fatah, President Abbas had the Palestinian parliament dissolved by the Palestinian Supreme Constitutional Court a few months later. The move was the latest in a series of decisions that effectively centralized power in the hands of Abbas—himself relying on a few unelected advisors—and relying less and less on elected bodies and officials and more on administrative bodies that could be controlled by loyalists. The Supreme Constitutional Court itself was a part of this trend, becoming operational in 2016 after Abbas appointed members into an organization initially created in 2006 but that had been an empty shell up until then.

***

A lot of names have been thrown around, and it may be that Abbas is looking to see what sticks and who is best positioned to replace him. What's notable is that all of the candidates have a similar profile: they're members of the Fatah old guard who rose through the ranks of the group decades ago and are unelected and unpopular. None of them would win a vote against other potential contenders, should free and fair elections be held in the West Bank and Gaza. But the process of selecting Abbas's successor is unlikely to be democratic and will rather resemble the selection of the new Secretary General of the USSR.

This is not a minor issue and could quickly become Israel's problem too. Abbas's reliance on older, unpopular men with little support, and his rule by decree through institutions that have grown increasingly illegitimate, means that an orderly succession is far from assured. Even if Abbas picks a successor, other leaders may well challenge his decision, denouncing his choice and claiming that only elections would be legitimate.

In that sense, one man appears to be better placed than others to succeed Abbas: Marwan Barghouti. Most polls suggest that, if the Palestinians were to pick their leaders democratically, Barghouti would win. That Abbas, through his principal advisor al-Sheikh, went to great lengths to try to persuade a detained leader whose freedom is limited not to run against him in a vote says much about the Palestinian president's own assessment of Barghouti's popularity and prestige.

In prison, where ideological oppositions generally take a backseat, Barghouti has also been able to improve ties with a number of imprisoned leaders from other Palestinian movements, including Hamas, the Palestinian Islamic Jihad and the Popular Front for the Liberation of Palestine. This would make him an even more dangerous candidate, one capable of going behind ideological lines to federate Palestinian groups, even without those groups' own approval. Barghouti's popularity is such that even Hamas had to pay lip service to the idea of potentially freeing him in a prisoner deal with Israel, although it is highly unlikely that the group will actually make good on its pledge, as Barghouti represents as much a danger to Hamas as he does to Abbas.

Armed with this popularity, it is not clear that Barghouti would refrain from contesting the appointment of any of the potential apparatchiks of the PA that will end up replacing Abbas.

In fact, he would be foolish not to: being elected as the new Palestinian president would represent his best chance at being freed. Of course, his detention means that his ability to shape the Palestinian discourse and politics has been limited and that he would not be able to campaign. Yet the mere image of a Palestinian leader 'campaigning' from an Israeli prison might prove to be the only electoral argument he needs.

Another of Barghouti's assets is his ties with the al-Aqsa Martyrs' Brigades, the loose network of Fatah-aligned gunmen that played a key role in the Second Intifada and has technically disbanded since. This could prove critical should the power struggle to replace Abbas not entirely play out in the ballot boxes. To be sure, it's not clear that Barghouti has managed to maintain networks that predate his imprisonment. The leadership of the al-Aqsa Martyrs' Brigades has also changed, passing to a newer generation, and may no longer be centralized. But Barghouti could count on old acquaintances and his image to cement a movement he knows well.

***

Barghouti is just one of the leaders who could challenge Abbas's successor. There are others who could also do so on the national level, but also smaller forces whose loyalty will need to be secured by any successor.

For many years, Israeli analysts and commentators assumed that the transition of power from Abbas to his possible successor would be relatively smooth—if undemocratic—and that Fatah would come together, meet behind closed doors and pick a successor or simply approve a previously agreed-upon heir to Abbas.

But the past ten years have shown that this is only one of the possible scenarios, and perhaps not the most likely. Beyond the existence of significant rivals to Fatah, such as Hamas, Abbas's decision to hold elections has also revealed a deep fracture within Fatah and within the PA. This raises the question of whether Abbas's choice will even matter, given how divided his own party is as well as his own unpopularity. It's not clear that being designated as Abbas's heir is an actual asset on the Palestinian scene. Even an organizational buy-in isn't guaranteed, not to mention a popular one. If Abbas is poison, receiving Abbas's blessing isn't exactly the dream start a new Palestinian president may want.

This raises some potentially disturbing scenarios. There is a risk that without a clear successor to replace Abbas—and even with one—several factions will engage in a struggle that may include violent clashes. As we've seen, several of the possible candidates for Abbas's succession have maintained ties to armed factions and will most certainly use these ties as leverage in the succession struggle. From his cell, Barghouti may use his ties to the al-Aqsa Martyrs' Brigades to force other possible successors to take him into consideration. Any Abbas successor would also have to secure support from Faraj for the simple reason that he rules over one of the best-trained security forces in the West Bank. Despite years of crackdowns from both Israel and the PA, Hamas has maintained a network of operatives in the West Bank and can count on significant support from at least part of the population, including student organizations. It has also been able to coordinate with other groups that also maintain a presence in the West Bank, including the Palestinian Islamic Jihad and smaller factions. The Gaza-based model of 'joint rooms' coordinating actions between various Hamas-supportive factions and the Islamic group could be replicated in the West Bank. Not to mention the emergence of new, disenfranchised groups such as the Lions' Den, made of militants from various affiliations whose allegiance is unclear.

Piling upon the ticking time bomb of Abbas's poor health and future death is another worrying trend: Palestinians are increasingly arming themselves, not just the young militants belonging to one of the factions but also criminal networks, family clans, all the way down to the average resident of the West Bank. The feeling that chaos is here, and that there is more to come, as well as the perception that the PA is failing day after day to keep its monopoly on violence and arbitrate mundane conflicts, has led to a worrying spike in the number of illegal weapons circulating in the West Bank.

The PA is very much aware of this. Ramallah's security forces have been discreetly tackling the worrying spread of illegal weapons. The crackdown on illegal weapons isn't simply meant to pre-empt political violence, as there is a real possibility of future chaos fueled by armed gunmen.

Political violence is not new to the Palestinian scene. The violent Hamas takeover of Gaza in 2007, after the group won the legislative elections, is perhaps the most well-known example, but it's not the only one. In the lead up to the 2021 elections and during the short-lived candidate-registration campaign, incidents of violence have been reported, including several targeting Fatah candidates. While those were relatively limited, there's no reason to expect that similar incidents won't happen again in the future, particularly if the existing rifts between the various factions grow even deeper over the course of the coming years. In areas that are now 'out of control,' such as the Balata or Jenin refugee camps, illegal weapons grew rampant, leading to increasingly deadly scuffles with criminal groups, up until the PA could barely operate in these areas.

***

This is a catastrophic scenario for Israel. At best, it raises the possibility of deep instability, unrest and violence for the decades to come. At worst, this mix of explosive factors could turn latent internal struggles in the West Bank into an actual civil war.

Israel will not be able to stay on the sideline of a conflict and will be pulled in. The geography of the West Bank and Israel makes it impossible for Israel to hesitate. This is something that many outside observers may not realize until they've visited the region and seen just how small this highly disputed area really is. If you were to drive from Nablus (deep in the West Bank) to Tel Aviv, you'd pass a point that ties everything together.

From this point, near the Israeli settlement of Alfei Menashe close to the Green Line and near the Palestinian city of Qalqiliya, you can see almost all of the Israeli coast, from Haifa to Ashkelon. A mere 15 kilometers separates the West Bank from the nearest coast, near the bustling high-tech hub of Herziliya.

In 2002, a Hamas-linked suicide-bomber carried out the deadliest bombings of the Second Intifada. He detonated his explosives inside a hotel in the city of Netanya, as guests were celebrating the Jewish holiday of Passover. Thirty were killed and nearly 150 wounded in what became known as the 'Passover Massacre.' What's just as striking is that the terrorist responsible for one of the deadliest attacks Israel had ever faced only had to walk from Qalqiliya to get to his target.

Israel has no space to wait and see what may come out of periods of instability or even civil war in the West Bank. A broad security collapse in the West Bank would raise significant threats to Israel. Should Hamas take over the West Bank, for instance, the group could easily turn these areas into launching pads for regular missile attacks. Except this time, cities like Netanya, or even Tel Aviv and its dense suburbs, would become the 'new' Sderot. In Sderot, an Israeli city near Gaza, residents have only seconds to run to the nearest shelter, meaning that every building in the city, from schools to bus stops, either has to have a bomb shelter or effectively is a bomb shelter itself. Tel Aviv would become the new Ashdod and its suburbs the new Ashkelon, two cities that suffered the brunt of Hamas's and the Palestinian Islamic Jihad's attacks during the 2020 and 2021 conflict.

Hamas could easily target the Ben Gurion Airport: the group did try to 'close the skies' of Israel multiple times in 2020 and 2021. But this time, these would not simply be words, given how close the West Bank is to Israel's main international airport.

***

The possibility of a broad collapse in the West Bank is also an important factor behind the paralysis of the PA. The current leadership in Ramallah knows very well that Israel has no interest in seeing the PA fall or of it being severely undermined. Even under the various Netanyahu mandates, the Israeli prime minister made sure to never truly endanger the integrity of the PA. He certainly toed the line and made it sound like each concession he made to Ramallah was under the guns of Washington to pander to his right-wing audience. But when the PA was on the verge of collapse, he authorized the transfer of the funds needed to cover expenses. He made sure to appear reluctant to do so, but he understood a truth about the unhealthy codependent relationship between Israel and the PA: a weak PA is better than no PA at all. He also felt that a strong PA was not in Israel's interest, as we'll discuss later in this book.

This truth has led the Palestinian leadership to increasingly wave the possibility of a 'doomsday' scenario where the PA would cease to exist to threaten Israel and extract concessions. Several

Palestinian officials have openly spoken about the possibility of withdrawing from the Oslo Accords or from parts of it. How this would work in practice remains quite vague, and is perhaps deliberately so, as most of those officials are simply making veiled threats. Withdrawing from the Oslo Accords would mean dismantling the PA, stopping the security coordination between the Palestinian security forces and withdrawing the Palestinian recognition of Israel.

The first two steps would have drastic consequences, forcing Israel to take responsibility for the nearly 3 million Palestinians who reside in the West Bank and to reoccupy major urban cities in the West Bank. The past two years, between 2022 and 2023, have given us a small taste of what this would look like: as Israeli operations in major Palestinian cities spiked, so did the number of militant attacks and deaths. The year 2022 was the deadliest for Palestinians since the Second Intifada—including both civilians and gunmen—and 2023 has been even worse. If the PA were to cease to exist, Israeli operations in the West Bank would grow, and a cycle of violence that's already difficult to stop would push both sides to the brink of another major confrontation.

The Palestinian leadership, including Abbas, is very much aware of this. Their threats are of course taken for what they are: a bluff. Dismantling the PA would amount to declaring Abbas's leadership a massive failure. His legacy would be to have put the final nail in the prospect of creating a Palestinian state through diplomacy rather than violence.

Even stopping the security coordination between Israel and the PA is extremely dangerous for Abbas. The Israeli army effectively acts as a bulwark against the rise of Hamas. Israeli forces have continued to arrest Hamas operatives and dismantle Hamas networks, not out of support for Abbas, of course, but in a way that helps him nevertheless. The minute Israel stops doing so, either the PA takes its stead, with the risks of creating even more divides between Palestinians, or they stop and give a free hand to Hamas—which is how Hamas climbed to power in Gaza.

***

The post-Abbas era is riddled with dangers for Palestinians and Israelis. The new Palestinian leadership will be faced with a stark choice. It may decide to continue Abbas's policy, pretending that the Oslo Accords are still alive while acting as little more than a glorified municipality. This carries the risk of placing more pressure onto an explosive situation that won't dissipate with time. Abbas at least had the legitimacy of being picked by Arafat, whose centrality in the Palestinian struggle was indisputable. Without a clear vision for the Palestinians' future, chances are that Abbas's successor will be challenged by those who do and have even less control than the PA does today.

Alternatively, the new Palestinian leadership may choose to pressure Israel through violence, 'peaceful resistance' or by declaring the collapse of the Oslo Accords and the PA. Barghouti himself made his opinion known when he said he felt 'Oslo was the greatest idea Israel ever had' as it 'let them continue the occupation without paying any of the costs.' Many Palestinians likely agree with him, though killing the Oslo Accords falls short of actually representing a vision of what the Palestinians' future would be without them. Some commentators have promoted the idea of a binational state, one that would see Palestinians and Israelis become equal citizens of a single state. But it's clear that this option still has few supporters on the Palestinian side and even fewer on the Israeli one.

All of these options present a significant risk of violence, be it because the Palestinian leadership will be unified by a new figure that will promote various pressure tactics or for the very reason that no unified leadership will emerge, leaving a void to be filled by warring factions.

At this critical moment, when the transfer of power is made, Israel will have a critical choice, of either presenting itself as a partner for peace or continuing to deal with the Palestinian issue solely as a security problem.

It will not be up to Israel to decide who will replace Abbas, or to salvage the PA. But Israel will have a choice to make, using the remaining years of Abbas's rule either to foster a change in public attitudes towards the peace process or to return to a policy of ignoring and even marginalizing the PA. This policy has long been that of Prime Minister Netanyahu, who has been criticized both inside and outside of Israel for lacking a vision and being mostly a 'status quo' premier. But I'd argue that his vision (whether right or wrong) is not short-termist but is in fact drawn from the very core of the Israeli right-wing ideology, and one concept in particular: the Iron Wall.

12

ISRAEL'S IDENTITY CRISIS

Protests in Israel in 2023 against a proposed judicial overhaul have put a spotlight on Israel's identity crisis. This 'judicial coup,' as it was named by its opponents, introduced a series of reforms aimed at reducing the power of the judicial branch and its ability to strike down laws and government decisions. In a system with few established checks and balances, the reform was seen by many Israelis as a way to rein in the main one, namely the Israeli Supreme Court. The court, through a process of judicial review, was viewed as guaranteeing that the broadly agreed-upon principles of the political game in Israel, and the nature of the state itself, would be respected. For Israelis who descended onto the streets for months, this was a 'door opening' move by one of Israel's most radical governments, a move meant to pave the way for other changes.

By any measure, this crisis is unprecedented. Never has the reality of Israel as a democracy been threatened from within. Nor have Israeli military reservists ever before threatened not to show up for military duty.

The unprecedented nature of the crisis is, however, deceptive, in that the crisis behind these dramatic developments has existed ever since the creation of Israel and in fact even before. It will also continue even after this moment has passed, because the fundamental factors behind the crisis will deepen rather than ease.

The tension comes from Israel's very nature as a Jewish and democratic state. This mere definition is a challenge in many ways, raising the question of whether Israel can in fact both remain democratic and Jewish. Segments of the Israeli population disagree on where to put the emphasis: Should the state focus on being democratic even at the cost of its 'Jewishness'? Or should it first and foremost protect its unique character as a Jewish state, sacrificing some of its democratic ideals? Even the nature of what a Jewish state is or should be is a matter of controversy: Is it a state for Jews—raising the question of the status of minorities— or a state ruled by Jewish religious laws (Halacha)? The multi-layered definition of what a 'Jew' is, whether it refers to someone belonging to the Jewish people, or one strictly limited to religion, certainly doesn't help.

These questions have never been truly resolved and have been left by the wayside for the sake of confronting a 'tough neighborhood.' Nothing embodies this identity crisis more concretely than Israel's lack of a written constitution, one that would clearly state and arbitrate between the various pillars of its own nature.

The 1948 Israeli Declaration of Independence did state that Israel was to draft a constitution by 1 October 1948, but the can was kicked further down the proverbial road: in 1950, the Israeli parliament decided that Israel would rule on a constitution 'chapter by chapter' rather than as a whole. From the first such chapter, or Basic Law, passed in 1958 (the Knesset) to the latest, namely the controversial Nation-State Law, passed in 2018, Israel is theoretically still writing its constitution, chapter by chapter.

Yet in this process, the mere concept of what a constitution is or should be got lost. Israel's 'Basic Laws' do not have the same status as an actual constitution and can more easily be changed. Most can be changed through a simple majority of sixty-one votes out of 120 in the Knesset. In fact, they have been changed for purposes as mundane as to allow a rotation between a prime minister and alternative prime ministers, or to award some ministerial powers to deputy ministers. The concept of judicial review, namely the Supreme Court's ability to strike down laws that do not conform to Basic Laws—a procedure the Netanyahu government sought to water down significantly—only emerged relatively recently in Israel's history. The Israeli Supreme Court came to it reluctantly until the 1990s, taking on a firmer role as the arbiter of Israel's quasi-constitutional laws in 1992. This led to a bizarre situation in which the role of the Basic Law was elevated and placed above others, yet without explicitly stating it, nor protecting those laws through tighter procedures.

Beyond that, there are some within Israel who have argued that regardless of the legal situation, Jewish religious laws are above any laws of the state. That's not to mention the fact that a segment of the Israeli law is religious: family law in Israel is governed by a mix of religious and civilian laws that give judicial power to religious courts. Civilian weddings do not exist, and divorces are settled in front of religious courts. Although rabbinical courts only govern a very limited segment of the broader corpus of laws, their mere existence is, for some, a step in the right direction, while it is too much for others, who prefer to marry outside of Israel.

Several changes have put even more strains on the gap created by a lack of agreement on these inherent tensions. Israel is still wrestling with the results of the 1967 victory, which left it in charge of a significant Palestinian population, as well as demographic changes, including the arrival of more religious minorities from North Africa and an ongoing demographic boom.

These questions were not dealt with initially because of a sense of urgency, and perhaps a lack of understanding of how important they would be in the future. But time hasn't made them less divisive, nor will it in the future. Israeli governments are starting to take over and fill this space, left vacant for decades: in 2018, the Netanyahu-led government passed a Nation-State Law that can best be described as a new preamble to a future Israeli constitution, one that has alienated Israel's minorities who felt it more clearly boxed them in as second-class citizens.

In 2023, the new right-wing government led by Netanyahu created a new 'Authority for National Jewish Identity.' The government also set up a new Jewish identity branch within the Israeli Ministry of Education. Both of these entities were slated to be headed by far-right religious figures with a narrow vision of said identity. Unsurprisingly, this raised concerns that Israel was going to redefine what it viewed as a Jew—a question most Jews themselves can't settle, as some choose to put more focus on the religious, cultural and national identities mixed within it. The joke 'two Jews, three synagogues' has always been true, and attempts to box Jews in, while leaving others to the side, is no laughing matter.

More clearly defining the Jewish identity would have a wide material impact on Israel both domestically and with regard to its relations with the wider world. The law of return, which defines who can receive Israeli citizenship, could be modified to more narrowly allow only those deemed to be Jewish by orthodox authorities to immigrate. Turning to a narrower religious vision of Judaism would also significantly damage Israel's relation with the American Jewish community, given the significant share of Reform Jews among them.[1] Given how important Israel's relationship with Washington is, this is no small impact.

***

Those questions were already relevant in 1948, and even before, as modern Israel emerged. They have yet to be tackled, and time has not made them easier to solve.

In fact, they will become both far more pressing and more complex as Israel's two main minorities, namely the religious ultra-Orthodox Jews and Israeli Arabs, grow and weigh on the democratic debate. This has also forced the largely silent secular-traditionalist majority to come out of its long slumber to defend its own identity. Not to mention that all of those separate segments within Israeli society are experiencing different types of identity crises.

According to a study by Israel's National Economic Council, by 2050 ultra-Orthodox Jews will represent around a quarter of the population. By the same year, Israeli Arabs will represent 20 percent of the total population. The political dynamic within those groups will, in turn, become far more relevant, including their position and ability to shape the narrative when it comes to the Israeli–Palestinian conflict.

With regard to the ultra-Orthodox or Haredim—the 'Fearful'—views of the conflict have changed drastically. For most of their history in Israel, the ultra-Orthodox parties have acted more or less as a lobby aimed at securing the economic welfare of their constituents and have been indifferent to any other political issue. The ultra-Orthodox view themselves as fighting to keep their identity, including by maintaining a clear separation from the rest of Israeli society.

In Israel, there is a spectrum of populations with different religious fervor, ranging from the secular to the staunchly religious and the traditionalists in between. One can easily study the size, style and color of the kippahs to establish who belongs to a certain stream of religious behavior (sometimes mixed with ideological beliefs). Yet because of this insistence on being separate from the rest of Israeli society, there is a divide between the ultra-Orthodox community and the rest of the non-Haredi Jews that goes beyond religiosity.

The Haredim have a difficult history with Zionism and the State of Israel, having largely opposed Zionism before it was created. This is in part due to the secular nature of the Israeli state, as well as the belief that Jewish sovereignty over Israel should only come with the arrival of the Messiah. Ultra-Orthodox parties have since embraced the State of Israel by putting an emphasis on preserving 'Jewish life' in the land of Israel. It is a different view from that of Zionism, which emphasizes establishing a national project in the land of Israel: ultra-Orthodox parties put the focus on preserving and fostering Jewish religious life in the land, with the democratic and even national project coming second. In other words, it has traditionally been less important for Haredi parties to preserve the State of Israel than what they see as the authentic pillar of Judaism, namely religious study and obedience to religious laws.

This has generally made ultra-Orthodox parties relatively indifferent to the Israeli–Palestinian conflict. Solving the conflict has never been at the top of their priorities. It also allowed for compromises and pragmatic views on the conflict. Rabbi Ovadia Yosef, one of the key political and religious figures of Israel's Sephardic Orthodox community, initially supported the Oslo Accords and joined Rabin's government for the sake of avoiding further conflicts. Rabbi Elazar Shach, another prominent figure influential among the Lithuanian stream within the ultra-Orthodox community, also took similar positions while also criticizing those among the Haredim who decided to live in settlements in the West Bank.

Without the support of the Sephardic ultra-Orthodox party, Shas, which was already chaired by its current leader, Aryeh Deri, it is unlikely that Rabin's government would have seen the light of day. The party's decision to abstain in the vote on the Oslo Accords in 1993 rather than opposing them paved the way for the implementation of the agreements.

Even before the accords, Ovadia Yosef had made his preference for life over land known. He came out in support of another controversial peace agreement: the peace agreement with Egypt that saw Israel relinquish control over the Sinai Peninsula. His religious argument was driven by a key principle in Judaism, 'Pikuach Nefesh,' which highlights the primacy and sanctity of life over all other principles. In Judaism, this principle states that human life comes first, and that any other religious principle can be disregarded if life is threatened. His view of the accords later changed as the signing of the agreement was followed by a wave of Palestinian attacks and as suicide bombers blew themselves up in Israeli cities.

But his position showed an emphasis on preserving life that could easily be called pragmatic, as opposed to the dogmatism outside observers may assume they would find when looking at the most religious community of Jews in Israel. Observers also generally assume that ultra-Orthodox Judaism has been fused with nationalism. While there is a strong religious-nationalist stream in Israel, the two do not necessarily mix well when it comes to the Haredi community—at least for now.

***

This relative indifference (or pragmatism) when it comes to the conflict is changing fast. Over the first two decades of the twenty-first century, religious parties have become staunch allies of Prime Minister Netanyahu and as such an instrument in his efforts to ignore the Israeli–Palestinian conflict altogether.

The ultra-Orthodox parties were not always allies of the right. Prior to becoming one of Israel's longest-serving prime ministers, and as Israel's finance minister, Netanyahu implemented ultra-liberal policies that alienated the ultra-Orthodox community. His rise to the premiership, however, saw him change strategy and curry the favor of those parties, understanding that they make near-perfect coalition partners: as long as their main concerns are dealt with, they rarely make any ask and act as dependable allies.

This alliance has been extremely beneficial to the ultra-Orthodox community, which plays an increasingly important role in Israeli politics. But this also carries with it the risk of changing the political nature of the community. Segments of the Haredi youth are increasingly espousing the ideology of the secular/conservative right and far right. The question of whether to support or remain indifferent to the State of Israel is becoming less and less relevant for younger Haredim whose parents and grandparents were born in Israel and have known no other reality.

In the 2022 elections, for instance, 10 percent of the votes in the highly religious town of Beitar Illit went to the far-right Otzma Yehudit list of Itamar Ben Gvir and Bezalel Smotrich, the two leading figures of the Jewish supremacist movements who became ministers in the Netanyahu-led government.

Smotrich himself, who is much more of a long-term thinker than the gun-waving Ben Gvir, saw the opportunity of expanding his electoral base by appealing to the more religious segments of the population. When he became finance minister, he claimed that his leading economic principle was the Torah. Citing a biblical verse that promises prosperity to those who obey God's commands, he said: 'If we follow the Torah, we'll be rewarded with financial abundance and a great blessing. That will be my economic approach.' As a finance minister, this certainly raised eyebrows. Yet it showed he was aware that the future of the Jewish far right was in this growing pool of young Haredim who may no longer listen to the promulgations of rabbis. The same disenfranchised Haredim who are looking at a new vision that more clearly embraces their identity not only as Jews but also as Israelis. Smotrich also showed he could still play on the field of more traditional religious parties, as he highlighted on multiple occasions his insistence on increasing stipends for Yeshivas.

Some of the Haredi leadership took note of the trend. During the protest movement against Netanyahu's judicial overhaul, *Yated Ne'eman*, one of the leading papers of Degel HaTorah, a party representing the 'Lithuanian' stream within the ultra-Orthodox community, warned against participation in counter-protests planned in Jerusalem. The article, which was expressly approved by the party's rabbinical authority, did not have any qualms with the content of the protest itself but rather with Haredi participation in a protest called for by right-wing parties. The author denounced a growing trend that sees Haredim increasingly embracing the right-wing views of non-Haredi parties. The article did not pull any punches, suggesting that those who participate would lose their Haredi 'identity' or 'citizenship' and castigating those who listen to the 'little Kahanist' in themselves—a clear reference to the Jewish supremacist far right.

This also represents a quintessential dilemma for the Haredi community: as it grows, gets more involved in Israeli politics and society, it will also be subject to growing outside influence. The Haredi parties still do not know whether they want to influence the outside or be protected from it—and whether they can do both at the same time.

These are only limited and early signs of a potential shift in the Haredi population. But in the future, the battle to redefine (or maintain) the identity of the ultra-Orthodox population will likely accelerate because of their demographic weight. For instance, with the ultra-Orthodox population growing to be a significant minority within Israel, housing issues may easily become political ones. Haredim have already had to find other areas than the more traditional religious neighborhoods like Mea Shearim in Jerusalem or Bnei Brak in Tel Aviv. Settlements like Beitar Illit and Modiin Illit, which are situated just beyond the Green Line—the border that demarcates Israel from the disputed territories of East Jerusalem, Judea and the West Bank—are an example of what may happen in the future. Attracted by lower housing prices, ultra-Orthodox Jews are poised to increasingly cross the Green Line to populate settlements in the West Bank, less as a result of an ideological shift than an economic one. If this is the case, then the parties that represent them may no longer be able to maintain their relative indifference to the conflict or ignore it altogether. Those aspiring to represent segments of the ultra-Orthodox, including far-right Jewish supremacist parties, will also have an easier time doing so.

The prejudice against those who drop out of the main path, as well as the efforts of the traditional ultra-Orthodox leadership to keep their community as is, may slow this change. Those among the ultra-Orthodox who quit Yeshivas, either to work or because they are conscripted into the army, tend to be cast away even by their own families. They tend to be viewed as failures who did not manage to adapt to the authentic Jewish way of life and dedicate their lives to religious study.

But as the community grows, forcing a change, what may first be viewed as a 'second-class' or 'failed' Haredim may increasingly become an alternative way of life that better fuses strict religious observance with nationalism. What's more, the ultra-Orthodox leadership may find it harder to criticize right and far-right political parties than it does the mostly secular left and center left: their alliance with the Israeli right and far right makes any public criticism far more difficult. And while the Haredi community has built a narrative of suspicion against the state and the outside world, it will be increasingly difficult to extend this narrative to right-wing parties, as ultra-Orthodox political leaders are making deals with them on a regular basis.

This is not to say that the nature of the ultra-Orthodox community will change as a whole. But with most of Israel in the midst of a latent identity crisis, it would be wrong to assume that the ultra-Orthodox community is simply going to avoid it. This could have significant consequences for the identity crisis Israel is facing and whether it can maintain the already delicate balance between its Jewish and democratic character while also pushing Jewish supremacist parties beyond the confined limits they have recently broken out of.

***

The Arab Israeli minority in Israel is also facing its own crisis of identity, just as they are poised to play a more significant role in Israeli politics due to demographics and political changes.

This identity crisis dates back to 1948. Israeli Arabs are, by nature, caught between two worlds, conflicted between their Palestinian identity and their Israeli citizenship (for those who are citizens). Even the term 'Arab Israeli' (at times Israeli Arab) is not widely accepted. Some identify as Palestinians, or Palestinian residents of Israel, in part due to their rejection of Israel as a whole, or because they want to emphasize this identity and origin. Others fully identify as Israelis or as Israeli Arabs. According to a 2020 poll,[2] 51 percent of non-Jews in Israel identify as Arab Israelis, 23 percent as Israelis, 15 percent as Arabs and 7 percent as Palestinians. This identity is shifting: a year earlier, more than double the number of respondents identified as Palestinians and almost double as Arabs. The impact of COVID-19, which saw Jews and Arabs pull together, with the Israeli Arab minority being praised for their work in caring for the ill (a considerable number of Arab Israelis work in the medical sector), may also help to explain these results. There is also a generational divide between the younger generations, which are far more aware of their Palestinian identity, and older generations who are more likely to define themselves as Israeli Arabs. This is in part because of the emergence of social media, which has broken the physical and mental barrier that may separate them from Palestinians in the West Bank or Gaza.

Arab Israelis represent one out of five residents of Israel. Those living within what Israel considers to be its borders and having Israeli citizenship represent 17 percent of the overall Israeli population. This excludes Palestinian residents of Jerusalem who live in the eastern part of the city and hold the status of 'permanent resident' yet do not have full citizenship.

Like the Jewish population, the Arab Israeli minority can be divided along different fault-lines—some more relevant than others. Religiously, Arab Israelis are divided between a Muslim majority and the Christian and Druze minorities. There is also a noticeable divide between northern Israel and central Israel, where

70 percent of Arab Israelis reside, and the south, which includes mostly Bedouin minorities.

While the Druze community has largely embraced Israel,[3] with Druze serving in the Israeli army or voting for Zionist parties, for instance, other Arab communities are still deeply divided over how and whether to participate in Israeli politics and Israeli life.

Two key developments in the 2010s have affected this internal debate among the Israeli Arab minority in Israel.

The first is the breaking of a taboo over forming any kind of alliance or partnership with Zionist parties in the Israeli parliament. The four main Arab parties have a history of division but had generally remained united in rejecting any visible and lasting coordination with a Zionist party, at least publicly, and thus did not play a role proportional to their actual representation in the Knesset. This is not to mention that around a quarter of the Israeli Arab electorate generally does not vote in national elections for ideological reasons, due to their rejection of Israel.

Up to 2022, this rejection was mutual: most Israeli Zionist parties shied away from making deals with Arab parties (again, at least publicly), for fear of alienating part of their electorate—with the exception of far-left parties like Meretz.

The 2018–22 political crisis, which saw Israel go through five snap elections, forced Israeli parties to consider new strategies and to go beyond their comfort zones. Most notably, Ra'am, representing the more religious stream of the four Arab Israeli parties, decided to join the 2022 government formed by Bennett and Lapid. Even before this unprecedented decision, Arab parties played a role in efforts to unseat Netanyahu, while Ra'am itself pondered for a time whether to join the embattled Israeli prime minister. But this is also the result of a deeper dynamic that predates the 2022 turning point and will likely continue to impact Israeli politics. Part of the Israeli Arab public has been oscillating between hopes for better representation and disillusion with Israeli politics and their own representatives.

Part of the Arab Israeli public has felt that they would never be correctly represented in the Israeli system. This is a perception based on material evidence, including economic marginalization, poor quality of service in Arab municipalities when compared to others in Israel and the exponential rise of crime in the Arab sector and perceived lack of response from the Israeli police. But this has also turned into a self-fulfilling prophecy: lack of trust in the government and hopelessness when it comes to the mere possibility of change stifled voter participation in national elections.

However, with time, Israeli Arab voters have also acted increasingly out of self-interest to try to improve their socio-economic conditions. A portion of the Arab vote went to Zionist parties, including mainstream right and left parties who positioned Arab candidates on their lists. This was a disappointing experience, as Arab members of the Knesset were barely heard and failed to address the many grievances of the Israeli Arab community.

In 2015, an increase in Israel's electoral threshold from 2 to 3.25 percent forced the four Arab parties to do away with their electoral differences. The electoral change required more votes than some of the four parties could expect, putting them at risk of no longer being represented in the Knesset. Some felt the change was deliberately aimed to bar Arab parties from being represented. Either way, it had the opposite effect, as it led to the creation of the Arab Joint List between the four Arab parties. This represented the aspirations of a majority of Israeli Arabs who failed to see the ideological differences between the parties (divided between the Islamist Ra'am, communist-leaning Hadash, and two nationalist parties, Balad and the more moderate Tal led by Ahmad Tibi). The list garnered more than 80 percent of the Arab vote and secured thirteen seats in 2015 and fifteen seats in 2020—an unprecedented development in Israel's history.

But even this turned out to be disappointing. Although the Joint List became Israel's third party, its inability to participate in any ruling coalitions meant it was doomed to act from the sidelines. The four parties also quickly went back to political bickering.

***

The decision by Mansour Abbas of the United Arab List (Ra'am in Hebrew) to join the Bennett–Lapid government came on the heels of these disappointing experiments but wasn't necessarily less frustrating. Although Abbas secured significant funds to better the lives of Israeli Arabs, some of the money was never disbursed. Ayelet Shaked, a justice minister and one of the key leaders of Prime Minister Bennett's party, effectively torpedoed efforts to invest more significantly in Israeli Arab communities while shooting down one of the key projects sponsored by Abbas, which would have provided electricity to houses built without a permit—a major issue in Israeli Arab towns.

In many ways, Mansour Abbas was a trailblazer, gaining respect among Jewish Israelis by breaking several taboos, such as recognizing Israel as a Jewish state and speaking about the Holocaust. Even so, this was not enough for some. As Abbas made clear he was breaking with those taboos, Itamar Ben Gvir accused him of playing a 'cute Teddy Bear number,' which the far-right leader 'did not buy.' Although Ben Gvir is unlikely to have been convinced anyway, his distrust of Abbas likely echoed that of part of the Jewish Israeli public, who will never truly believe that Arab Israelis can make solid partners.

But perhaps more important is the fact his first tenure wasn't necessarily convincing enough to Israeli Arab voters. It did not break years of disillusionment. His game-changing decision to put a focus on the betterment of socio-economic conditions at the expense of a more ideological line did not pay off in a way that would legitimize the risk. Some may argue that his tenure was too short to truly make a dent in decades of neglect, but this argument is unlikely to convince most Israeli Arabs.

In the short term, it may well have shown that those deciding to abstain were right not to bother. The elections that followed the collapse of the Bennett–Lapid government showed decreased voter participation among Arabs, which could suggest most are disillusioned by this first governmental experience. At the same time, Ra'am, the only party out of the four that decided to participate in the previous government, did fare relatively well when compared to others. It also may have an edge, demographically: while Israeli Arab votes were mostly split between the various parties in northern and central Israel, in the Bedouin communities of the south 75 percent of the votes went to Ra'am in 2022. This is notable given that Bedouin communities are poised to represent a greater share of Israeli Arabs in light of the significant gap in the average number of children born to Bedouin families (around 5.3 in 2019) and the rest of Israel (closer to two).

A poll held after the Bennett–Lapid coalition collapse also showed that nearly 70 percent of Israeli Arabs wanted Arab parties to be in future coalitions.[4] However, the same polls also showed that the Israeli Arab community was almost evenly split over whether voting changes anything, and that a slight majority felt Abbas's decision had not paid off.

What's certain is that the de facto exclusion of Israeli Arab parties from Israeli politics is no longer a given. The trends I've described show that there is certainly a willingness to engage with the political scene, if only to better the lives of the Arab minority in Israel.

Whether Israeli Arab parties will successfully influence Israeli politics is key to Israel's future, particularly as these efforts come amid a second potentially transformational development: the sectarian riots of 2021, which the Israeli police commissioner called the worst in decades.

The riots broke out during the 2021 conflict with Hamas in Gaza, boiling over after weeks of tensions in Jerusalem that had already seen a spike in attacks by both Jewish and Arab Israelis in an already tense city. The violence was most visible in mixed cities with both Arab and Jewish residents. While some of them were at times touted as 'models' of Jewish–Arab integration, violent incidents of sectarian violence shattered this myth. In Lod, crowds of Arab residents burned cars, three synagogues and several shops. Other incidents of Arab violence were reported in Acre, Ramle and Haifa. In parallel, several strikes, including in the construction sector, were called by Palestinian trade unions, impacting Israel.

Jewish Israelis quickly joined the fray. One incident saw an Arab driver get beaten up, on live TV, in the city of Bat Yam south of Tel Aviv as a crowd of Jewish Israelis were making their way to the Arab-populated city of Jaffa. In Lod and Acre, Jewish Israelis also targeted Arabs, as well as symbols of coexistence. This led to the launch of an unprecedented policing operation in Arab-populated areas of the country. The operation, dubbed 'Law and Order,' saw the deployment of border police in several of those cities, with clashes widening and hitting Arab-majority cities, including Jisr az-Zarqa along the coast and the so-called 'Arab triangle'—an Arab-populated area close to the border with the West Bank that includes the city of Umm al-Fahm. A theater that promoted co-existence was torched in Acre, and a house firebombed in Jaffa.

***

These sectarian riots are sometimes referred to as the 'unity protests' or 'unity Intifada.' This reflects the perception—or perhaps more accurately the hope—that the protests represented a turning point. According to this narrative, the riots were the sign of a growing alignment between Arab Israelis, or in this case Palestinian citizens of Israel, and Palestinians. A manifesto was released online, arguing that Arabs from the river to the sea were 'one people and one society throughout Palestine.'

This is true to an extent. The riots were the sign of deep religious sensitivities surrounding the holy sites in Jerusalem and the longstanding perception that Israel has broken the status quo there. The Sheikh Jarrah controversy stemming from the expulsion of residents of several buildings in an area of East Jerusalem also resonated within the Israeli Arab subconscious: the expulsion evoked the 'Nakba' (Catastrophe) that saw many Palestinians become refugees during the 1948 Independence War in what most Palestinians believe was a deliberate effort to expel Arabs.

Although fears of a repeat are exaggerated, one can't blame the Israeli Arab public for unconsciously or consciously expressing or acting upon those fears: Jewish supremacists—including those who entered the Israeli government in 2023—have effectively advocated expelling Arabs. Far-right leader Bezalel Smotrich famously said that Israeli Arabs were 'citizens of Israel, for now at least.' On a deeper level, the ambiguity of the Jewish nature of the state also contributes to those fears.

These issues won't disappear. This was perhaps the most significant such outburst but not the first: the Second Intifada in the 2000s also led to riots, and so did more specific issues related to Bedouin communities in the south.

It is not clear that these fears represent enough of a unifying factor to claim that the geographic and mental division between those living in Gaza, the West Bank, Jerusalem and Israel has now been shattered. No similar riots were seen during other rounds of violence between Israel and Gaza-based factions, nor during spikes in tensions in Jerusalem.

But there are unifying factors, and they will be accentuated or eased depending on whether Israeli Arabs are able to weigh in on Israeli politics. The 'unity Intifada' narrative may also push radical groups like Hamas to show even more inflexibility, as it believes the chances have increased of reconquering Palestine 'from the river to the sea.' Radical Palestinian groups may seek to destroy what they see as the 'gray area'[5] that allows Israeli Arabs to live a life as both Arabs and Israelis.

What is notable is that this eruption of violence came just as Ra'am, through the voice of Mansour Abbas, ran a campaign that explicitly advocated joining a ruling coalition—which he eventually did after temporarily pausing negotiations due to the violence. This raises the question of whether other factors may have influenced this spike in violence, including a reaction to the decision to join the coalition, which may have deepened the internal debate within the Israeli Arab community.

Israeli Arabs are fighting a different struggle from the Palestinians: while the Palestinians have sought statehood, Israeli Arabs have sought equality within an Israeli state. The past decade and a half has shown that there is a thirst among a broad segment of the Israeli Arab public for participation in Israeli politics. They have also shown that failures to integrate will accentuate the pull of those arguing Israeli Arabs will never be Israelis and should embrace efforts to eradicate the 'Zionist state' altogether.

***

These demographic trends will pile upon existing divides that compound Israel's identity crisis. On the one hand, the democratic influence of the secular-traditionalist majority in Israel is poised to be challenged by the growth of the Arab and ultra-Orthodox communities. On the other hand, the weight the secular-traditionalist Jewish majority bears, be it with regard to military service or their contribution to the state budget, will increase. This is a topic in itself, often dubbed the 'sharing of the burden' (i.e. the burden of serving in the army, paying taxes etc.).

By design, military conscription in the ultra-Orthodox and Arab sectors is limited, as both Arabs and ultra-Orthodox are exempt from military service. There are significant exceptions, including an increase in the number of ultra-Orthodox who do serve in specific units, including Nahal Haredi, or even elite units outside of it. Druze serve in the army, and a portion of the Bedouin community volunteers for service, generally being drafted into the Bedouin scout unit. But overall, the 'burden' of serving in the military largely falls on the secular-traditionalist majority.

In terms of fiscal burden, in a country where taxes are relatively high and disparities in salary particularly high (including between Israel's 'start-up nation'/tech sector and the rest), the secular majority will increasingly bear an outsized portion of the fiscal weight.

These disparities may change and won't always follow the broader secular versus religious fault-line. In fact, an increasing number of ultra-Orthodox, particularly women who are generally the breadwinner of the familial unit, are taking high-tech jobs. The overall number of ultra-Orthodox who participate in the workforce has also increased dramatically over the past two decades: in the early 2000s, only one out of three ultra-Orthodox men and half of the women were employed, whereas since around the mid-2010s half the men and more than three-quarters of ultra-Orthodox women participate in the workforce. Yet this trend has now largely plateaued. Though employment rates between Haredim and non-Haredim have converged, there is still a significant gap.

This will raise the question of whether the state can and will make-up for the resulting financial gap, or let employment rates mechanically increase, as the percentage of ultra-Orthodox in Israel continues to grow.

To be clear, both possibilities are not exclusive, and a mix of workforce integration and rising state subsidies is the most likely scenario. But this is a recipe for societal tensions, particularly when considering how the Israeli political system encourages clientelism, giving outsized weight to minorities within governmental coalitions.

This was particularly clear under the Netanyahu-led government that was formed in December 2022: in May 2023, the religious and far-right-backed Israeli government passed a budget that included significant handouts for religious students and cities, as well as one of the highest amounts of discretionary funds allocated to Netanyahu's coalition members. A record-breaking 14 billion shekels (1.5 percent of the budget and more than the budget for higher education) was disbursed by the state for discretionary use by members of the coalition. This is more than four times the amount of previous discretionary funds. These funds were meant to ease growing tensions between the Israeli prime minister and his partners, including religious parties who had sought to pass a new military exemption law for Yeshiva students.

They also included significant additional spending for the Yeshivas, and for ultra-Orthodox institutions not regulated by the Education Ministry and that do not teach topics such as math or science. This is despite multiple warnings that Israel needs to find a way to better integrate ultra-Orthodox into the economy. According to economic forecasts, Israel stands to lose around 5 percent of its GDP in a decade should it not better integrate ultra-Orthodox into the workforce and double that in twenty years. These forecasts should warrant some realization that the Israeli 'start-up nation' and economic miracle isn't guaranteed in the future.

The opposition rightfully described the spending as a bribe, but it is a bribe that is very much incentivized by the system. Although Netanyahu's main opponent, Yair Lapid, criticized the system, he did not change it during his tenure as prime minister, perhaps because the Israeli political system, which relies on proportional representation, encourages such practices.

The question is whether the secular-traditionalist majority will start acting like another minority, one that seeks to defend its interests in the same way that other minorities do, or continue to be largely divided between right and left. The secular–religious divide has long been discussed and certainly plays a role in Israeli politics. But among the secular-traditionalist majority, the right/left divide largely prevailed over any such consideration.

This may no longer be the case, not because the right versus left divide has disappeared but because the secular versus religious divide has gradually taken precedence. And like the rise of the ultra-Orthodox, some parties are betting on this divide. Avigdor Lieberman, for instance, who traditionally appealed to the Russian minority, took a largely anti-religious turn to attract voters beyond his typical electorate—with limited success. Lapid, the leader of the center-left Yesh Atid, also began his political career questioning the perceived lack of equality between secular Israelis and ultra-Orthodox.

More importantly, the protest movement triggered by Netanyahu's planned judicial overhaul was the first sign that this secular-traditionalist majority, long silent, was becoming aware of the need to defend the model it feels is best suited for the country. For the first time, broad segments of the Israeli population realized that democracy needed to be defended, and that there was in fact an alternative model to the liberal society they've lived in. This model was that of a conservative-driven anti-liberal movement, one that views enshrining the supremacy of the Jewish majority as critical to the survival of the state—even if this means tampering with democracy.

This may be a turning point in Israel's history, as the anti-government protests can be seen as a 'big bang' for political groups defending Israel as both a Jewish and democratic state. Although the passing of one of the various reforms put forth by Netanyahu in July 2023 can be seen as a setback, the impact of the protest movement may be far broader. The crisis has seen a flurry of new grassroots groups emerge, from the Kaplan Force[6] to the 'Brother in Arms' movement of military reservists, or the 'high-tech workers against the reform.' Those groups were created for the purpose of organizing protests and planning joint actions, yet they also turned into independent platforms for discussions. This political 'big bang' can be compared to the 2011 'Social Justice' protest movement, which denounced the high cost of living in Israel and propelled new leaders and local parties. Although the social justice protest did not significantly alter the political landscape in Israel, it certainly gave an impetus for parties to focus on the economy and the high cost of living. The wave of weekly demonstrations denouncing the judicial reform in 2023 are more far-reaching in that they materialize and are a more concrete expression of the non-religious majority's need to defend their vision of Israel—one that may indeed need to be defended in the coming decades.

This was also the first time Israelis started to explore and get more intimately acquainted with the ins and outs of Israeli democracy, beyond the periodical—but increasingly frequent—elections. Average Israelis got an in-depth look at the power of the Supreme Court, the inconsistent nature of Israel's Basic Laws, the appointment process of judges and the importance of legal advisors within government ministries.

They discovered that what they may have taken for granted, Israel's democracy, was built on moving grounds, rather than stable pillars. For the first time, Israelis truly became interested in the rules of the game and how those rules may be bent to the point that the table itself may break.

***

The crisis of identity is independent from the Israeli–Palestinian conflict in the sense that it would exist even if the conflict was solved. But it isn't separate: the Israeli–Palestinian conflict has at times deepened this crisis, and this identity crisis serves to either fuel or ease the conflict.

In many ways, the impulse of the practitioner or thinkers of the peace camp comes from this crisis. Leaders like Rabin, who signed the Oslo Accords, Sharon, who oversaw the Gaza disengagement, or Olmert and Livni, who participated in some of the previous far-reaching efforts to reach an agreement with Palestinians, were all in one way or another motivated by this crisis.

All of them had concerns over whether Israel could remain both Jewish and democratic while ruling over another people. All of them saw separation—in the form of an agreed-upon process or a unilateral one—as a way to preserve this delicate balance. Demography was one of the key drivers of their decision-making: without some form of separation, Israel would have either had to lose its Jewish nature, as Palestinians would form a majority, or its democratic nature, as those ruled by Israel would not have the same rights.

Those in favor of peace talks argued that if Israel is to preserve its Jewish majority while also remaining democratic, then creating a Palestinian state was not an option so much as the only option available. This argument conveyed the message that those supporting peace were not only pragmatic but realists.

This is nearly the opposite of the image the peace camp has among growing segments of the Israeli population today. The idea of peace has shifted from a pragmatic concept meant to solve a factual issue to a romantic idea that will never materialize, with those who hold such views being seen as naive at best, or at worst as traitors who are not interested in preserving Israel's Jewish nature.

There are a number of reasons why this trend is unlikely to disappear in the future. The first relates to the sidelining of the conflict with Palestinians in Israeli media and in the political scene. Israelis voted five times between 2019 and 2023. In these five elections, views on the Israeli–Palestinian conflict never played a critical role. The polarization around the pro- and anti-Netanyahu camps certainly played a role in masking other issues, but regardless political parties rarely put forth their views on how to solve the conflict as a key selling point.

Even in a post-Netanyahu era, it's not clear that this will change. There are other deeper factors that explain why Israeli society has moved away from this pragmatic view of peace.

One of them has to do with interaction with Palestinians. Most Israeli Jews can be divided into two in this regard, the first being those who live within Israel's Green Line, who have virtually no interaction with Palestinians, and the others who live in the West Bank and view Palestinians with suspicion. The erection of the security barrier—which is at times a fence, at times a wall— has led to a noticeable reduction in Palestinian attacks inside the

Green Line, but it has also added to the existing separation of the two people.

The second has to do with how Israelis view democracy. While most Israelis, including Israeli Jews, say they want the country to remain a democracy, they also generally agree that Jews should have 'more rights' than others and do not appear to see this as a contradiction.

The Israeli Democracy Index, published by the Israeli Democratic Institute (IDI), notes a consistent trend in this regard: according to the IDI, since 2018 the share of respondents who agree with the statement that 'Jewish citizens of Israel should have more rights than non-Jewish citizens' has climbed consistently, from 27 percent in 2018 to 49 percent in 2022. Another 2020 poll showed a large majority of Jews agreed or somewhat agreed with the statement that to be a 'real' Israeli, one must be Jewish.[7]

This reflects a major misconception about what a Jewish state should be, one that will have consequences in the future. It is also one that may be entrenched in the future, given how divided Israeli education is between various branches and 'tribes.' Not all of those branches put the same emphasis on democratic principles.

More broadly, there is a clear decline in the number of Israelis who think Israel can, in fact, be both Jewish and democratic. This has always been a difficult balancing act, but the disillusionment with the idea of an equilibrium between the two is concerning. It may encourage segments of the population to pick sides between a democratic Israel and an alternative some analysts have dubbed 'Judea,' a biblical reference to the Kingdom of Judea.[8] This is still very much a theoretical divide, but it is one that has become relevant to describe this multifaceted crisis of identity, one that may either be resolved or accentuated.

How this crisis of identity plays out will have far-reaching consequences, both domestically, with regard to the Israeli–Palestinian conflict, and beyond. The idea that Israel can advance normalization and ties with the Arab world while its 'backyard is on fire'—as the US ambassador described it—is doubtful. Similarly, Israel's enemies, including Iran, have clearly been emboldened by the crisis Israel experienced in 2023. Attacks guided by Iran took advantage of what the Islamic Republic saw as an inherent and festering weakness. The Iranian supreme leader, Ayatollah Ali Khamenei, even went so far as to boast that, given the situation in Israel, the 'Zionist entity' would no longer exist a decade from now.

This is risible, coming from a country that has so evidently failed its own population. Yet the crisis in Israel is real, and the nature of Israel, as a state and an identity for its citizens, is a question rather than a fact. If looking from the outside, Israel is a ship in a storm, looking from the inside, it is also a ship in a storm, with a storm in the ship.

13

THE PATH OF DESPAIR AND DISILLUSION

In 2017, as President Trump was preparing to formally recognize Jerusalem as Israel's capital, many analysts and journalists were predicting that chaos would ensue—a chaos that would not only engulf Jerusalem, Israel and the Palestinian territories but also the region as a whole. The reasoning was that, by doing so, President Trump was crossing a red line, one of the many theoretical red lines in the region.

The proverbial 'Arab street' would not let that pass, and violence was sure to break out across the region. After the announcement, the Arab League promptly released a statement warning that Trump's announcement 'deepens tension, ignites anger and threatens to plunge the region into more violence and chaos' and declared that it would seek to have the announcement condemned by the UN Security Council—which unsurprisingly did not happen given that Washington has veto power. Hamas released the usual statement indicating that by recognizing Jerusalem as Israel's capital and moving the US embassy, formerly situated in Tel Aviv, to Jerusalem, Washington was 'opening the gates of hell.'

The subtle metaphor of fire erupting was also used by the leader of Israel's far-left party, Meretz, who warned the move could spark an 'unnecessary explosion,' and by the head of the Arab Joint List (a coalition of four Arab Israeli parties that existed at the time), who called President Trump a 'pyromaniac who could set the entire region on fire with his madness.' Opinion pieces denouncing the catastrophic consequences of the move descended upon Western media outlets, with longtime Middle East commentator Robert Fisk claiming that 'mad presidents do mad things.'

The US embassy issued security advice and recommended that its staff avoid the Jerusalem Old City, a typical hotspot for violence—particularly the Damascus Gate, which has seen multiple stabbings over the years.

Yet, to most commentators' surprise, the Palestinian response was limited. Protests did erupt in the West Bank, rockets were fired, but to any longtime observer of the conflict, this really could have been any other week in the region. The explosion so many had predicted did not materialize.

On cue, pro-Israel Hasbara commentators claimed that,[1] once again, most of the world had blown the threat of a 'Palestinian explosion' out of proportion. Trump's move, they explained, was a simple recognition of an actual fact: Jerusalem is indeed the capital of Israel.

Beyond the commentaries, and the narrative warfare that has long plagued this conflict, the lack of a Palestinian response was in fact quite notable. The American declaration showed that Washington was moving away from a diplomatic formula that had become the norm, decades after Washington had played such a critical role in brokering the Oslo Accords. The lack of a Palestinian response was all the more striking, but perhaps not for the reasons commentators on one side, or the other, had highlighted.

Incidentally, the absence of Israeli rallies in the streets of Jerusalem or elsewhere was an unnoticed parallel to the muted Palestinian response. Sure, Israelis were pleased with the decision, but no one saw it as an earth-shattering moment, despite a clear effort by the Netanyahu government to depict it as such for bonus domestic points.

The Palestinian apathy matched that of Israelis. This is not good news.

This apathy is dangerous. It is the sign that neither side truly sees a solution to the conflict. For Israelis, the recognition of

Jerusalem as Israel's capital changes little. While Israel still engages in a substantial PR effort to boost its image, most Israelis have bought into the idea that nothing good will come from the outside world, and that the conflict with Palestinians will not be resolved by statements, recognitions and grand diplomatic gestures.

While the Oslo Accords deeply divided Israeli society, the US recognition of Jerusalem, which should have united all segments of the Jewish Israeli population, was met with half a smile at best—a shrug for most.

In 1993, Israelis were divided on peace. Two decades later, they are indifferent, and this is worse.

The same can be said of the Palestinians. What some Israeli and pro-Israel commentators saw as some sort of victory—the implicit admission that the Palestinians had 'lost the will to fight'—is the result of something far more dangerous: despair. It is not that Palestinians did not care, but rather that they have lost direction and a sense of how to turn anger into a political vision. In the previous chapter, I argued that the vision proposed by President Abbas, one that still pretends the Oslo Accords are alive and kicking, has flatlined before our eyes.

But the vision of his and Fatah's main rival, Hamas, has also failed to create any form of consensus. Hamas is also facing a crisis of its own. The idea that the group will eventually destroy Israel, or that it will 'drive the Jews' to the sea, has been proven, time and time again, to be unrealistic. Hamas has certainly improved its military capabilities and is now capable of firing more rockets and firing them deeper into Israel. It can use blueprints from Iran to carry out drone attacks. On 7 October 2023, it used all of those capabilities to capture Israeli towns and shatter the idea that Israel was safe.

But it got very little from the two last major rounds of violence in 2014 and 2021. After a two-month war in 2014 and an eleven-day conflict in 2021, the group has yet to offer a clear path to Palestinian statehood, or at least acceptable conditions in Gaza. The 2023 attacks also brought nothing but ruin to Gazans, and while they certainly blame Israel for the widespread destruction and death, there is so much misery that Hamas is sure to be blamed as well.

Hamas's own 'vision' is unclear and marked by deep internal contradictions. The 7 October attacks marked the bloody resolution of an inherent contradiction within the group. Since it came to power in Gaza, in 2007, Hamas has been torn between its two identities. On the one hand, there is Hamas's core identity as an insurgent and self-portrayed 'resistance' group. This is the group that fires rockets at Israel, the group that carries out terror attacks and the group that eventually murdered civilians on Simchat Torah. On the other hand, Hamas is also a political party, a government. This is the group that administers Gaza, is responsible for providing for the more than 2 million Palestinians living in the Gaza Strip. A group that wants to be viewed not only as 'one of the many' Palestinian factions but as the Palestinian faction that will, eventually, rule over Palestine—'from the river to the sea,' as the slogan chanted by many who ignore its meaning goes. In 2012, I discussed this issue with one of the Israeli intelligence officers who closely monitored Hamas, and he said something that turned out to be quite prophetic: when push comes to shove, if Hamas were forced to choose between these two identities, it would always pick its core identity as an insurgent group. If governing Gaza eventually meant undermining its image as a resistance group, then Hamas would return to what it was initially.

One of the leaders who sought to resolve this contradiction is none other than the mastermind of the 7 October 'al-Aqsa Flood,' as Hamas named it: Yahya Sinwar. Sinwar rose to power in 2017 after spending twenty-two years in an Israeli prison. He was viewed by some in Israel as a pragmatist, by others as a hardliner. When he was elected as Hamas's Gaza chief in a secret internal vote by the group, his popularity in Gaza was largely intact. He was not one of the corrupt Hamas leaders living in luxury outside of Gaza, nor was he one of the leaders who managed to live in (relative) luxury inside Gaza. His popularity was untouched by the slow erosion of Hamas's image in Gaza due to the group's inability to solve the economic and humanitarian crisis in the Strip and its growing reliance on violence and repression.

But he was very much aware of the contradiction and how Hamas's image as a resistance group had been tarnished by its inability to deliver as a government. He initially engaged in a new strategy, following the US recognition of Jerusalem as Israel's capital. Piggybacking on what was meant to be a series of peaceful protests, dubbed the 'March of Return,' he encouraged border riots. Palestinian protesters regularly held demonstrations near the Gaza fence, with Hamas using 'confusion units' to carry out attacks, including sending hundreds of incendiary balloons into Israel, placing IEDs along the border, carrying out sniper attacks and at times firing rockets. The goal was to put as much pressure on Israel while still staying below the threshold of war. But this, once again, led nowhere. Israel made limited concessions that were consistent with Netanyahu's own strategy, which was to keep Hamas afloat in Gaza—and thus keep the Palestinians divided.

Sinwar had even hoped that at some point he would be in a position to force Israel into a broader agreement: a *hudnah*, or religious truce. Such an agreement would freeze the Gaza theater for a decade. Israel would agree to significantly boost the fledging Gazan economy through the building of large infrastructure such as a seaport, new energy plants and so on. In exchange, Hamas would agree to stay 'quiet' in Gaza—though it likely would have continued to expand its operation in the West Bank, hoping to dislodge President Abbas. Under Netanyahu, Israel always made a point to pretend to consider this proposal only to eventually reject it or let it die a natural death. Netanyahu needed Hamas to survive but not to thrive.

At the same time, Sinwar explored a different option. A path of unity with Hamas's main Palestinian rival: the Fatah-controlled PA of Mahmoud Abbas. Sinwar was prepared to go to great lengths to secure a token unity government: he even offered a return of the PA to the Gaza Strip. The PA would take over civilian duties in the Gaza Strip, pay the salaries of the many civil servants Hamas has hired since it took over and thus make its symbolic return to Gaza. This was a significant offer, more than a decade after Hamas had literally thrown Fatah officials from the roof of Gaza's highest buildings.

But, of course, there was a catch.

Abbas saw through Hamas's offer and preconditioned any return of the PA to Gaza on the dismantling or reintegration of Hamas's military wing into Palestinian security forces. Hamas refused: this would defeat the main purpose of the offer, which was to protect Hamas's military wing. The 'model' Hamas proposed has often been described as the 'Hezbollah' model, as Hamas would retain all of the leverage over a powerless civilian authority. The return of the PA, in name at least, would give Hamas much of the freedom it lost when it became the de facto government of the Gaza enclave, by removing the need to care for Gazans. Hamas would have continued to fire rockets and carry out attacks, galvanizing Palestinians while letting the PA handle the consequences and accusing Ramallah of collaborating with the enemy.

Then came the last attempt Sinwar made at resolving Hamas's own contradictions. In 2021, he launched another operation, dubbed 'Sword of Jerusalem,' by firing rockets at Jerusalem at a time of extreme tensions due to the expulsion of Palestinians from a neighborhood of the city and tensions around the holy sites in the Old City. This led to an eleven-day war that Sinwar likely saw as a way to force Israel back to the negotiating table and break the geographic divide between Gaza and the West Bank. Hamas was no longer fighting for Gaza but for the whole of Palestine. It was launching a war in the name of al-Aqsa, a religious symbol of unity. It hoped that by doing so, Palestinians in the West Bank and Israel would rise up, embracing its vision of resistance. And in many ways they did. Riots broke out in Israel, Hamas colors were raised in Ramallah and chants praising Sinwar and Mohammed Deif—the head of the al-Qassam Brigades, the military branch of Hamas—were heard across the West Bank. But years later this had all but disappeared, and Hamas was still stuck inside a territory it was unwilling and unable to manage without moving away from what made it so successful in the first place—'resistance.'

In the same year, Sinwar was challenged directly by a little-known figure inside Hamas and only re-elected as the group's Gaza chief after several rounds of internal votes. This was a wake-up call for Sinwar. Four years after coming out of Israeli prison, with his popularity untouched, he had failed to bring about the radical change he had initially aimed to foster. Reports have suggested that the 'al-Aqsa Flood,' the Hamas 7 October massacre, may have emerged around that same period, aiming to return Hamas and the Israeli–Palestinian conflict to a state the Hamas leadership in Gaza preferred: a state of permanent war.

***

This is not to say that Hamas doesn't want a political role. These negotiations were the result of debates within the group over the best path to achieve political dominance in the Palestinian arena.

Hamas is effectively playing the long game, trying to first position itself as the sole representative of the Palestinians. This places it in a difficult position in the sense that it means Hamas's foremost enemy isn't necessarily Israel but Fatah. Hamas has effectively kicked the can down the road and postponed any debate on whether violence can truly achieve statehood for the Palestinians for the sake of replacing Fatah as the voice of the Palestinians.

The fragilities and latent crisis within Fatah and the Fatah-controlled PA, as well as the fact that Hamas is not viewed as a legitimate representative of the Palestinians by most, mean that the group has largely been given a pass on presenting its vision of the future.

The group has instead focused on less far-reaching objectives. Over the past decade, and even more so over the past two to three years (2021–3), the group has been less focused on Gaza and more focused on breaking the divide between the Palestinian enclave it controls and the West Bank.

When looking at the series of escalations that took place in Gaza over the 2010s and early 2020s, a growing pattern has emerged: most of them can be traced back to events in the West Bank and Jerusalem. The 2014 war can be traced back to the kidnapping and killing of three Jewish teenagers in the West Bank. This led to weeks of tensions as Israeli forces carried out operation 'Brother's Keeper,' one of the most extensive anti-Hamas operations in the area. Even to this day, Hamas is still looking to recover from this operation, using every tool it has to rebuild its presence in the West Bank despite regular Israeli and Palestinian raids. The connection is even clearer regarding the 2021 conflict, as Hamas took a decision to fire rockets at Jerusalem as tensions were simmering over the expulsion of Palestinian residents of Sheikh Jarrah, in East Jerusalem. Even Hamas's local ally, Palestinian Islamic Jihad, adopted this strategy, reacting to the arrest of one of its leaders in the West Bank in 2022 by issuing threats from Gaza, triggering a two-day conflict and firing hundreds of rockets in 2023 after the death of one of its former spokespersons in the West Bank, Khader Adnan, in Israeli detention.

The trend is clear: Hamas is seeking to break out of its isolation in Gaza and views the West Bank and Jerusalem as a theater that will be far more critical to its future. The group may be faring better than its counterpart in Ramallah, but that is a low bar and a deceptive conclusion. Although the group can certainly profit from acts of violence in the West Bank, it cannot control them.

***

This is because the real 'winner' of the increasing violence between Israel, Hamas and Fatah is despair. Neither Fatah nor Hamas is capable of fully directing or capitalizing on the Palestinian people's frustrations and anger. Neither of them has been able to seize some of the opportunities that have arisen to really build anything credible or offer a vision to replace the broken Oslo Accords. Violence may help Hamas stay afloat and certainly gives it an advantage in the long run, but violence has consequences that Hamas has been unable to mitigate. And while the group can fuel violence, it can't stop it or direct it in a way that gives the group actual leverage over Israel.

The waves of violence that Israel has experienced may have been fueled and sometimes triggered by Hamas, but they also often take on a life of their own. The 2015–16 'Knife Intifada' is a good example of this phenomenon. This series of attacks included several deadlier and more organized attacks, including a shooting attack inside a bus in Jerusalem and a shooting attack inside the Beer Sheva bus station, both of which may have been planned. Those high-profile attacks were also carried out by Palestinians in their thirties, as opposed to the vast majority of attacks carried out by Palestinian teenagers, with no clear militant background.

The wave of attacks was not the result of a decision by a single group. This is not to say that there was no incitement behind them, but the attackers were mostly what we're now accustomed to call 'lone-wolves,' that is, attackers with only tenuous connections to a militant group.

The cycle of violence also fueled itself, with one attack inspiring the next. Some attackers sought to avenge previous attackers killed by Israeli forces. Others even had family connections, lived in the same village or studied in the same school. In the era of 'virality,' copycat attacks have become a norm. This is a trend neither Fatah nor Hamas can control.

Israel also found those attacks more difficult to foil—they take little to plan and as a result are far more difficult to pre-empt. Much in the same way that lone-wolf attackers in other countries have generally flown below the radar of security services, Palestinian attackers have done so too. The Israeli security services subsequently got better at tracking potential attackers by using social media and flagging those who were posting speeches and posts that could point to an upcoming attack. The use of such tools may be controversial to outsiders, yet in Israel they've become quite common, for they are the only relatively effective tool to identify potential attackers. But they barely register in the long run.

In a way, this wave of Palestinian militants embodies the despair of their generation. They are disorganized and aren't acting in anyone's name but still generally reference nationalistic and religious reasons for their actions.

Where the first decades of Palestinian militancy were organized and carried out by ideologically indoctrinated individuals, this new wave of attacks is the product of a generation that has lost hope that anything will truly change and has turned to violence not in the hope of changing anything but as an end in itself.

The lack of leadership also rules out negotiations: the absence of a unified voice, or anyone to talk to, leaves the issue to be dealt with as a security rather than a political issue. We will see below that, while this trend of fragmentation in the Palestinian landscape has come naturally, it has also been encouraged by Israel.

***

The following years will offer an opportunity to break this dangerous slide towards despair and offer a new vision for Palestinians or solidify it by making violence the only alternative. Hamas's objective is clear: the group is seeking to become the sole representative of the Palestinians, eclipsing a weak and collapsing PA. It is fostering a return to a 'permanent state of war' from which it will eventually emerge on top—not necessarily as the victor defeating Israel but as the sole organization still capable of speaking in the name of Palestinians. By launching the al-Aqsa Flood, Hamas has effectively returned to its roots as an insurgent group.

Despair plays into the hands of those advocating violence because violence removes the need to offer an actual vision of what the future of the Palestinians looks like. Hamas will seek to build the critical mass it needs to give the final *coup de grâce* to the Fatah-controlled PA.

This is one scenario. Hamas bets that whatever replaces it in Gaza will be weak. While cynical, this is not unrealistic: the Israeli government has struggled to think or even plan for what will come after the military operation it launched in the wake of the Simchat Torah massacre. Some have advocated for a return of the PA, but this poses significant problems. The authority is weak, unable to control the territory under its supervision in the West Bank. It is also unpopular and viewed by many Palestinians as an extension of the Israeli occupation. Discontent has already erupted during the war, with some protesters in Ramallah who came to denounce Israel quickly turning their anger against Abbas.

If the PA returns to Gaza on the back of a deadly Israeli military operation, it will most likely reinforce all of the trends that have led to its current state of paralysis. To solve this, Abbas has made one key precondition: he would only agree to a return of the PA as part of a comprehensive peace effort. This demand is reasonable when considering the risk the authority would take if the path towards peace was still shut as it returns to Gaza.

That is of course if Israel allows it. Netanyahu has made it very clear he does not want the PA back in Gaza, infuriating Washington and many of Israel's remaining Arab partners, who backed this solution. Instead, Netanyahu has sought to explore more 'exotic' solutions. This includes a return of Abbas's archrival in Fatah, Mohammed Dahlan—a man who was kicked out of Gaza in 2007 and who has made a name for himself as an opportunistic figure with a penchant for shady deals, including an attempt to mend ties with Hamas while portraying himself as a rigorous anti-Islamist figure to his main backer, the UAE. Netanyahu has also explored a 'bureaucratic' government, either backed by the UN or by Arab countries. Some of his far-right ministers have explicitly called for the displacement of Palestinians. All of these solutions are a nightmare. Even without considering the moral aspect of displacing Palestinians, doing so would send shockwaves throughout the Arab world that could easily destabilize Arab regimes that Israel considers to be 'moderate.' Egypt and Jordan would be at risk of collapsing and being replaced by regimes that would likely break ties with Israel. The PA would likely disappear, giving way to a chaos Hamas would be able to exploit.

But Netanyahu is ready to risk this for the sake of continuing on his path of offering an 'alternative to peace.' This 'alternative to peace' has been formulated in action by Netanyahu. Although the Israeli leader is increasingly the slave of changing circumstances, as he is fighting for his own survival and legacy—and to remain out of jail, as the Israeli prime minister is also facing several trials on charges of corruption and bribery—there is in fact a philosophy that supports the policy adopted by the embattled Israeli prime minister.

This philosophy has long defined the Israeli right's view of the Israeli–Palestinian conflict and still does today: the Iron Wall.

***

Understanding the concept of the 'Iron Wall' requires looking back to a time before the birth of Israel. Ze'ev Jabotinsky, the father of Zionist Revisionism, theorized the concept in an essay of the same name in 1923 and then in a second called 'The Ethics of the Iron Wall.' Jabotinsky was responding to his main opponents at the time, namely left-wing Zionist figures. He became one of the intellectual and philosophical founders of the right wing in Israel. Netanyahu himself is the son of Jabotinsky's former secretary.

In his short essay, Jabotinsky was taking aim at the idea that the Arabs of Palestine and of the region in general would accept an Israeli state for the sake of economic development and prosperity. He was criticizing those he called the 'utopians' who believed that Arabs would sooner or later view Israel as a vector of prosperity and end up accepting it.

As he puts it in one of the most striking parts of his essay:

> To imagine, as our Arabophiles [left-wing Zionists] do, that they [Arabs living in Mandatory Palestine] will voluntarily consent to the realization of Zionism in return for the moral and material conveniences which the Jewish colonist brings with him, is a childish notion, which has at bottom a kind of contempt for the Arab people; it means that they despise the Arab race, which they regard as a corrupt mob that can be bought and sold, and are willing to give up their fatherland for a good railway system.

In hindsight, his criticism of left-wing Zionism was nothing short of prophetic. Jabotinsky saw the naivety of his political opponents, recognizing that, if the role were reversed, the Jewish people would not have abandoned what they would consider their lands for the sake of better infrastructure and comfort. Jabotinsky viewed and clearly described himself in that essay not as an idealist but as a realist. As he says: 'That is our Arab policy; not what it should be, but what it actually is, whether we admit it or not.' This a prescient criticism of the left-wing founders of the Israeli state, whose ideological forefathers thought there could be peace through development but who ended up fighting some of Israel's deadliest conventional wars.

Jabotinsky's criticism of the 'utopians' gave birth to the concept of the 'Iron Wall' or the 'Wall of fire': the view that Israel would never be accepted by its neighbors unless it became a real power, and that it would be in a state of 'perpetual war.' The Arabs, be it in what was called the Palestine Mandate at the time or the region as a whole, would not accept Israel, and Israel would need an 'Iron Wall' to defend itself against those that rejected it. According to Jabotinsky, '[i]t is only when there is no longer any hope of getting rid of us, because they [Palestinians/Arabs] can make no breach in the iron wall,' that there could be an agreement.

THE PATH OF DESPAIR AND DISILLUSION

The debate that led Jabotinsky to formulate his ideology regarding the conflict still shapes Israel's national narrative today. The two concepts of peace via economic growth and peace by strength are two seemingly opposite points in a line that encompasses most of the Israeli political spectrum. Some of Jabotinsky's criticism of the left also matches the criticisms of today's Israeli right, including his description of left-wing thinkers as 'utopians' who refuse to live in the real world.

But more importantly, it forms the basis of a narrative of 'survival through strength' that still permeates the Israeli right wing and even broader Israeli society as a whole. The 'Iron Wall' is the idea that Israel should never relent, and that through sheer strength and its continued ability to exist despite everything, it will ultimately vanquish Arab rejectionism. That Israel is now surrounded by walls and fences and created the 'Iron Dome' certainly serves that image of the fortress in an ocean of hostility, or as one former Israeli prime minister called it, the 'villa in the jungle.'

This explains Netanyahu's vision and his acceptance of the status quo. Jabotinsky theorized the idea of peace through power, and Netanyahu is one of his successors. In many ways, the Abraham Accords have further comforted the Israeli right in its perception that strength alone will be enough to break Arab rejectionism. After all, Israel had to give up little to get normalization agreements with countries that appear to realize that Israel is here to stay. This fits with the Iron Wall narrative and is a source of comfort for those who reject any sort of compromise with the Palestinians.

***

But Netanyahu's vision goes beyond the idea of an 'Iron Wall.' Jabotinsky was not against an agreement per se—he simply stated what he saw as the facts, that an agreement was impossible and that Arabs across the region would fight Israel. 'What is impossible,' he said, 'is a voluntary agreement': 'As long as the Arabs feel that there is the least hope of getting rid of us, they will refuse to give up this hope in return for either kind words or for bread and butter, because they are not a rabble, but a living people.' These words didn't rule out peace but placed any peace agreement in a distant future in which Israel's neighbors, as well as the Palestinians, would have accepted Israel as a reality that cannot be overcome.

Netanyahu's vision, and that of his ideological kin, is one where this distant peace does not exist, and one in which Israel actively acts to erode the parameters for peace. This explains a longstanding Israeli effort to marginalize the PA and maintain the divide between Hamas and Fatah as well as that between the West Bank and Gaza. In Netanyahu's mind, this serves as Israel's best asset, helping it fend off any pressure to agree to the resumption of peace talks. Should Israel be faced with pressure to negotiate a deal, it will argue that 'there is no partner for peace.' The Palestinian divide ensures the enduring defeat of the Palestinian camp for lack of legitimate and acceptable representation. In negotiations, two voices for one people is already too much.

This is also representative of the perception that time is on Israel's side. In a way, this is correct: Israel is becoming an economic power in constant development, while attention on the conflict declines as other regional and global issues take precedence.

Trump's peace plan was tied to this vision. Trump put things simply: the Palestinians lost and need to draw the consequences from this defeat. 'To the victor, the spoils' would have been a better name for the 'Deal of the Century' (or its official name, the Peace to Prosperity Plan). Paradoxically, Trump's plan also mixed right-wing beliefs that a 'winner had emerged' with the same naive hope the forefathers of the Israeli left supported by offering 'prosperity' in exchange for territorial concessions and an admission of defeat.

This childish vision was a caricature of Netanyahu's strategy but certainly not far from it. Incidentally, it also makes the exact same mistakes Jabotinsky saw in his left-wing opponents. It is based on the idea that somehow the Palestinians will at some distant point in time have to come to terms with their defeat. In the same way that the pre-Israel thinkers missed the possibility that Arabs would not abandon their identity and what they perceived as their land for the mere sake of economic prosperity, the right wing feels that somehow they will now be ready to swallow their alleged defeat. Effectively, this vision is one that counts on the rise of a Palestinian leadership that can accept an unfair settlement, despite clear proof that the Palestinian leadership has been unable to even consider what some would view as 'fair settlements' over the years. The current leadership, under President Abbas, has also shown that weakness is detrimental to a settlement. Only a strong Palestinian leadership can accept the compromises a fair deal would entail. Only a strong Palestinian leadership can secure public buy-in for those conditions—which is ultimately the only guarantee that such a settlement will hold in the future. Now imagine how strong, secure and popular the Palestinian leadership would have to be to go beyond necessary compromises to accept they have effectively 'lost.' It would require the kind of leadership we haven't seen so far. It would also effectively contradict the idea that the Palestinians have in fact 'lost.'

In many ways, the Trump Peace to Prosperity Plan gave us a vision of the future according to the most hardline view in Israel. It was a plan that marginalized and sanctioned the Palestinian leadership in Ramallah in a bid to convince them to accept a diminished state. It was also a vision that paved the way for the annexation of the West Bank, something Netanyahu himself understood as he pushed for a plan to annex parts of the West Bank.

It is unclear what this annexation plan would have entailed, though there was speculation that the Israeli prime minister was looking at annexing around 30 percent of the West Bank. The main idea was to use the lack of a united leadership and response to the plan on the Palestinian side to unilaterally annex the parts of the West Bank the agreement said would be Israeli.

The annexation plan never materialized. In the summer of 2020, amid signs that Netanyahu would go through with annexation, the UAE and Israel announced they would normalize ties. Abu Dhabi conditioned the agreement on guarantees that Israel would not go through with annexation, offering a win-win situation that both Netanyahu and the Emirati leadership could present to their respective audiences.

But this idea of taking unilateral steps is poised to re-emerge. With the conflict entering a long 'status quo' phase, Israeli leaders have been tempted to take unilateral steps that they feel are in Israel's interest for the sake of separating from the Palestinians. A direct line can be drawn between Sharon's decision to disengage from Gaza and Netanyahu's plan to annex the West Bank: both of them stemmed from the same perception—that the Palestinian leadership is incapable or unwilling to reach a settlement and would be unable to abide by one. As a result, Israel needs to take unilateral steps to disengage from areas where its presence is not sustainable and strengthen its presence in areas where it is. The temptation is to then withdraw beyond this 'Iron Wall' and let Palestinians fend for themselves.

The issue is that time and time again this idea of unilateral separation has shown its limits. The Gaza disengagement, which was unilateral and did not include any sort of engagement with the Palestinian leadership, directly led to the rise of Hamas. Similarly, unilateral measures in the West Bank are liable to benefit radicals within the Palestinian landscape, just as the traditional Palestinian leadership is facing a latent legitimacy crisis. The collapse of this traditional leadership, which is in part tied to Israel's unwillingness to re-engage and the Palestinian leadership's own failure to accept fair proposals, has in fact pulled Israeli forces deeper inside Palestinian cities. The number of Israeli operations in Palestinian cities like Nablus or Jenin has risen exponentially as the PA lost control over swathes of the West Bank. This is a symptom, for the illness is far more widespread.

But this vision has one key element: it requires little from Israel and from Israelis. It does not require any painful concessions or the agreement of a majority of Israelis—as a peace agreement would. It requires only inertia and indifference, two powerful forces. This is why the conflict with the Palestinians no longer ranks as a top issue in the many elections that have been held in Israel since 2015. This is also why Israelis may not have celebrated the US recognition of Jerusalem as Israel's capital, or the Trump peace plan, which was clearly tilted in Israel's favor. At this point, it is not that Israelis embrace the vision offered by proponents of the 'Iron Wall'; it's that they do not care anymore.

14

THE SPACE FOR HOPE IN A SHRINKING 'UNIVERSE OF POSSIBLES'

Looking at the future, several key scenarios could emerge in the coming decade. The first is the traditional two-state solution, with separate Palestinian and Israeli states. The second is the continuation of the status quo. The third is an Israeli move to annex parts or all of the West Bank, without giving the same rights to Palestinians as Israelis. The last one is the creation of an alternative to the two-state solution in the form of either a one-state solution or two states within a confederation.

Solutions to the conflict are rarely presented in that way to Palestinians or Israelis. A 2021 RAND study,[1] in which Palestinians from the West Bank and Gaza as well as Israelis were presented with similar paths led to depressing results, as most Israelis preferred the status quo, while most Palestinians found none of the solutions to be acceptable.

However, interestingly, merely framing the conflict in that way, with an eye to the future rather than the past, also changed each side's perceptions. The conflict is rarely presented in that way, with a look to the different future scenarios. Even an honest conversation on the topic rarely steers clear of devolving into endless arguments about the past in which each party tends to frame itself as the victim of the other.

All of the solutions mentioned earlier are problematic and often rejected when considered separately. They only become realistic when put together, as the overall 'universe of the possible.' Effectively, unless someone can come up with new creative endgames to the conflict, these are the only possibilities, whether parties to the conflict are ready to accept them or not. Expecting a new solution to appear with time, effort or violence is like throwing a six-faced dice and expecting the number seven to come out. The route to one of these endgames can be long, more or less painful, but the endpoints are there, unless the parties believe they can erase the other.

Perhaps the most likely outcome is the continuation of the status quo, though the dynamics I have discussed on both sides means that this would not truly be an endgame but a transitory phase for one of the other outcomes.

The dynamic we discussed in the Palestinian arena, namely the slow descent towards despair and radicalization, as well as the wave of unprecedented violence unleashed during the 7 October attacks and their aftermath, makes keeping the status quo unlikely, as the PA could collapse or be taken over by radicals advocating violence. Israel would likely continue to expand its settlements in a way that will make it even more difficult for Palestinians to envisage a viable Palestinian state.

There are currently more than 600,000 Israelis in the West Bank, beyond the Green Line. Most of them—an estimated 500,000 or around 80 percent—live in major settlement blocks situated close to the Green Line. These are not necessarily ideological 'settlers' as some may imagine—though living and staying beyond the Green Line is clearly a political statement—as many of them have been driven there by affordable housing prices and proximity to the main urban areas. This economic rather than political reality explains how 'successful' those settlements are in attracting Israelis when compared to the other smaller settlements situated deeper inside the West Bank.

More importantly, that most Israelis in the West Bank are living in close proximity to the border meant previous plans for 'land swaps' with a future state of Palestine were realistic—though not necessarily easy to sell to either side. According to the 2003 Geneva Initiative, for instance, Israel and a future state of Palestine would exchange less than 5 percent of their respective territories, all of which would be situated along the Green Line, making geographical and demographic sense.

But the realities on the ground are changing to the point that this idea of separation may no longer be viable. Since 2003, the number of settlements situated deeper inside the West Bank has increased. At least 100,000 Israelis are living in these smaller settlements, 120 of them being legal under Israeli law and around 150 being deemed illegal even according to Israeli law. The new government formed by Netanyahu in December 2022, which includes far-right settler figures such as Smotrich, has worked hard to expand these settlements—as they are the true 'two-state solution killers.'

Evacuating all of the settlements would be a daunting task: in 2005, during the Gaza disengagement, Israel only had to evacuate 8,000 settlers from twenty-one settlements. While the evacuation may have been swift, the mere process itself deeply divided the country. The consequence of the Gaza withdrawal, the rise of Hamas and the 7 October massacre will not help in creating support for such a withdrawal. The Trump plan was also the result of this conclusion and sought to avoid as many evacuations as possible. Yet looking at the map proposed under Trump's 'Deal of the Century' makes it clear such a Palestinian state would not be viable or truly sovereign in any sense of the term. What Trump proposed was a plan to symbolically upgrade the PA to a state, in name only. This is a proposal no Palestinian leader can accept.

At the same time, maintaining support for the status quo, namely avoiding steps that would kill the two-state solution, will become increasingly difficult. Settlements situated deep inside the West Bank are far from the average Israeli's eye. These settlements are important and discussed only by those supporting their expansion. The settlement issue has become a way for right-wing politicians to secure the support of far-right parties, without experiencing any sort of domestic backlash. International pressure on Israel not to create 'state-killer' settlements has disrupted some of the most daring attempts at killing a future Palestinian state, but counting on the outside world to keep a close eye is a dangerous bet.

**

The status quo 'route' is one that leads not only to a series of conflicts but that also pushes both sides to consider how they can defeat the other rather than how they can solve the conflict.

Yet other solutions to the conflict are just as unrealistic. One of them, pushed mostly from the outside, is the idea of creating a binational state.

This is not so much a plan as a way to pile pressure on Israel: much of the (largely academic) intelligentsia supporting and writing about this vision tend to overlook the clear opposition of both sides. Their main goal is to make a political point and highlight that Palestinians are now living in a 'one-state' reality, a reality of 'apartheid' in which Israelis and Palestinians have different rights. This South African narrative is, in that sense, less about proposing a solution than making a statement.

The key obstacle to solving the Israeli–Palestinian conflict is creating the political space to reach a solution that is relatively well defined. It is about political support rather than political engineering. Proposing a binational state would not solve this key issue, as polls continue to show strong opposition to such a state on both sides. At the same time, it would remove the framework most Israelis and Palestinians view as most viable. Building a new state, in which both Palestinians and Israelis would feel equally represented, would require trust between the two parties, and public support for a peaceful resolution and for coexistence, that far exceeds that needed for a two-state solution.

There are no signs that we're on a trajectory to secure such levels of trust. In other words, those who are so quick to pronounce the two-state solution 'dead' have yet to find one sign that the binational solution they are proposing is 'alive.'

What's more, those proposing the creation of a 'binational state' are generally the same people who pronounce the two-state solution—the only realistic solution to the conflict—to be dead. In that, they are unwittingly helping Israel's far-right parties, who very much believe that the two-state solution isn't dead and are working towards making this 'death' into a reality. The truth is no solution dies, and using metaphors to describe a process makes for dangerous shortcuts.

***

This shrinking 'universe of the possible' is worrying, to say the least. As this universe shrinks, the possibility of major corrections, in the form of either brutal spikes of violence or political decisions that are difficult to reverse—such as the annexation of all or parts or the West Bank, or the collapse of the PA, for instance—all become more likely.

Thirty years after the Oslo Accords, we've rolled back so far that the fight for hope is no longer about finding the correct parameters for peace but rather about convincing both sides that peace is desirable in the first place. It may sound absurd to outside observers, but the case needs to be made for peace.

This not only requires brave leadership on both sides but also a realization that the opposite case, the case for war, is being made on both sides, and that in many ways its supporters are winning.

Palestinian terrorism, and years of dealing with the conflict by adopting a security-oriented approach, has narrowed much of the debate in Israel. It's not a debate on values, political philosophy or the possible future of Israel's democracy if the conflict remains unsolved but solely one envisioned from the security point of view.

But the debate on values and identity that has only just started in Israel may recenter this debate towards the question of who Israelis want to be, what the nature of the state is and whether it is compatible with the current status quo. When a country searches for its identity, it certainly looks at its past, but it also looks to its future and where it wants to be in the coming decades. This is where solutions can be found: by placing each realistic outcome next to each other rather than as separate alternatives.

15

JUMPING INTO THE UNKNOWN AFTER THE 7 OCTOBER MASSACRE

On a quiet morning of 7 October, more than 1,000 Palestinian militants mostly from Hamas but also from smaller factions broke into Israel, using a series of coordinated attacks to bypass the security fence. In the following hours, they massacred at least 1,200 Israelis in border communities as well as a nearby music festival, making no distinction between civilians and soldiers, children, women and men, Jews and Arabs. In response, Israel declared war on Hamas and launched an unprecedented operation initially focused on the northern Gaza Strip, where a significant portion of Hamas's military arsenal—including rockets, fighters and tunnels—is situated.

In doing so, Hamas sought to shatter the status quo and move away from an eternal cycle of violence and 'quiet' towards what one of its officials called a 'permanent state of war.'

It is too early to say whether the group will in fact succeed. The Israeli operation in Gaza has progressed relatively quickly. On the military level, the Israeli army has been able to use several lessons it drew from previous fighting with Hamas, as well as better coordination between its branches, to more effectively defeat Hamas's main defenses.

At the same time, the death toll in Gaza is unprecedented. There is no need to rely solely on the Hamas-run Ministry of Health—which tends to make no distinction between civilians and militants. Satellite images show extensive damage to entire neighborhoods, including Beit Hanoun and Rimal. Israel also operates in very densely populated areas, such as al-Shati. Urban warfare is always ugly. It is a zero-sum game between the risks you are willing to have your forces take and the danger you are placing on the civilian population. The question of who is to blame for this is not what interests me here. The battle of narratives is a tiring exercise that often precludes cold and rational analysis of what the future entails. This narrative battle has also been a convenient replacement for those, on both sides, who have no idea of how to solve the conflict. Pointing fingers is certainly easier than pointing towards a solution.

In these situations, making sense of what comes next becomes both more pressing and more difficult, especially given the PR battle that has plagued this conflict. The real question is: Where does this take us?

The first path is clear: more chaos and more violence. This is the most obvious route, and there are unfortunately many factors that will be conducive to it. On the Israeli side, the 7 October attacks have shattered the idea that one people can live side by side with the other, even when protected by a USD1 billion security fence. The irony is that many of the communities that were attacked were actually some of the last bastions of the Israeli peace camp. During the attack, as her community was being invaded by Hamas terrorists, Vivian Silver was on the phone with an Israeli radio station, arguing passionately about the need for peace. Her body was identified more than a month later. Several other family members of victims have warned against using their pain to bring death to innocents in Gaza. They've been steadfast in their commitment to peace, as the ultimate solution to this conflict. But to many other Israelis, this is naive. That Silver argued for peace moments before being killed will be deemed as proof that she was wrong to call for peace, that there can never be peace. This is an anecdote, but one that sums up quite well how even the voice of the victim is drawn into the torrent of hatred and fear that follows terror attacks of this magnitude.

The attacks have shattered Israel's sense of safety, which is not a good place to start rebuilding peace. It has also threatened to shatter the few spaces in which Jews and Arabs coexist. To be sure, a poll showed that the Arab Israeli sense of belonging to Israel has increased following the attacks, rather than decreased.[1] This is perhaps explained by the indiscriminate brutality Hamas used against Israelis, regardless of their faith. But amid few signs of resilience, these attacks aimed to break society apart and have done so in many pernicious ways. In Jerusalem, some Israeli Jews did not feel they could send their children back to kindergartens in which Arabs worked. Streets were empty both in West and East Jerusalem, and the few spaces of coexistence disappeared.

On the Palestinian side, the extensive Israeli bombing will leave scars that will resonate far beyond their immediate—and already ghastly—impact. Northern Gaza may be unlivable for years to come, fueling the narrative that Israel sought to trigger a 'second Nakba.' In the West Bank, the aftermath of the 7 October attacks was marked by the wave of settler violence that followed and efforts to displace Palestinians, with settlers disguising themselves as Israeli soldiers or carrying out attacks while the Israeli army watched and did nothing. This is no coincidence, as the settler movement in Israel saw this as a historic opportunity to advance their cause. They, too, are interested in a state of permanent war. Once again, the divide is not between Palestinians and Israelis so much as it is between those who think they can win the conflict and those who think it should be solved.

In Gaza, Israel has no good options. Bringing back the PA would perhaps be the most rational solution, but it is still a risky one. The PA is already losing control of the West Bank. Returning to Gaza on the back of a massive and destructive Israeli operation will be a death blow to its credibility. Any genuine effort to restore stability would also have to include a resumption of peace talks. Terror groups like Hamas are rarely defeated solely by military means, and an investment in peace talks will be necessary to reinvigorate a moribund PA before it dies or is taken over by more radical streams within Fatah. The PA has also conditioned its return on the resumption of peace negotiations—which is justified.

But bringing the PA back also clashes with the interests of Netanyahu, who is looking to keep the Palestinians divided and to fend off pressure to resume peace talks. In multiple speeches, Netanyahu said that he would not bring the PA back to Gaza, infuriating both the pragmatic Arab camp and the United States. The embattled Israeli prime minister will try to force other Arab countries to pitch in and perhaps build a technocratic transition government supported by Arab troops. By doing so, the fundamental contradiction in the Abraham Accords and efforts to decouple the Israeli–Palestinian conflict from the Arab–Israeli conflict will re-emerge: if Arab partners agree, they will have once again missed an opportunity to solve the Israeli–Palestinian conflict. This is not where we're going, as several of Israel's Arab interlocutors have been clear they want the PA back in Gaza and have preconditioned any help on such a return.

This could lead us away from the path of despair and preserve the path of hope. Although it is still too early to say, there may be people on both sides who understand we cannot do the same thing again and again and expect a different result. Anger at Hamas for what it brought to Palestinians and anger at Netanyahu and his stream of right-wing politics may help remove some of the numerous obstacles to peace. In history, this would not be the first time a very brutal spike in violence leads to peace.

PART 4

ISRAEL'S COLD WAR

16

FAILED STATES, SUCCESSFUL IRAN?

A series of destabilizing and transformational developments have turned Iran into a king among ruins. In just two decades, a mostly isolated Iran has been able to expand at little cost as the Middle East experienced a series of crises. The US invasion of Iraq, the Arab Spring and the emergence of ISIS have all removed the barriers to Iran's expansion.

By carefully investing in a series of non-state but powerful allies, Iran has positioned itself for success as states crumbled in the Middle East. First, overthrowing Iran's main enemy along its western border, the American invasion of Iraq opened the way for an Iranian expansion westward. Iran had long cultivated Shiite opposition movements, most of whom had found refuge in the country. They would form the base of an expanding Iranian footprint in the country. Despite the US presence in Iraq, Iran still controls several key Iraqi militias that have in turn formed an important political bloc vying for influence over the Shiite community.

Iran would later take advantage of the Arab Spring to widen this initial investment westward. In Syria, Iran was quick to side with its natural ally, Bashar al-Assad, at a time when dictators were falling elsewhere. In Yemen, Iran quietly expanded its ties with the Houthis, a Shiite minority settled in northern Yemen, close to Iran's main regional rival, Saudi Arabia.

The third stage came with the emergence of ISIS, which provided Iran with an opportunity to mobilize sympathetic elements in Iraq and Syria. As Iranian-backed troops advanced and destroyed the 'Caliphate' the jihadist group had built across the Iraq–Syria border, Iran effectively built a ground corridor that extends from its western border all the way to its first foreign venture: the Lebanon-based Hezbollah.

Iran has been able to project its influence outside its border at little cost. To do so, it has relied on key patterns and strategies that can be replicated in the future. This is concerning for Israel given that the region is in the midst of a broad crisis that started with the Arab Spring but did not end with the Arab Winter that followed—as I mentioned at the beginning of this book.

One of the factors behind Iran's success has been a unifying narrative that places Israel at the center of Iran's attention: the Axis of Resistance. This Axis of Resistance narrative posits that Iran and its allies are resisting the encroaching influence of the 'Great Satan,' the United States, represented in the region by the 'Zionist Entity'—or 'Little Satan.'

This is a powerful narrative, one that can be traced back to the Lebanon Civil War and the subsequent intervention of Israeli forces in the country and the occupation of southern Lebanon. Iran has chosen this narrative as opposed to other core values and identities that make it unique. Tehran understands, for instance, that if it were solely to use the religious Shiite 'angle,' this would largely limit its ability to collaborate with non-Shiite actors, in a largely Sunni-dominated region. Support for the Palestinian cause as well as anti-imperialist/anti-American positions is far more mobilizing than a narrower Shiite-centric narrative.

At the same time, this narrative has also been damaged by Iran's and its proxies' own actions. While Iranian and Iranian-supported forces have touted their intention to destroy Israel, in deeds they've been mostly busy killing Syrians, Iraqis and Yemenis while crushing any attempt to reform Lebanon. The road to Jerusalem—or al-Quds, as per Iran's terms[1]—is quite sinuous, with stops in Mosul, Damascus and Sana'a.

This is because, at its core, the Axis of Resistance narrative is meant more as a rallying cry to expand Iranian influence across the region than as an urgent call to eradicate Israel. To be clear, Israel is viewed as an enemy, but one that has been useful to rally support outside of Iran—just as the fear of Iran served Israel's efforts to normalize ties with the Gulf.

Still, the cracks in the Iranian narrative have been wide and consistent. In a matter of a few years, Iranian forces and local proxies have participated in several crackdowns, including on Syrian rebels as well as pro-democracy protesters in Iraq and Lebanon. They have positioned themselves as a reactionary force keen to stamp on Arabs, and one that does little to serve the cause of the Palestinians. The hypocrisy has, to a certain extent at least, been revealed.

But it does not matter as long as some still believe in this narrative, or pretend they do, and as long as Iran maintains what's really at the core of its projection capabilities: brute force by an armed minority in a failed state. Some have posited that Iran's arrival is often preceded by state collapse. Others have suggested that Iran's arrival precipitates such collapse. Both are true: Iran often gets involved in countries that are unstable, and its presence further worsens that initial instability. Iran has seen the opportunity I described earlier, but it has also made sure to bet on non-state actors as a bulwark against any possible change, should the state manage to rebuild itself.

States that have experienced a form of collapse and civil war in the Middle East broadly follow two opposite models: the Algerian model and the Libyan model. The Algerian model, referring to the Algerian Civil War that gripped the country in the 1990s, saw the Algerian state re-emerge at the end of it, as a centralized entity, capable of maintaining its monopoly on the use of violence. This is despite the length of the conflict, as well as the appearance of some local militias during the conflict.

The opposite model is that of post-Gaddafi Libya. Following the death of the Libyan leader in October 2011, the state swiftly collapsed, ruled by a mosaic of militias. The government has since split between two rival entities vying for legitimacy. But even at times when it was unified, sub-state actors, namely local militias, stamped on any state authority to the point that on several occasions militiamen actually entered the parliament.

Iran made the bet that, as states failed across the region, they would come out of the crisis looking more like Libya than Algeria. It appears to have been a winning bet, as Algeria is the exception rather than the rule. Civil wars tend to leave lasting divides, particularly when the central authority fully collapses and when sectarian divides have already split the country into a mosaic of different interests and groups who have an easier time killing each other than working together.

This dynamic has propelled Iran out of the confines of its own borders and into significant swathes of the Middle East, with the main question being whether it can both maintain its influence, just as its unifying narrative is being challenged and calls for change resurface, and even expand it by taking advantage of future crises ahead.

Notably, the fact that Iran is a 'king among ruins' and one whose crown depends on decrepitude also means that Israel's environment will remain dangerous, even if Iran's influence was suddenly to disappear.

***

The other central question is whether Iran's fragilities will catch up to it. The Islamic Republic of Iran—Iran's formal name—has been experiencing internal turmoil that has raised doubts over whether it can survive the next decade. Protest movements have frequently hit Iran. Since 2009, those outbursts of unrest have expanded both in frequency and in other ways.

The 2009 protests, following presidential elections hardliner Mahmoud Ahmadinejad claimed to have won, were the first in a now long series of protest movements that have accelerated over the past ten years, and particularly since 2017. Significant waves of protests have been recorded almost every year since 2017. But beyond their frequency, each movement broke a significant barrier, whether it be geographic or socio-economic. Recent movements have hit segments of the population that were not involved in the 2009 protests, for instance. The socio-economic protests of 2017–18 centered on primarily conservative cities like Mashhad or Isfahan, prompting Ebrahim Raisi, a conservative leader who later became Iran's president, to support some of the grievances expressed by the protesters. The 2022–3 wave of unrest, often known by its main motto, 'Women, Life, Freedom,' also broke several barriers: while previous protests focused mostly on socio-economic issues, including prices, this protest hit at the heart of Iran's religious core. High inflation, water shortages and meager and often corruption-ridden pension schemes have all been triggers of protests in Iran. But this movement hit differently, raising questions about the rule of the 'judges' or Valayat al-Faqi, a system that places ayatollahs at the center of decision-making.

And although other protests had also seen slogans calling for the demise of the regime, those grew far wider during the movement prompted by the death of Mahsa Amini, who was beaten to death after being detained by Iran's religious police. The protests broke out of the Kurdish heartland, from where Amini hailed, and expanded across Iran, as the gender segregation imposed by the Iranian regime is something all Iranian women have experienced.

This is not to say that Iran's demise is bound to happen. The Iranian regime has developed a widespread counter-revolutionary expertise that it has exported abroad—including in Syria, Iraq and Lebanon—before bringing it back home. This expertise relies on brutal repression carried out by the IRGC and the Basij, two powerful paramilitary forces. Throughout the protests, these two repressive arms of the state carried out widespread acts of violence against protesters, ranging from the use of live ammunition during protests, torture and rape against detainees, to public hangings. For a revolution to succeed, these two forces need to be weakened, either by internal conflicts or by decreased morale. They have never truly shown any real signs that this is the case, despite a power struggle at the top of the Iranian state. Their brutal repression also means they know exactly what their fate would be if they were to falter, showing that nothing unites a repressive regime more than shared crimes.

But the regime does not solely rely on repression. It has learned to use other more insidious tactics, including counter-protests, mass surveillance and economic retribution, to divide an increasingly hostile Iranian public.

When looking at the future of the Iranian regime, it is hard to overstate the importance of its alliance with a rising autocratic axis, led by China. Beijing faces similar challenges to Iran. The Chinese Communist Party also seeks to curtail democratic aspirations and is perhaps the closest to solving the quintessential problem autocratic regimes have faced over the centuries: their tendency to fall due to internal troubles. Beijing believes that, as an authoritarian regime, it has tools other failed regimes never had. These include the ability to spy on its citizens and exercise intimate control in a way that has never before been possible—until now. This digitized repression, and the tools of cyber-control, are indeed expanding at a dizzying pace. What's more, Beijing understands that autocratic regimes have a better chance of surviving when they band together: revolutions tend to cross borders, and publics within democratic regimes often view democratic aspirations abroad with sympathy, mechanically encouraging a tendency to support nascent pro-democratic movements.

In other words, China will have an incentive to bolster Iran and export its 'techno-dictator starter kit' not just out of the 'goodness of its heart' but because it preserves its own interests. The Iranian regime understands this and has already been investing in surveillance tools, including the installation of 15 million cameras across twenty-eight cities in Iran, including Tehran. Those cameras were provided by Tiandy, a Chinese company responsible for developing several key AI-powered facial recognition technologies, including those used against the Uyghur minority, among others. Tiandy is also believed to be developing technologies that would help authorities recognize protesters even at night, which could prove central to a more effective crackdown on demonstrations of unrest. Chinese telecommunication companies have also widened their presence in Iran, amid speculation they are streamlining surveillance processes through key control centers capable of monitoring a great number of cellular conversations.

***

In just a few years, Iran has shown itself to be capable of projecting significant power abroad while being fundamentally weak. It has used failed states to expand its power through sub-state actors while at the same time experiencing crises that could see it become a failed state itself—if it isn't one already. This paradox also explains the divisions and debates we've seen regarding attitudes towards Iran. Those who believe the Iranian regime is on its deathbed have insisted that we should not give it any breathing space and attack on every front until it finally collapses. This is a policy often described as 'maximum pressure.' On the other hand, those who feel that Iran is here to stay, at least for the foreseeable future, have worked to determine how to engage with Iran to limit its power, compartmentalizing the various issues and addressing them in different ways.

Although far less public, this same debate has also affected Israel. What's clear is that for Israel, countering the threats posed by Iran, be it its nuclear and ballistic missile programs, regional influence and network of proxies, are at the top of its regional priorities: although Iran is 1,000 kilometers away from Israel, it has become a 'not-so-distant' enemy, operating along at least two of Israel's borders.

17

A NOT-SO-DISTANT ENEMY

In 2012, I sat not far from the Merom Golan kibbutz with a journalist covering the war in Syria. In front of us, the forest was burning. Several mortars had struck the border between Israel and Syria. The Israeli military declared the area a 'closed military zone': for the first time, the Syrian rebels were attacking the Quneitra border crossing between Israel and Syria. This was the first time the Syrian Civil War directly affected Israel.

Southern Syria was the heart of the Syrian rebellion, the wave of unrest initially triggered by the arrest of several Syrian children in Daraa. The Syrian opposition would quickly establish itself along most of the border with Israel, forcing Israel to look much more closely at a border that had so far—and despite Syria and Israel being officially at war—been quiet.

Israel would respond by offering limited support to the Syrian opposition through an operation dubbed 'Good Neighbor.' The aim of this operation was not to actively support regime-change in Damascus but to maintain a good relationship with local opposition movements, ensuring they would not turn against Israel. To some extent, this operation was successful, and the area controlled by the rebels remained relatively quiet, as opposed to the northern part of the Syrian Golan, which remained loyal to the regime, and a southern pocket later held by a group affiliated with ISIS. But this relative quiet dissipated as the Syrian rebel presence collapsed in 2018.

In the wake of the Russian intervention in Syria, and the later battle of Aleppo in 2016, the Syrian rebellion started losing its foreign backers. Regime-change in Damascus was no longer within reach. The regime's bloody 'Reconquista' reached the south this year.

In parallel with advances of troops loyal to Assad, Russia also brokered a deal with the United States and Israel, which would guarantee the creation of an 'anti-Iran' buffer zone in southern Syria. In exchange for tacit support for the Russian presence, and a pledge to turn a blind eye to Assad's return, Moscow guaranteed that Iran and its proxies would not be allowed to operate along Israel's border with Syria.

Whether Israel truly believed the arrangement would work in the way it intended isn't clear. What is clear, however, is that those who did believe Russia would make for a good partner were proven wrong relatively quickly, as Iranian militias quickly emerged in southern Syria, despite Russia's pledge.

Moscow deployed a very limited number of soldiers to southern Syria. According to the various reports in the Russian media, there was likely never more than 1,200 soldiers deployed in the three main provinces of southern Syria. This is nothing compared to the 10,000 soldiers participating in the UN Interim Force in Lebanon (UNIFIL) in charge of implementing a buffer zone in Lebanon—a mission they have failed to accomplish. To be sure, the Russians have also attempted to build their own force in southern Syria by attracting former rebels into a newly created Eighth Brigade, led by former rebel commander Ayman al-Awdah. The Eighth Brigade was itself part of a broader Assault Corps set up within the Syrian army. Moscow's objective was to start rebuilding the Syrian Arab Army (SAA), which has effectively collapsed after a decade of conflict, with Assad's forces now consisting mostly of a mosaic of diverse militias and foreign forces. This is an arduous task and one that Moscow had little experience in. Russia has never been in the state-building business. While Israel may have bet on Moscow to avoid a 'Libyan Scenario' and return Syria to the central state it was, this bet largely failed—even before the war in Ukraine, which would shift Moscow's priorities.

The Eighth Brigade did attract a number of local Syrians, due to a combination of limited economic prospects and the perception that the brigade could perhaps act as a buffer against Iran as well as several other regime units who started arresting former rebels. To almost no one's surprise, the Syrian regime had, indeed, started to break the 'reconciliation agreement' it initially signed with the rebels, ramping up a campaign of arrest against 'criminals' with the aim of rooting out the remnants of the rebellion.

The only checks on Iran's influence, incidentally, didn't come from Russia but rather from local Syrians themselves. The Iranian encroachment and attempt to recruit locals into newly set up Syrian groups—part of a broader Iranian-backed 'Syrian Resistance' network—was met with its own kind of resistance from the locals. Iranian recruitment efforts backfired, with attacks against Iranian and Hezbollah officials being reported regularly up to the present day.

While this shows that local resentment towards Iran can serve to delay the entrenchment of the Islamic Republic in the Syrian south and its proxies, Israel shouldn't count on it. Iran and its proxies have been able to operate along Israel's border, carrying out a number of direct attacks against Israel. In November 2020, for instance, Israel discovered several explosive devices planted along the fence with Syria and retaliated by carrying out airstrikes. This was the latest attempt by a Hezbollah-controlled cell dubbed the 'Golan File' to carry out attacks against the Jewish state and likely isn't going to be the last.

This isn't a small development and could present a strategic threat to Israel in the coming years, should no solution be found. Iran and Hezbollah's goals in southern Syria are clear: they are seeking to build a second 'southern Lebanon,' one that would further expand the threat stemming from Hezbollah's massive rocket arsenal south of the Litani River to the border with the Israeli Golan Heights.

The difference would be that, whereas Hezbollah feels constrained in southern Lebanon due to the cost a possible war with Israel would inflict upon its supporters, the same cannot be said of southern Syria. The group would have far more leeway to carry out attacks from Syria than it has in Lebanon, and the Israeli north could find itself facing a drizzle of rockets comparable to that seen in Gaza or coming from Lebanon before the 2006 war.

What Iran is effectively building isn't just an extension of south Lebanon into Syria but a platform through which it can more easily attack Israel without bearing the cost or taking the same risks.

The infrastructure Iran and its allies have built in Syria isn't as extensive as that Hezbollah set up south of the Litani River in south Lebanon. But this could change, forcing Israel to once again be pulled into southern Syria, up until an actual ground intervention may even be needed.

This 'second southern Lebanon' that Iran is building in southern Syria is the closest tip of a much broader Iranian-led spear that aims to encircle Israel with a 'ring of fire' made of Iranian proxies. Iran has not only penetrated the border with Israel but effectively built a 'land corridor' through which its influence and militias can circulate almost unchecked. Israel has in turn been drawn into a war it initially chose to ignore.

When the Syrian Civil War erupted, Israel made a conscious decision to stay on the sideline of the conflict. There were advocates of an Israeli intervention on humanitarian grounds, particularly after Assad used his chemical arsenal (which had been built for the sake of deterring Israel) against his own people, but those calls were quickly dismissed: Israel had no business siding with the rebels or the Syrian regime, according to decision-makers at the time. It was a case of 'better the devil you know' than the one you don't: while Assad was certainly no friend of Israel, he had still maintained the 'quiet' along the border ever since the Yom Kippur War (1973). The radicalization of elements within the Syrian opposition and the emergence of jihadist groups including the al-Qaeda-tied Jabhat al-Nusra and ISIS certainly gave further grounds to those advocating in favor of Israel's neutrality in the conflict.

Geopolitics hates a vacuum, and Syria was no exception. The conflict not only attracted jihadist groups; very early in the Syrian conflict, multiple rumors and signs suggested that Iran was getting involved in the civil war, initially through its Lebanese proxy, Hezbollah, and possibly by sending members of the Basij force, an Iranian paramilitary group versed in the 'art' of suppressing revolutions and quelling dissent.

Years later, the Iranian presence has become far more visible. The Iranian intervention itself has shown Tehran's ability to wage a counter-insurgency war, and at times a conventional one, while still maintaining a relatively low exposure. This was mostly achieved through the use of local proxies and auxiliaries that took the brunt of the cost of the conflict.

Initially, the Lebanon-based Hezbollah was at the forefront of the war, deploying thousands of soldiers in the nearby country. Two years after the beginning of the civil war, Hezbollah showed what it was capable of by carrying out a large-scale operation to expel rebels from the area of Qusayr, near the border with Lebanon. The group was no longer staging the kind of guerilla warfare that had been seen in 2006 but was taking on the role of a conventional force pushing out armed rebels who were using the border region as a staging ground for attacks deeper inside Syria.

The most effective Hezbollah units, including the equivalent of the group's shock troops, the Radwan unit, took part in some of the most decisive battles of the civil war, including the later stage of the battle of Aleppo in 2016—dubbed the 'mother of all battles.' By that time, Iran's footprint in the country had expanded significantly. The Aleppo battle saw the deployment of the Iranian Artesh, Iran's conventional army, as opposed to the IRGC, Iran's main paramilitary force.

Still, most offensive operations were carried out by other more 'expandable' units. In southern Aleppo, this included two distinct formations, namely the IRGC's Fatemiyoun unit, made up of Afghan nationals, most of whom had fled the conflict in Afghanistan to settle in Iran, and the smaller Zainabiyoun unit made up of Pakistanis. The former was at the forefront of key battles in southern Aleppo in 2015–16, as was made clear by research at the time into the losses and death notices released by the IRGC and the funerals held in Iran. Beyond that, Iran could also count on several Iraqi militias, which were mostly deployed in eastern Syria to fight ISIS and have remained there ever since.

In a matter of a few years, Iran's presence in Syria had grown to be not only visible to the naked eye but also critical to the Syrian regime, turning the tide of a war Assad may have lost, even before the intervention of another key Syrian ally—Russia.

***

Iran's 'Shiite Jihad' to fight rebels and Sunni jihadists alike had laid the groundwork for a deep Iranian entrenchment in Syria, one it has used to cement its presence even after the more active phase of the Syrian conflict has ended. When looking at Iran's expansion in Syria, this is often what's discussed.

But Iran's influence goes far beyond the more 'flashy' and identifiable militias made of foreign fighters and Farsi-speaking soldiers. As one of Assad's main allies, and the first to intervene militarily in Syria, Iran also played a critical role in shaping Assad's response to the emerging conflict. One of the key issues Damascus initially faced was the rising number of defections from within the ranks of the Syrian military. At the beginning of the civil war, the SAA saw its numbers shrink, with Sunnis (who formed the backbone of the opposition) defecting en masse. Other officers and soldiers wavered, as they received orders to clamp down on fellow Syrians. Even those who remained were viewed with suspicion and marginalized.

To help stop the bleeding, Iran set up a parallel network of local militias. Tehran particularly invested in those who were either supportive of the regime or fearful of the growing radicalization of segments of the rebellion. Indeed, as segments of the rebellion radicalized, minorities, including Druze and Christians, feared they would be a natural target. Others, such as the Alawites, were also supportive of Assad, as Assad himself hails from the Alawite community.

The National Defense Force and Local Defense Force were born. These paramilitary forces used existing pro-regime networks, such as the Shabiha militias, as well as local dynamics as a pillar to create flexible troops whose loyalties wouldn't falter.

Iran, including General Qassem Soleimani, had a direct role in forming, funding and equipping these revamped militias. Iranian investments in cash, as well as Hezbollah's victory in Qusayr, also played a role in attracting recruits to the units, which were at times better equipped than the official Syrian army.

In this case, Iran showed its ability to plan ahead. Not only did the arrival of those forces reverse a dangerous dynamic that saw the Syrian army melt like ice but it also served as a long-term vector of influence in Syria. What Iran built was a mosaic of forces that was entirely Syrian and would likely remain in place even as the conflict in Syria wound down. Beyond that, Tehran invested in areas of future interest, including by setting up forces in strategic areas: this is the case, for instance, with the Golan battalion, mostly based around the village of Hader, just a few kilometers away from the border with the Israeli Golan. Local loyalties enabled the creation of local cells that could be used to stage attacks against Israel.

But the Iranian penetration didn't stop there. As part of its program to 'advise and support' the Syrian army, Iran and its Lebanese proxy also sent local advisors to a number of SAA units. During military operations, they would serve both to support the SAA and to streamline communication with other pro-regime units. Outside of military operations, this network of contacts was easily turned into one of influence that paralleled the organization of the Syrian army. This was particularly the case in southern Syria: Israel warned members of the SAA's 90th Brigade, which is responsible for the Quneitra Province bordering Israel, not to cooperate with Hezbollah. At times, the IDF has also released pictures of high-ranking members of the SAA meeting with Hezbollah officials, including Hajj Hashem, the Hezbollah commander of the southern front. Yet it is no surprise that the two collaborate: Hezbollah has been deeply embedded in the unit for years now.

In that sense, the Syrian Civil War provides a textbook example of how Iran exploits crises to build non-state actors. Those same actors cannot easily be removed: some of them are outside actors (such the IRGC Fatemiyoun and Zainabiyoun Brigades), but others are very much a part of it. That is not to mention that the state relies on these non-state structures to continue to exercise sovereignty while at the same time being influenced by them. Maher al-Assad, Assad's brother, has long been known to be a close associate of Iran, providing the regime with access to the very top of the Syrian state: the Assad family.

As a result, an initially reluctant Israel was pulled into the Syrian conflict. Over the years, Israel has been playing a game of 'whack-a-mole' with Iran in Syria, hitting Iranian positions in areas of Syria only to see it reappear somewhere else.

Initially, the Israeli military tracked and destroyed shipments of missiles and equipment bound for Lebanon. Iran was (and still is) using Syria as a gateway to Lebanon, seeking to arm Hezbollah with weapons, including precision-guided missiles, that could play a significant role in a future third Lebanon war.

The campaign quickly turned to local outposts and warehouses used by Hezbollah and the IRGC. As early as 2014–15, Israeli strikes targeted warehouses and offices on the outskirts of Damascus International Airport. Syria's main international airport outside of Damascus had become the main headquarters of the IRGC in Syria. The 'Glasshouse,' a building within the compound of the airport hosting high-ranking Iranian officers, would be targeted a number of times. Even today, the airport is regularly hit, with Israeli strikes often coinciding with the arrival of Iranian planes suspected of transporting weapons and weapon-making equipment.

The campaign was successful in inflicting damage and delaying the Iranian entrenchment. But Iran reacted by further expanding its operational area to more distant regions of Syria. Whereas the Damascus route, from the Syrian capital and into Lebanon through Qalamoun, was the main route used in the early years of the conflict, the Israeli campaign forced Iran to look elsewhere and start 'diversifying.'

Iran had by then secured access to most key Syrian bases, including major air bases such as the Tiyas air base, which sits close to the city of Palmyra in central Syria. The base would become another key staging ground for Iran and its proxies and has been the target of nearly a dozen Israeli strikes including one against a drone control center in 2018 prompted by the sending of a drone into

Israel. That Iran had penetrated several key Syrian bases meant they could be used as entry points for the shipment of Iranian weapons.

The fight against ISIS also brought to life a grand Iranian project. As the group's so-called 'Caliphate' was defeated in 2017, Iranian-backed militias from Iraq and Syria met for the first time at a key border crossing point, along the Iraq–Syria border: the cities of al-Qaim, on the Iraqi side, and Albu Kamal, on the Syrian side. Iranian militias would remain in this critical border area long after the fall of the 'Caliphate.' They built new bases, including underground storage bunkers, and controlled the main border crossing. Through this porous border area, Iranian shipments could easily circulate by trucks and be transferred from Iran's westernmost border all the way to Syria and Lebanon. This land corridor also enabled unimpeded movement from Iran, all the way to Lebanon, the Syrian coast and the border with the Israeli Golan. Soleimani, the man behind this grand ambition, would regularly pop up on one or other side of the border—before ending his regional tour buried by a US-fired missile near Baghdad Airport. This 'land corridor' links together all of Iran's efforts, and its consequences go far beyond providing an alternative route to weapons shipment. Iran views it as a safe haven where it can invest economically and both cement and project its influence.

This also means that Iran now has easier access to the Syrian coast and thus the Mediterranean. Although Iran has yet to use this access as a platform for attacks and power projection, the Iranian entrenchment along its own coast, and that of northern Yemen, could be replicated to further expand Iran's ability as a tactical nuisance (at least initially). Alongside its drone and ballistic missile programs, Iran has also helped its proxies acquire anti-ship missiles as well as explosive-laden naval drones, some of which have been used by the Houthis in Yemen.

In the aftermath of the Aleppo and Idlib offensives to dislodge rebels in 2016, Iran also established a significant presence in northwestern Syria. As the Iranian presence grew significantly between 2015 and 2016, Iran used its proxies to cement its influence in this area, with the Aleppo International Airport soon becoming another hub for smuggling. After all, the same planes that brought in Shiite fighters to defeat the rebellion against Assad could just as easily bring in weapons. But the Iranian takeover did not stop there. The Syrian regime had long maintained a number of military industries near the town of as-Safirah, south of Aleppo. This specific area became a staging ground for the Fatemiyoun (Afghan) brigade mentioned earlier during the battle of Aleppo. Yet Iran had other ambitions and viewed the strategic military industries as an important node that could be used to gain experience and even build locally made weapons directly in Syria.

The Safirah military industries were not the only military complex to be taken over by Iran. In fact, a similar trend emerged in almost all the areas under Assad's control, either with or without the Syrian president's assent. Iran was making its presence felt in key military facilities, including those belonging to Syria's Centre d'Etudes et de Recherches Scientifiques or Scientific Studies and Research Center (SSRC).

Despite its innocuous name, the SSRC is a cover for Syria's chemical and ballistic program, suggesting that Iran was investing in and possibly acquiring knowledge and expertise from its Syrian partner.

This was a serious development for Israel, and the Jewish state invested significant resources in understanding Iran's intention and mapping out its activities. The Syrian chemical and ballistic weapons program largely shrank during the civil war as a result of a 2014 agreement that stripped Assad of a significant part of his chemical arsenal, as well as the fact that Assad had used a portion of his arsenal against his own people. Yet the Syrian regime still maintains significant capabilities and know-how that could be useful for Iran. Before the war, Syria maintained one of the largest and most diverse chemical weapons arsenals. The program included several facilities across the country, particularly around Damascus as well as in the Homs and Hama provinces. Those facilities were subsequently hit a number of times by suspected Israeli strikes, but the impact on knowledge transfer remains difficult to estimate. Iran and its proxies have most likely been able to acquire some of the know-how by parasitizing Syria's chemical weapons program and could replicate the kinds of attacks that have been used against rebels and Syrian civilians. Those attacks would require vectors (aircraft or missiles) that can be destroyed, and the consequences of those attacks may not be as drastic as some may fear. However, their psychological impact isn't negligible, particularly considering that in recent years Israel's enemies have largely sought to defeat it by targeting its home front.

In addition to the Syrian chemical weapons program, Iran also took over segments of the country's missile program. The IRGC started working on building weapon-manufacturing plants that would see missiles not only being transferred through Syria but also being produced and possibly improved in Syria.

The building of facilities resembling missile-production factories in Iran began to attract media attention as early as 2017–18. The Iranian activities around the Syrian SSRC also suggested that Tehran may be able to use Syria's expertise in improving ballistic missiles to retrofit some of the missiles already produced with more accurate guiding systems, including those in possession of its main ally in Lebanon: Hezbollah.

This was no small threat: in a future war with Hezbollah, the number of precision-guided missiles the Lebanese group is capable of deploying would be critical and could lead to significant damage to the Israeli home front and military.

A conflict with Hezbollah would be very different from what the Israelis experienced in Gaza or in the Second Lebanon war. The group has since acquired one of the largest missile and rocket arsenals in the world, with these sites being deeply embedded in villages in southern Lebanon. Whereas Hamas was, for instance, able to fire between 200 and 600 rockets per day, Hezbollah would fire at least double these numbers, with the assessment that the group has expanded its capabilities and could fire between 1,200 and 2,000 rockets.

The accuracy of those rockets is also important: whereas Hamas fires unguided rockets, the Iranian precision-guided missile program could see Hezbollah fire a small but notable number of accurate missiles. This would present a significant challenge even for Israel's air defenses—some of the best and most combat-ready in the world. It is almost certain that Hezbollah will seek to overwhelm Israeli air defenses by firing hundreds of 'dumb' rockets, alongside a couple of precision-guided missiles targeting Israeli air bases and military facilities or even key civilian installations.

This could push Israel to start prioritizing which projectiles it shoots down and which it has to let through. One thing Israel civilians may not be aware of is that the Iron Dome and the rest of Israel's air defense is first and foremost meant to protect the Israeli military and particularly its ability to strike back. In other words, when faced with a choice between intercepting a missile fired at Tel Aviv, and one fired at its airbases, the military would protect the latter.

This is of course a scenario Israel would like to avoid. The threat has been mitigated in part, with Hezbollah only being assessed to have limited access to precision-guided missiles, but the game of whack a mole is far from over. Each time Israel misses its shot and fails to prevent weapons transfer, the future threat and casualty count of a potential war with Iran or Hezbollah grows.

***

The land corridor Iran is building isn't the only investment it has made in the region. Closer to Israel, Tehran has also sought to weigh in more directly on the Israeli–Palestinian conflict. Years of dispute with Hamas over the Syrian conflict, prompted by Hamas's own decision to side with the Syrian rebels, have disrupted some of the ties Iran had built with the rulers of Gaza. Although relations have since eased, with Hamas making up with Assad, Iran drew lessons from the previous period and has sought a closer ally.

Tehran found the perfect one in the Palestinian Islamic Jihad, a group whose leadership is based in Damascus and Beirut. Since its inception in 1981, the Palestinian Islamic Jihad has been shaped by the Iranian Revolution and the ideology Iran has used to project power—the Axis of Resistance. However, the group has also had to be sensitive to Gaza's own dependence on Egypt, which shares a border with the Palestinian enclave. Just like Hamas, the Islamic Jihad has long needed to balance its pro-Iranian agenda with Cairo's own suspicions vis-à-vis Iran. This changed in 2018 with the election of Ziyad al-Nakhalah as the new head of the Palestinian Islamic Jihad following the death of his predecessor, who had suffered a stroke. Al-Nakhalah decided that the time was ripe to even more closely align with Iran and take on a more prominent role. This matched Iran's ambitions to be able to more directly foment unrest and destabilize the West Bank and Gaza.

As a result, the Palestinian Islamic Jihad has been the target of several rounds of violence in Gaza, including the November 2019 Operation 'Black Belt' that started with the killing of one of its main commanders, Baha Abu al-Ata, in Gaza. In 2022, Israel launched another operation in Gaza, dubbed 'Breaking Dawn,' specifically against the Palestinian Islamic Jihad. The next year, Israel carried out a new operation dubbed 'Shield and Arrow' comprising a series of targeted assassinations against the group—killing Abu al-Ata's successor—after the group threatened to respond to the death of one of its former members in Israeli detention.

Hamas stayed on the sidelines of those conflicts, underscoring the group's understanding that the Islamic Jihad had taken on a life of its own and was both an ally in the struggle against Israel and a rival in the struggle for leadership and control over the Palestinian scene.

Perhaps more worrying for Israel, the last two of those conflicts originated from the West Bank, highlighting the group's ambition to break out of Gaza. The 2022 operation 'Breaking Dawn' was launched after the arrest of Bassem al-Sa'adi, a senior Islamic Jihad member in the West Bank. The 2023 operation 'Shield and Arrow' was launched after the death of Khader Adnan, a former Palestinian Islamic Jihad spokesperson who died in Israeli custody while on a hunger strike.

This is no coincidence: just like Hamas, the Palestinian Islamic Jihad also understands that the battle for the future of Palestinians, and of the conflict with Israel, will be waged in the West Bank rather than Gaza. The same realization has dawned on Iran itself: in a public statement, Iran's Supreme Leader Ayatollah Ali Khamenei said that while 'Gaza is the center of Resistance,' it is 'the West Bank that will bring the enemy to its knees. And good progress has been made in this region so far.'

Khamenei's statement reflected a change that was already evident years before, as Iran sent help to local groups in the northern West Bank. Tehran also encouraged the Islamic Jihad's presence in areas that were already largely unchecked and where the PA was largely unable to operate—including Jenin and Nablus. The Palestinian Islamic Jihad worked with other groups, including disenfranchised members of the al-Aqsa Martyrs' Brigades (a group affiliated with Fatah but that took on a life of its own), to cement its presence in the northern West Bank, giving Iran another vector of influence in the Israeli–Palestinian conflict. As with other proxies, Iran and Hezbollah likely provided the Islamic Jihad with know-how, including on how to manufacture large explosives and perhaps even explosive-laden drones. One large-scale mine would be used against a state-of-the-art armored car in Jenin in June 2023, wounding seven Israeli soldiers during a raid.

Once again, Israel reacted by launching an operation, this time in Jenin itself. In a two-day operation internally called 'House and Garden,' elite IDF units stormed Jenin, dismantling a network of explosive labs, improvised explosive devices, command centers and tunnels.

The intention was clear: to exploit the weakness of the PA and ensuing security vacuum, to create a 'mini-Gaza' or new 'southern Lebanon'—but this time, within the West Bank. I mentioned earlier that some cities in the West Bank are a mere walk away from the densely populated Israeli coast. Iran and its Palestinian allies certainly took note.

Iran is often considered a 'distant' enemy, but due to a series of transformative events in the region since the US invasion of Iraq in 2003, it has managed to extend its arm and surround Israel with a network of proxies—a 'ring of fire.'

The goal may not only be to slowly strangle Israel and tie it down: it may well be part of a deeper strategy, using the Israeli–Palestinian conflict as well as anti-American sentiment across the region to project Iranian influence. If Iran were to emphasize its identity as a Shiite nation, it would quickly find limits to its regional power in a largely Sunni-dominated region.

But by building a broader and more 'inclusive' narrative, mixing anti-Israel and anti-American ideologies with anti-imperialist rhetoric of the kind often touted by the far left, Iran has broken the mental dams just as geopolitical obstacles to its expansion turned to dust. Iran invested in local proxies that can thrive in a region in crisis, turning from a distant threat to Israel to an intimate one.

18

AN INEVITABLE COLLISION?

At the beginning of 2023, for the first time, the Israeli army mentioned the risk of a 'multi-front war' as a real possibility in its yearly risk review. Israel was no longer envisioning separate conflicts against Iranian proxies but a major Israel–Iran war that would engulf the region and see its troops operate in multiple theaters. The scenario that was considered, and for which the Israeli army later trained during an exercise dubbed 'Firm Hand,' would see Israel face a conflict of a scale it not seen since 1973. A few months later, the 7 October massacre by Hamas made this threat even more real as Iranian proxies in Lebanon, Syria and Yemen—and perhaps also Iraq—started firing missiles at Israel.

Not that Israel hadn't prepared for such a scenario before. The idea that Iranian investments in Lebanon, Syria, Iraq and Yemen could see Israel being pulled into a major regional war was hardly new. But in 2023, it felt less like a theoretical training scenario and more like a distant but real possibility. Around the time of the Jewish Passover holiday, Iranian proxies gave Israel a taste of what a multi-front scenario would look like. An Iranian drone crossed into Israel from the north. Days later, one of the most significant rocket barrages since the Second Lebanon War was fired from Israel's northern neighbor, with another rocket attack being reported from Syria a few hours later. Israel blamed the attack in Lebanon on Hamas's relatively new networks of operatives in the country. But the message was received: Iran was showcasing its ability to challenge Israel on various fronts and to change an equation that had seen Iran mostly absorb Israel's blows in Syria. Later, a report by the *Wall Street Journal* would confirm that this set of attacks, which took place amid grave tensions in Jerusalem and the West Bank, came at the behest of the new commander of Iran's Quds Force, General Esmail Ghaani. The pieces of various puzzles, each significant on their own, were coming together to form a new integrated threat, offering Tehran the ability to challenge Israel and pull it into a conflict the likes of which it hasn't seen in decades.

This raised the broader question of whether such a conflict was inevitable. Israeli forces have been trying to maintain a delicate balance between the need to act forcefully against Iran and its proxies and the necessity to keep tensions below a certain threshold. This concept is often discussed as the 'campaign between the wars' in reference to the latent conflict with Syria and Egypt, in the various periods in-between wars in Israel. Some have referred to this campaign, perhaps more accurately, as a 'conflict to avoid a war.' The goal is indeed to prevent Iran from growing strong enough to feel confident about launching a war. It means imposing a cost on Iran's regional activities, preventing it from entrenching further and delivering game-changing weapons that would alter the current equation. As part of this 'conflict to avoid a war,' Israel has carried out hundreds if not thousands of operations, mostly in Syria but also in Iraq, in the Red Sea and in Iran itself. In a sense, airstrikes against weapons shipments in Syria, mysterious explosions at weapons depots in Iraq and acts of sabotage against nuclear installations in Iran are all part of this campaign between the wars. They all serve to push back the clock of a major confrontation, yet they also all carry the risk of triggering one.

This has raised the question of whether a collision is in fact inevitable. As Iran dots Israel's border with new threats, the Jewish state has so far managed to pull back from the brink and inflict significant blows on Iran and its proxies. But looking at the trend, and despite an extremely efficient campaign waged by Israel, the facts are there: Iran has still been able to expand its footprint, perhaps not in the game-altering ways it sought but certainly in a way that causes alarm.

Understanding this complex threat requires some knowledge of the main pieces of the puzzle and how they contribute to the overall risk of collision. Some of those pieces have already been discussed, including Iran's parasitic influence in Syria, which has seen it form the beginning of a 'southern Lebanon' near the Golan. Others stem from its proxies in Yemen, which could challenge Israel's freedom of navigation in the Red Sea, or Iranian proxies in Iraq, which have proven relatively efficient foot soldiers for Iran's ever-growing ambitions.

But two pieces stand as perhaps the most significant: Iran's most important regional venture, in the form of its Lebanese ally Hezbollah, on the one hand, and the Iranian regime's own nuclear appetite on the other. Both are the centerpiece of this new threat, on top of which additional elements are added to form a coherent strategy.

***

In Israel, a third Lebanon war is often discussed not as a mere possibility but as a certainty. The idea that Israel will, once again, find itself pitted against Hezbollah, one of its fiercest and most competent enemies, is viewed not as a question of if but rather of when. Yet this perception that war is just around the corner isn't as evident as one may think while also being far more terrifying than the casual talk of a third Lebanon war may make it sound to the average Israeli.

A full-scale third Lebanon war would be far more devastating than the wars Israelis have seen in previous decades. In terms of scope and the predicted number of casualties on the Israeli side, a third Lebanon war would be closer to the Yom Kippur War than the Gaza conflicts or even the Second Lebanon war.

The Hezbollah Israel fought in 2006 isn't the same organization it would face in a future conflict. The group now has one of the largest missile arsenals in the region and in the world. Estimates put Hezbollah's arsenal at between 100,000 and 150,000 missiles and rockets. The group would also be able to fire missiles and rockets at a rate far superior to that of Gaza's Hamas, for instance: Hezbollah may be able to fire between 1,200 and 2,000 rockets and missiles per day, and perhaps significantly more during the first days of the war. This is on a scale Israel simply hasn't experienced before, making Hezbollah's rocket arsenal perhaps only second to Iran's nuclear ambitions when it comes to the most pressing threats facing Israel.

To compare, during the 2014 conflict, Hamas and other Palestinian groups fired more than 4,500 rockets in around two months. In 2021, during the eleven-day conflict in Gaza and Israel, the group fired a similar number of rockets, albeit at a rate of fire far superior to that of the 2014 conflict, with an average of around 400 rockets a day. On 7 October, during the first twenty-four hours of the war, Hamas and other groups fired an unprecedented 4,300 rockets, with the number later falling significantly.

In the early stage of the 2021 war, Hamas even claimed to have launched more than 100 rockets at once at Tel Aviv. This unprecedented attack gives a sense of how different things would be should a third Lebanon war break out, for they would be a recurring feature of the conflict. On a daily basis, Hezbollah would be capable of firing three times the number of rockets fired by Hamas during the May 2021 conflict. What's more: it could do so for weeks and months, effectively crippling the Israeli economy and leading to significant casualties.

The sheer number of missiles would put a strain on Israel's air defenses. Israel has one of the best and most experienced air defenses in the world, but this is also because the threat matches the expertise.

Beyond that, the group is likely to use a number of other strategies unavailable to Hamas drawing from the experience of other Iranian proxies. This includes what I've called a 'mix and match' strategy, one mostly implemented by the Iran-backed Houthis in Yemen against Saudi Arabia. The Iran-backed Yemeni rebels have at times been able to pierce through the Saudi air defenses and hit targets deep inside Saudi territory by using a mix of different types of projectiles: ballistic missiles, cruise missiles and drones that have different flying patterns and require different interception vectors, involving different air defense systems. By mixing those weapons, launching two or three different types of projectiles, the attacker can hope to bypass even sophisticated defenses. Israel took note and started training on how to repel those attacks, but this is an additional challenge on top of the sheer number of projectiles in Hezbollah's arsenal.

Hezbollah is also believed to possess around 2,000 drones, having exhibited these weapon systems a number of times and even built some airstrips for the purpose of launching them. Hezbollah is also known to have a number of ballistic missiles, some transferred from the Syrian arsenal (from the Scud family) and others produced either in Lebanon or transferred from Iran.

These missiles are of particular concern to Israel, and many of the Israeli strikes in Syria were tied to an effort to hinder an Iranian-led effort to improve Hezbollah's ability to pinpoint and destroy targets inside Israel. Over the 2010s, Hezbollah and its Iranian masters engaged in a large-scale program meant to improve the accuracy of missiles already within the Lebanese group's possession so that these missiles could strike precisely at specific targets. To do so, the Lebanese group received expertise from Iran as well as Syria.

Hezbollah's Precision-Guided Missile Project (PGMP) partly relies on its older Syrian sister, the SSRC, which Iran partially took over, as mentioned in the previous chapter.

Iran also regularly sends industrial equipment meant to provide Hezbollah with ways to independently improve the accuracy of its missiles. One such piece of heavy industrial machinery was the target of a daring Israeli operation in the heart of Beirut in 2019. Using the cover of the night, an Israeli commando used explosive-laden quadcopters to eliminate equipment sent by Iran that would have served to repurpose unguided missiles and significantly improve their accuracy. Given the threat these systems represent, it is no surprise that Hezbollah's PGMP has been in the crosshairs of the Israeli military.

Stopping it is at the top of Israel's priorities, and for good reason.

In case of a war with Hezbollah, the amount of missiles and variety of systems the group possesses, despite Israel's ongoing campaign of airstrikes in Syria, would test Israel's air defenses in a way no other group has.

The possibility that the group will seek to carry out pinpointed strikes against specific targets in Israel, including sensitive military and civilian sites, adds another layer of complexity. Hezbollah's Hassan Nasrallah has issued a variety of threats over the years, including against the Dimona nuclear reactor and the Haifa ammonia plant.

Those threats are meant to strike fear in the minds of Israelis, but they also reflect the group's ability to carry out accurate strikes, some of which may be successful, particularly if precision-guided missiles are fired alongside dozens, if not hundreds, of other unguided missiles targeting Israeli cities. Among others, the group is poised to take aim at Israeli air bases, which would be critical in the following war effort as Israel mounts its own offensive against the group. Hezbollah would also seek to inflict significant damage on critical infrastructure, including the Ben Gurion Airport, energy facilities and offshore gas platforms. The group has made clear threats against Israel's gas infrastructure, and Israel has responded by testing a naval version of the Iron Dome.

Perhaps as worrying for Israeli civilians is the fact that Hezbollah's firepower will also force Israeli air defenses to prioritize these critical targets over Israeli cities. Should Hezbollah fire missiles at air bases and Israeli cities in a way that overwhelms Israeli air defenses, the Israeli military is likely to prioritize Israel's air bases.

This principle is common knowledge within parts of the Israeli military. On the military level, it makes perfect sense to protect the country's ability to respond to a threat, including its military air bases. But this may not be so obvious to the average Israeli. In fact, the Israeli army has made little effort to prepare the Israeli public for what 'prioritizing the protection of Israeli air bases,' for instance, may mean in terms of civilian casualties as Hezbollah rockets fall unchecked on unprotected Israeli cities.

The Israeli public is largely accustomed to seeing Iron Dome batteries being placed to protect civilian targets: despite Hamas's claim, including during the previous conflict, that it specifically targeted a number of air bases (Palmachim and Tel Nof, among others), the group never successfully did so. The threat posed by Hezbollah, however, is of a different scope and far more serious than that of Hamas, suggesting these sorts of choices may in fact have to be made on a daily basis.

As a result, a third Lebanon war may result in hundreds of civilian casualties, something the Israeli public, again, may not be prepared for.

***

The scope of the threat posed by Hezbollah's rocket, missile and drone arsenal will also impact the way a third Lebanon war will unfold in Lebanon itself. Contrary to previous wars in Gaza, when Israeli air defenses could absorb some of the blows and relieve at least some of the public pressure on the political elite to react, the Israeli government will be forced to quickly up the ante. If a conflict breaks out, it will escalate almost immediately, with both sides trading the heaviest blows in the first hours and days of the conflict.

Hezbollah's rate of fire means that Israel will have to quickly go after its rocket arsenal through both a ground and air campaign. The group has entrenched itself in a network of bunkers and tunnels south of the Litani River—the area of southern Lebanon where the group is most active—but also north of it. Should a conflict break out, Israel is liable to immediately enter southern Lebanon and hit the country with an unprecedented air campaign that will target both Hezbollah and Lebanon, given the group's deep entrenchment in the country.

But the conflict may not initially play out the way it did previously. Hezbollah itself has evolved and may rely on different tactics. Nasrallah has warned of an operation to 'Free the Galilee'— in reference to Israel's northern region of Galilee. While this is likely hubris, the Israeli military does take the threat of a possible Hezbollah incursion very seriously. The IDF assesses that during the first days of the conflict, the group will seek to carry out incursions in Israel's territory, including against the various villages and the kibbutzim border, the Blue Line (the de facto border between Lebanon and Israel). The group regularly monitors the movement and positions of the IDF through a network of observation posts, some famously posing as local posts of an environmental NGO known as 'Green without Borders,' as well as operatives posing as 'shepherds' and through the use of small quadcopter drones.

The conflict may start with Hezbollah incursions meant to delay the entry of Israeli forces while also striking a blow against Israel's home front. These incursions can be carried out directly above ground or using tunnels dug from Lebanon into Israel. Israel is preparing for such a possibility: after years of denying that tunnels were being dug across the border, in 2018 Israel launched Operation 'Northern Shield' with the aim of eliminating that threat. The operation started in December 2018 when Israel exposed a large tunnel from the Lebanese village of Kafr Kela, which is believed to be an important 'defensive' node for Hezbollah close to Israel's northernmost city of Metula, and ended in January 2019.

Although operation 'Northern Shield' did lead to the discovery of at least six 'attack' tunnels (tunnels crossing into Israel), not all of them may have been discovered. Despite the presence of UNIFIL, Hezbollah's activities along the border remain largely unchecked, and the group will be able to rebuild its underground network. In fact, it is most likely that some remain: in Gaza, the IDF deliberately left some 'attack' tunnels while monitoring them to thwart any future attacks and collapse them when needed. The same tactic is sure to be used in Lebanon. Still, the Israeli military is prepared to face a number of 'hostage-taking' situations in border communities, which would significantly hamper the initial war effort.

Hezbollah has also gained significant expertise in near-conventional operations and special ops. The group first showed its ability to carry out large-scale military offensives when it led the battle of Qusayr, mentioned previously. Hezbollah would later also carry out a counter-insurgency operation in Lebanon itself, near the border town of Arsal. Since then, the group has shown off its 'conventional' capabilities on multiple occasions during military parades. Some of them, such as the use of old armored personnel carriers, are irrelevant to a fight with Israel. But the group has also developed 'rapid intervention' units, including quads equipped with anti-tank missiles, meant to quickly be deployed to stop the advance of armored columns.

This is not the only asset Hezbollah could use both in its initial effort to 'conquer the Galilee' and during the course of a conflict. The group's elite 'Radwan' unit, which is close to elite commando/special force units in most countries, has been involved in several operations in Syria, including offensives against the Syrian opposition. Perhaps more worryingly for Israel, the unit is also believed to have operated closely with Russian special forces during a number of operations in the eastern Syrian desert and in Aleppo, where it likely gained further insight into the tactics employed by regular military forces. Training and operating alongside a conventional force, including special forces, may have provided it with significant expertise that can be used in initial attacks against Israeli border communities.

***

The rapid escalation suggests that a conflict will play out in days, rather than weeks. Effectively, neither side can really achieve any sort of strategic victory over the other: despite its expanded capabilities, and claims that it will 'conquer the Galilee,' Hezbollah cannot hope to destroy Israel. Similarly, given the size of Hezbollah and how deep it is embedded in Lebanon, inflicting a decisive blow against the Iran-backed group is not a realistic objective, unless Israel is ready for a prolonged occupation of Lebanon. The occupation of southern Lebanon showed even this would be unlikely to lead to Hezbollah's destruction, and in fact may have done just the opposite.

The cost of the operation in lives and in economic terms will be disastrous, particularly for Lebanon. Israel has warned multiple times that it would take Lebanon 'back to the Stone Age.' This is in part a talking point that's mostly meant for deterrence, to underscore the extreme risks an ill-advised Hezbollah escalation entails. But it also reflects the likely reality of a conflict, particularly a protracted one. Israel will look to quickly destroy Hezbollah positions and military arsenals deeply embedded in civilian areas, with public pressure mounting to put an end to the rocket attacks on Israeli civilians. Lebanon is already a de facto failed state, with staggering levels of inflation and a political deadlock that has gone from bad to worse. Hezbollah's influence in Lebanon means it would have to justify such a devastating war to its own public, which has shown signs of war weariness, as well as the other main communities in Lebanon, who are slated to suffer from a war they have not chosen. Anti-Hezbollah sentiment is rising in Lebanon, in part because of the perception that the group may have been involved in the Beirut port explosion of August 2020. Some notable incidents are likely to have worried Hezbollah, including a series of attacks against Hezbollah supporters as well as a protest denouncing the firing of rockets by Hezbollah outside of a Druze village in southern Lebanon. Although Hezbollah largely remains in control, it is not foolish enough to think that this situation is set in stone, especially in the complex and degraded Lebanese environment.

In other words, while the amount of destruction on both sides is almost certain to be extremely vast, neither side can truly hope to achieve more than a tactical victory. They will have much to lose and little to win.

In a way, this is close to the Cold War doctrine of 'Mutually Assured Destruction' (MAD), when both the Soviet Union and the United States had far more to lose than to win in a direct confrontation.

Evidently, the situation between the two is different, since neither side has the means of annihilating the other—or in the case of the nuclear-armed Israeli side, means that would realistically be used. But the dynamic is the same, and there are clear incentives on both sides not to go beyond a certain threshold.

This is why one should always be skeptical of the claim that a third Lebanon war will happen again. The dynamic that has held so far since the 2006 Second Lebanon War has generally prevented a broader conflict.

At the same time, it is true that this 'MAD-like' dynamic has been eroded. The accumulation of weapons on Hezbollah's side could incentivize Israel to intervene now rather than waiting until Hezbollah has effectively changed the 'rules' of the dangerous dance Israel and the Iran-backed proxies are entangled in. Perhaps more importantly, after 7 October, many in Israel's border communities near Lebanon, who have been evacuated in the first week of the war, would not want to come back unless the threat coming from Hezbollah is neutralized. After all, the 'al-Aqsa Flood' operation carried out by Hamas is a copy of what Nasrallah had in mind when he spoke about the 'conquest of the Galilee': thousands of Hezbollah commandos from the Radwan force would cross into Israel, taking border communities and creating hundreds of hostage-taking situations, as thousands of Hezbollah rockets rained down on Israel. After 7 October, this is not a threat Israel can easily dismiss.

But the question of when a line has been crossed—that is, estimating when Hezbollah has accumulated 'too many' of these weapons—is difficult to answer. Covert actions and the 'campaign between the war' have a far better risk/benefit ratio in that sense. Triggering a war with Hezbollah to remove its military capabilities is akin to triggering a nuclear war for the sake of removing the adversary's nuclear arsenal. This makes a deliberate escalation into war less likely, though not impossible, but wars are not always desired, and miscalculations can quickly escalate into a full-blown conflict.

What the 7 October conflict has also shown is that even in the midst of one of the worst regional escalations, and despite daily tit-for-tat attacks, the mechanism of deterrence has worked well, so far, to prevent a conflict. But Iran's ambition of expanding its front against Israel threatens to tip the scale in a way that increases the chance of a conflict, and the change in threat perception in Israel certainly encourages more pre-emptive actions. That's not to mention the other potential external: Iran's own nuclear program.

***

Most outside observers and Israelis may have a misleading sense of what an Israeli strike against Iran's nuclear program would look like. This is in part due to Israel's own history. Since its inception, Israel has carried out two major operations against two separate nuclear programs: Operation 'Opera' to destroy the Iraqi nuclear reactor 'Osirak' delivered by France to Saddam Hussein in the 1980s, and operation 'Outside the Box,' which led to the destruction of the nuclear reactor in eastern Syria in 2007.

In many ways, both operations were quick and painless. Both operations also give a deceptive picture of what an Israeli operation against the Iranian nuclear program would look like. The Israeli attacks against Iraq and Syria were carried out at a time when both the Iraqi and Syrian nuclear programs were in their infancy. As such, a decisive blow could be dealt through a complex but relatively swift and pinpointed operation. One facility would need to be destroyed, in one strike, dealing a decisive blow to the nascent nuclear programs.

An Israeli attack against Iranian nuclear facilities would, however, be very different from these previous strikes. The Iranian nuclear program is far more advanced and far closer to a nuclear breakthrough than its regional predecessors. The Iranian program also consists of multiple facilities, all of which can be rebuilt if one of them is destroyed.

Should an Israeli attack focus on only one or two of these facilities, the results would likely be only a minor setback for the Iranian nuclear program. In April 2021, for instance, an attack—which some Iranian officials blamed on Israel—targeted chains of centrifuges within an underground section of the Natanz fuel enrichment plant. It is still unclear what may have caused the attack, and more specifically whether this was a form of direct sabotage using explosives or a cyber-attack.[1] The attack resulted in a power failure that affected both the main electrical network and the emergency generators, prompting centrifuges to shut down. Centrifuges are used to enrich uranium, which needs to be processed for civilian and military purposes. They do so by spinning at extremely high speed to separate uranium components. Suddenly shutting them down would result in significant damage to the centrifuges, suggesting that a high number of centrifuges may have been damaged in the 2021 attack. Whatever means were used, the attack was a success. And yet, according to Iran's own claims, and reports by the UN nuclear watchdog, since 2021 Tehran has continued to accumulate uranium at a high pace, showing that a single strike is unlikely to have the desired impact.

The Iranian nuclear program is decentralized by design: the Iranians have sought to ensure their program can survive Israeli strikes. The Syria and Iraq strikes benefited from a key element of surprise that is off the table when it comes to an attack against Iran. Iranian facilities, particularly the uranium enrichment plants, have been built in bunkers deep inside Iran's mountains. This includes the Fordow fuel enrichment plant, which is built 50 to 80 meters underground, and the Natanz fuel enrichment plant, which is being extended to include even more deeply buried enrichment facilities. These two plants, as well as at least half a dozen others, are at the top of Israel's 'shopping list' if it ever gets in the business of more overtly going after Iran's nuclear program. Excavation works at a number of sites suggest that this will continue over time, making it far more difficult for Israel to destroy these facilities without a proper upgrade to its capabilities.

To reach these targets, Israel will need to use dozens of 'bunker-busters,' the nickname given to a series of mostly US-made bombs capable of digging past ground and metal to reach deeply buried targets. This is a challenge in itself, as Israel does not possess the latest version of US-made bunker-busters: in fact, the latest generation of bunker-busters (also known as 'mother of all penetrators') are so heavy that most planes (including all of the aircraft in Israel's arsenal) are incapable of carrying them. Israel will have to use smaller bunker-busters that are still so heavy that each Israeli plane carrying them would only be able to fire one such weapon before having to go back to base hundreds of kilometers away. As a result, the mere payload needed to strike the deeply buried fuel enrichment plant mentioned above would require dozens of planes. In addition to these main targets, Israeli planes would also have to strike hundreds of other targets, including air defenses, air bases, nuclear-related facilities and military sites across Iran. The distance Israel has to cross is another key challenge, requiring careful planning and the use of refuelers—airplanes carrying fuels to avoid trips back and forth from Israel to Iran.

To be clear, this does not rule out an Israeli attack, nor a successful one. But it will not be the 'quick and painless' option some may anticipate. Such a strike would require hundreds of planes, thousands of sorties and trigger a regional conflict of the sort Israel has not seen since the 1973 Yom Kippur war.

The word 'strike' itself is deceptive: an attack against the Iranian nuclear program would look far closer to an actual 'war,' one that would not be confined to Iran or Israel. Israeli planes would likely have to carry out several days of strikes, if not weeks, depending on the goal of the strike and how much of a blow Israel would seek to inflict upon Iran's nuclear program.

This largely shifts the risk versus benefit ratio, particularly when considering that Iran, and its proxy Hezbollah, will respond. Although Hezbollah's Nasrallah claimed in a speech in February 2022 that, should Israel attack Iran, the group would not necessarily be involved, this is unlikely to be the case. The claim is meant to maintain a semblance of independence in the eyes of an increasingly weary Lebanese public. The truth is that the very purpose of Hezbollah's gigantic missile and rocket arsenal is to respond to an Israeli attack against Iran. Iran did not invest in Hezbollah's missile arsenal out of the goodness of its heart, or in this specific case, hatred of Israel, with vast efforts being made to equip the group with one of the largest stockpiles of missiles and rockets in the world. This is one of Tehran's strategic assets, at the heart of Iran's deterrence vis-à-vis Israel: deterrence not only against an Israeli attack against Lebanon but also against an Israeli attack against Iran's nuclear facilities.

If a war were to break out, this Iranian investment would serve to undermine Israel's campaign of airstrikes against Iran's nuclear program. Hezbollah will use the precision-guided missiles it has acquired to carry out pinpointed strikes against air bases across Israel in an effort to jeopardize Israel's air operations. As an Israeli official once put it, it is possible to imagine that an Israeli aircraft that would take off to strike Iran would return to a base that has since been struck by Hezbollah's missiles.

More broadly, this also raises the threshold of what an Israeli attack should achieve. I have mentioned the possible cost of a war with Hezbollah. In geopolitics, cost must be matched by higher benefits, and an attack against Iran would not deviate from this principle. This means that an Israeli attack would likely seek to maximize the damage inflicted on Iran. In other words: if Israel does strike Iran's nuclear facilities, it won't pull any punches. The result will be devastating for Iran and its proxies because Israel would have no other choice but to strike with as much conventional power as it can muster.

This also raises the question of whether Israel would actually want to pursue this course of action. The risks are tremendous: Israel would be engaged in a likely multi-front war that will bring about all of the 'elements of the puzzle' (or what some have called Iran's 'ring of fire') against Israel: Israel could find itself involved in weeks-long campaigns of airstrikes in Iran, a war with Hezbollah, as well as clashes on the Syrian front and possibly in Gaza and the West Bank. Although not an existential war, it would require resources similar to prior wars of survival.

At the same time, given how challenging such an operation is, there are no guarantees that Israel will be able to fully destroy Iran's nuclear program. To be clear, Israel has the ability to set the Iranian program back by at least a couple of years, destroying enrichment facilities, centrifuge-making plants, heavy-water production sites and so on. The Iranian regime would see the war it sought to bring closer to Israel suddenly being waged within its own territory, something it has sought to avoid at all costs. The IRGC and Ayatollah Khamenei are fully aware that they sit on a volcano at home, and that a war with Israel could have unintended and unpredictable consequences.

And if Israel is to pay the cost of a multi-front war, there is also no guarantee that the Jewish state will stop simply after destroying Iran's nuclear program: if it can, Israel will likely also seek to damage the Iranian regime's ability to maintain control over an increasingly resentful population. As is always the case, help from Israel could backfire, giving the regime another reason to use violence against its own people—but here again, the trajectory of such a conflict would be unpredictable.

***

Iran is slowly raising the temperature on Israel, hoping that by gradually building up its proxies and 'ring of fire' around Israel, it will expand its ability to challenge Israel while deterring the Jewish state from responding too forcefully, including against its nuclear program. In a way, Iran's strategy is almost a parallel to Israel's 'campaign between the war.' This is a high-risk game, in which both sides seek to gain a lead over the other while avoiding a full-scale confrontation that remains riddled with massive risks and unpredictability.

The question for Israel will always be one of limits. Going back to the slow-cooking metaphor, Israel does not want to find itself getting cozy in gradually hotter waters, to suddenly discover those same waters are boiling. The question of the 'limit' will always be a difficult one, and understanding when Israel needs to act even more forcefully is always a complex issue to decide on.

But the collision with Iran is not inevitable.

French thinker Raymond Aron said of the Cold War confrontation between the United States and the USSR that it posed a unique dilemma in that 'peace is impossible, and war improbable.' This well-formulated equation, which explains the long impasse of the Cold War, also applies here. Peace is impossible as long as the Iranian regime remains in place. But war is also improbable because the cost of a full-blown confrontation is too high, particularly when compared to what each side can hope to achieve.

Perhaps, just like the Cold War, the most plausible outcome isn't a 'final confrontation' but rather a continuation of both sides' 'campaign between the wars' and a slow attrition that will see one of the two rivals falter.

19

AN EMPIRE AT RISK OF COLLAPSING UPON ITSELF

With each wave of protests in Iran comes those who have long dreamed about the fall of the Islamic Republic, an oppressive regime that has clearly lost the support of a great majority of Iranians. According to some of the more reliable polls—which should still be viewed as just a general measurement of popularity—80 percent of Iranians do not support the Islamic Republic.[1] The Iranian regime is embroiled in a series of crises that certainly pose greater risks than before.

Yet those who see each revolt as a future revolution are focusing on the wrong side of the issue. That the Iranian people have long been opposed to their own government is no secret. But the Iranian regime does not rely on popular support, or at least not from most Iranians. Among the 10 to 20 percent of Iranians who still support the regime are those who have a vested interest in maintaining it and are willing to shed blood (theirs, but mostly that of their compatriots). Iran has built a powerful counter-revolutionary force in the form of the IRGC as well as the Basij paramilitary force. These have proven time and time again that they were ready and even at times eager to crack down on any signs of dissent, killing hundreds of protesters if needed. In 2019, they killed 1,500 protesters.

If the regime is to collapse, the cracks will come from outside of this minority, but perhaps more importantly from within it. Looking at fallen authoritarian regimes, it is clear that divisions, hesitations and internal rivalries have all played a central role in allowing outside pressure to gain critical mass. As long as those on the frontline of the regime's internal struggle for survival are ready to die or perhaps more importantly kill in the regime's name, the chances of a successful revolution are low.

The Iranian regime has shown little hesitation in shedding blood. Even during the latest protest, which has seen Iranian forces fighting not only its own people but women protesters, the apparatus as a whole held firm—killing and arresting the brave protesters who dared challenge them. Executions were carried out and reached new levels of cruelty, as those arrested were generally told not to make a fuss so as to broker a deal with the authorities, before being executed under cover of night. Their family members were often harassed and detained in a likely effort to make an example out of them and show that the punishment extended beyond the 'culprit.' This is a regime that, like many others, is developing more sophisticated ways to silence its own people. That the Iranians have in fact not been silent is a testament to their bravery and the widespread detestation the regime inspires.

But a closer look also shows cracks, perhaps not the kinds that will lead to a collapse in the short term but certainly weaknesses that show that Iran is not impervious to pressure from its own population. In 2021, the already thin veil of 'democracy' that has always accompanied the Islamic Republic was promptly removed. Direct elections in Iran were always tightly controlled: the Guardian Council, an entity largely controlled by the Iranian supreme leader, is tasked with 'vetting' candidates—making it impossible for anyone not first greenlit by what's effectively the Iranian deep state to run in the first place. Yet up until 2021, there was a choice (as superficial as it may be) between two main camps, namely the conservative/hardliner camp and the 'moderates' or reformists. Outside commentators have claimed that this divide is artificial, and to an extent it is, given that the Iranian government and president are not the main decision-makers on a number of issues. Still, those two camps have ideologically different positions that have enabled some debate.

But in 2021, the Guardian Council effectively barred any credible challenger to Raisi, an Iranian cleric close to Ayatollah Khamenei best known for his participation in a series of executions of opponents in the 1980s. Raisi became president in 2021 in elections that, even compared to the usual Iranian standards, were a farce.

This is not without risks given that direct elections allowed Iranians to express some frustrations and that the decision to sideline reformists created tensions within the political landscape that are still felt to this day.

But these tensions may only be minor compared to what's ahead, when the real decision-maker in Iran will need to be replaced: the Islamic Republic's supreme guide, Ayatollah Khamenei. The Iranian leader, who is eighty-four years old at the time of writing, is in fragile health. In 2014, he underwent a successful prostate cancer operation yet has since been rumored to be ill on multiple occasions.

Khamenei has yet to name a successor, and technically this task will fall upon the Assembly of Experts, another clerical body within the Iranian regime. President Raisi is positioning himself as a clear contender, but his candidacy will be contested by others. This includes Khamenei's own son, Mojtaba, who was recently named an 'ayatollah'—a religious title seen as necessary to succeed his father. Raisi's inability to avoid waves of unrest in the country may have boosted Mojtaba's chances or those of other hopefuls. However, a succession from father to son would not be without risks, recalling the dynastic principles of the previous regime the Islamic Republic replaced following the 1979 Revolution. What's clear is that Khamenei's passing will be fraught with risks for Iran, with multiple candidates jostling for power.

Unexpected scenarios should not be ruled out. The principle upon which the Islamic Republic was built, namely Velayat al-Faqih (the rule of the judges or clerics), is increasingly contested even from within the Iranian regime. The protests prompted by the death of Mahsa Amini have shown how despised the system of religious control and gender apartheid have become. A trend has even seen young Iranians film themselves knocking the turbans off clerics in the street—in addition to the year-long trend that saw Iranian woman publicly remove their veil in defiance of the regime. At the same time as the Islamic Republic is becoming even less popular, it is increasingly relying on the IRGC and Basij militia even more. The IRGC govern their own segment of the economy and represent the long-arm of the Iranian regime.

It is not beyond the realm of possibility that the Islamic Republic will change but not necessarily for the better, not becoming more democratic but toning down the religious aspect at its core. Behind closed doors, figures within the regime are leaning into a model that would give less power to a clique of dying clerics and more to a number of military and paramilitary officials less driven by ideology than the interests of their own class. This new Iran would be just as cruel and retain the 'Axis of Resistance' ideology but be more nationalistic than Islamist.

Another group that could see Khamenei's succession as an opportunity are the reformists, who feel they've been undeservedly marginalized to help Raisi's ascension. Some figures within the reformist camp have expressed support for some of the protestors' demands and have called for the core of the Islamic Republic to be revamped. They are unlikely to get any significant support from Iranian protesters, who see the reformist camp as tarnished by its collaboration with the regime. But the reformists have been close to the centers of power of Iran and could weigh on its future succession struggle.

Overall, this means that Khamenei's passing will raise profound questions beyond the mere name of the supreme guide's successor. Iran is approaching a crisis of its own making, one that is unlikely to pass without some form of change, either from within or from without.

CONCLUSION

THINKING ABOUT THE FUTURE

In a region that has changed so drastically over a relatively short period of time, thinking about the future is a dangerous and, often, vain exercise. Who could have predicted 9/11 and the ensuing War on Terror? Any plans made in the Middle East beforehand would likely find themselves to be trash-bound after the attacks. Who could have predicted that the suicide of a street vendor in Tunisia would end up unseating a long-time dictator in Egypt, prompting a NATO intervention in Libya or triggering a civil war in Syria? Who predicted the 7 October massacre and the way it has reshaped the region?

But while we may be powerless to predict, we are able to anticipate. No one could have predicted the exact time and process that we now call the Arab Spring. But the elements that led to it were there—and still exist today. The future is discernable when it comes to major trend lines. Breaking points, the likes of which are mentioned above, are harder to date but are still visible to the naked eye.

All of those characteristics, which blur any attempt at thinking about the future, are even more pronounced for Israel. The region is changing in a way Israel cannot control, while Israel itself is changing in a way those participating in that change can't predict. Israel and the Jewish people's long quest for survival have also left mental scars. Those further weigh on their ability to project in the future: for Jews, thinking about the 'future' has often been limited to a binary question of survival or collapse.

But in the midst of all this uncertainty, we can paint two broad paths, similar to those presented in the article mentioned in Chapter 4, written in Hebrew by the Emirati ambassador to Washington just before the Abraham Accords. In this article, which appeared on 12 June in the leading Israeli newspaper *Yediot Aharonot*, Ambassador al-Otaiba warned Israelis that they faced a choice between a path of isolation, one that began with the annexation of parts of the West Bank (a plan promoted by Netanyahu at the time), and another path of engagement. The first path would 'harden Arab views of Israel' and 'overturn all of Israel's aspirations for improved security, economic and cultural ties with the Arab World.' The other path was one of engagement around 'shared concerns about terrorism and aggression' between two countries with diverse economies and deep relations with the United States.

The Emirati ambassador was looking more specifically at the opportunity that was ahead to break the longstanding status quo in the Arab–Israeli conflict through a groundbreaking normalization agreement. But the two paths he implicitly described are a good mental framework to think about Israel's future. Israel can choose to take a path of engagement. This will be a long and difficult path, for the region is changing, and friendships between leaders aren't as durable as friendships between peoples. But the opportunities are there to build the infrastructure that will more solidly attach Israel to the region, the roads that hopefully someday people will use to cross borders and make peace with their feet. We should not expect a massive engagement but one that starts from above and provides the space necessary to deepen the ties from 'top to bottom.'

But Israelis need to be aware that one can easily fall from one path to the other. In 2020, Israel chose a path of engagement with the region when Prime Minister Netanyahu signed the Abraham Accords and dropped his plans to annex part of the West Bank. While stunningly transformative, this doesn't mean that the choice

CONCLUSION

is made and that the voices calling for isolation have quietened down. In fact, they have, to a noticeable extent, grown louder as Israel's crisis of identity also grew deeper.

We're in a moment of both great hope and immense despair. The Abraham Accords can pave the way for tremendous opportunities if Israel is able to successfully navigate a changing environment marked by doubts over the US commitment to the region and more complex relationships between various blocs. But Israel also needs to avoid learning the wrong lesson from the accords: although 'Palestinian fatigue' is real, it is not as widespread as some in Israel may think. The wave of unrest that followed the 7 October attacks and the Israeli operation in Gaza certainly serves as a reminder that sympathy for the Palestinian cause is real, both inside the Middle East and abroad. More importantly, whether the world ignores it or not, Israel's conflict with the Palestinians will not disappear. Geography is, in that sense, very much destiny. Any crisis affecting the Palestinian territories, including the upcoming Palestinian leadership crisis, will only take seconds to become Israel's crisis.

Despair and a lack of unity on the Palestinian side have profoundly shaken the bonds between the Palestinian leadership and its people. Those celebrating this as good news, abiding by the proverbial 'divide and conquer' motto, may be proven wrong at a considerable price—and in fact already have. But here again, where there is despair, there is also hope for change: as leadership change approaches, and with it a struggle to redefine Palestinian objectives, Israel can extend a hand and provide renewed engagement.

The current political set up and the war that broke out on 7 October, starting with a massacre of Jews unseen since the Holocaust, certainly aren't conducive to such a move. But Israel itself is in a moment of flux. A new generation is rising up to redefine priorities that have so far been narrowly limited to security. The Israeli–Palestinian conflict is one that has suffered from this approach, at times denounced by those in charge of Israel's own security. Putting values back at the top of the agenda and taking a more long-term approach may dissipate the dark clouds that have unfortunately amassed over years of the status quo.

Lastly, and perhaps more importantly, this natural reluctance to think about the future prevents us from doing so in another critical way: not as a predictive exercise but as a simple way to envision a different world from the one in which we're living. Thinking about the future isn't so much an exercise in crystal ball-reading as it is one of course correction or course confirmation.

The Israeli–Palestinian conflict is in dire need of people who think about what will come next and what should come next, as well as the gap between the two. People who are not looking for petty arguments to convince an external audience. We've been debating this conflict for as long as it has existed: both sides have come up with their arguments, and we know them all. Repeating them for a new generation won't help settle the debate, but it will preclude us from settling the conflict itself.

When I was a child, learning chess, I was taught a very simple lesson but one that would stay with me for life. Always start by envisioning where you want to be. Not the moves you made, the mistakes now painfully obvious or the opportunities not taken. Visualize the endgame. Imagine what it could look like, and don't let yourself become a prisoner of 'the next move.' Then move gradually back from this place, one step at a time, to the place where you are.

The same approach needs to be applied to this conflict. Both sides need leaders capable of envisioning where they should take us and how. By not thinking about the future, we often find ourselves trapped in the present, a present that we feel we know and control, but one that often ends up controlling us.

The future can scare. We often feel helpless to change it. But it will never be as scary as the one we may face should we sleepwalk into the many pitfalls placed before us.

ACKNOWLEDGEMENTS

This book would not have been possible without the support and invaluable contribution of a number of incredible people, including:

My wife, Elisa, who has been encouraging me and helping me all the way, from discussing the angle of the book to picking options for the cover, or just being the amazing and courageous person that she is—and tolerating me for reasons I have yet to figure out.

Michael Dwyer, my editor, who perfectly embodies the spirit of Hurst, the curiosity and passion for knowledge and its diffusion that has been the 'brand' of this unique publishing house. Michael took a chance in publishing this book, given how controversial but also well-covered this topic can be. I feel like this approach and openness is not unique to my own case, but is the mission he has given himself—a worthy mission he fulfils every day.

The Hurst Team, including Daisy and Alice, who have been wonderfully patient, dedicated and understanding, while working to make the book what it certainly wouldn't be without them.

The CEO of Le Beck, Tony, who has always been challenging me with new questions I would never have thought of, and ready to discuss any topic with the same passion.

I would also like to dedicate this book to Sigal Levy, who was killed at the Nova Festival by Hamas. Sigal was on a mission to help at-risk youth at the time when Hamas terrorists descended upon the music festival. May her memory be a blessing. As one released hostage from the festival said: We will dance again.

NOTES

2. THE RETURN OF GREAT POWER COMPETITION

1. MBZ was then the crown prince of Abu Dhabi and has since become the UAE's president.

3. PALESTINIAN FATIGUE?

1. Arab Opinion Index, 2017–18, Arab Centre in Washington, https://arabcenterdc.org/wp-content/uploads/2018/07/Arab-Opinion-Index-2017-2018-1.pdf
2. Zogby Research Services, 'The Annexation Debate,' https://static1.squarespace.com/static/52750dd3e4b08c252c723404/t/5f7dbd0f49f01a0aa9ccec15/1602075922724/Annexation+Update+v1.pdf

4. A DEEP DESIRE FOR ENGAGEMENT

1. Zogby Research, 'The Annexation Debate,' p. 14.
2. Channel 12 poll conducted on 16 August 2020.

6. SECURITY TIES

1. Citizen Lab, https://citizenlab.ca/2012/10/backdoors-are-forever-hacking-team-and-the-targeting-of-dissent
2. The Pegasus Archives, Citizen Lab, https://citizenlab.ca/tag/pegasus

7. THE CROWN JEWEL

1. David Pollock, 'A Third of Saudis Want Business with Israel Now, Even without Formal Ties; 'Muslim Rights' Top List of Public's Terms for Full

Normalization,' Washington Institute, 18 September 2023, https://www.washingtoninstitute.org/policy-analysis/third-saudis-want-business-israel-now-even-without-formal-ties-muslim-rights-top
2. The Hamas attack was carried out on the Jewish holiday of Simchat Torah.
3. The full interview can be viewed here: https://www.youtube.com/watch?v=cE6lUOHNGxU

9. TRADING PEACE FOR QUIET

1. 'The Palestine/Israel Pulse: A Joint Poll (January 2023) Conducted by Program Head Dr. Nimrod Rosler of the International MA in Conflict Resolution and Mediation,' Gershon H. Gordon Faculty of Social Sciences, Tel Aviv University, https://en-social-sciences.tau.ac.il/resolution/pulse-jan-23

10. THE PALESTINIAN 'AUTHORITY'

1. Palestinian Center for Policy and Survey Research, Public Poll no. 85, https://www.pcpsr.org/en/node/920

11. CHAOS IN THE POST-ABBAS ERA

1. Palestinian Center for Policy and Survey Research, Public Poll no. 81, https://www.pcpsr.org/en/node/854

12. ISRAEL'S IDENTITY CRISIS

1. Reform Judaism (as opposed to Orthodox Judaism) includes multiple streams, all of which put more of an emphasis on the need for Jewish religious practices to evolve and include additional modern values, such as the importance of gender equality, for instance.
2. 2020 Pluralism Index, Jewish People Policy Institute, http://jppi.org.il/wp-content/uploads/2020/04/2020-Index-English.pdf
3. Though it still faces discrimination.
4. 'Arab Society: Special Election Survey,' Israel Democratic Institute, 2022, https://en.idi.org.il/articles/46164
5. A concept initially theorized by ISIS in relation to the Muslim community in the West and mentioned in one of the group's publications to justify the 2015 Bataclan attacks in Paris.
6. In reference to Kaplan Street in Tel Aviv where most protests took place.
7. 2020 Pluralism Index, Jewish People Policy Institute.
8. Jewish tribes were divided, then, between the Kingdom of Israel in the north and the Kingdom of Judea in the south (around Jerusalem and south of it).

13. THE PATH OF DESPAIR AND DISILLUSION

1. *Hasbara* or 'explanation' in Hebrew refers to Israel's public relations effort.

14. THE SPACE FOR HOPE IN A SHRINKING 'UNIVERSE OF POSSIBLES'

1. Daniel Egel et al., 'Alternatives in the Israeli–Palestinian Conflict,' Santa Monica, CA: RAND Corporation, 2021, https://www.rand.org/pubs/research_reports/RRA725-1.html. Also available in print form.

15. JUMPING INTO THE UNKNOWN AFTER THE 7 OCTOBER MASSACRE

1. Tamar Hermann and Or Anabi, 'Flash Survey: Israelis Support Immediate Negotiations to Release the Hostages while Fighting Continues,' Israel Democratic Institute, 10 November 2023, https://en.idi.org.il/articles/51431

16. FAILED STATES, SUCCESSFUL IRAN?

1. Itself deriving from the Palestinian name of the city.

18. AN INEVITABLE COLLISION?

1. Considering Iranian facilities are generally in closed circuits, a mix of human intervention and cyber-attack can also not be ruled out.

19. AN EMPIRE AT RISK OF COLLAPSING UPON ITSELF

1. Including a 2019 poll by the Group for Analyzing and Measuring Attitudes in Iran, led by Ammar Maleki, which can be found at https://gamaan.org/wp-content/uploads/2019/04/gamaan-referendum-survey-report-english-2019.pdf

INDEX

Abbas, Mahmoud, 34, 44, 125, 126–7, 128, 130, 131–2, 133, 134, 135, 136–7, 138, 139, 141, 142, 145–7, 149, 152, 181, 183–4, 193
Abbas, Mansour, 166–7, 170
Abdullah, King of Saudi Arabia, 89
Abqaiq and Khurais attacks (2019), 17, 18, 19, 20, 75, 76, 95–6
Abraham Accords, 2–3, 20, 33–4, 38, 39, 40, 45–6, 52, 55, 56, 57, 58, 252–3
   boost in trade, 111
   defense relations, 62–3
   expansion of the normalization process, 85–6
   global companies investment, 107
   Gulf–Israeli relations before, 64–5
   impact on PA, 126–7
   impacts, 65–5
   Iran's expansionism and, 63–4
   new countries, 85
   potential candidates, 59–61
   Riyadh and normalization dynamic, 41–2, 86–9, 95, 96
   security ties, 67–84
   US involvement, 61–2, 64, 66
Abu al-Ata, Baha, 227
Adnan, Khader, 227
ADQ, 114, 115
Ahmadinejad, Mahmoud, 210
'Air Sinai', 46
'al-Aqsa Flood', 182, 185–6, 188, 241
al-Aqsa Martyrs' Brigades, 135, 136–7, 145, 148, 149, 228
al-Aqsa Mosque, 54, 55
al-Alawi, Ibrahim Nasser Mohammed, 70
Alawite community, 220
Albu Kamal, 223
Aleppo International Airport, 223
Aleppo, 223, 239
Aleppo, battle of, 216, 219, 224
Alfei Menashe, 150
Algeria, 209, 210

INDEX

Al-Manarah Square, 138
al-Aloul, Mohammed, 142, 145, 146
al-Qaeda, 218
al-Qaim, 223
al-Shati, 202
Amazon, 105
American Jewish community, 59, 87, 97, 158
Amini, Mahsa, 211, 249–50
Amir-Abdollahian, Hossein, 28
Ansar Bayt al-Maqdis, 11
'anti-Iran' buffer zone, 216
Arab Joint List, 166, 179
Arab League, 59, 179
'Arab NATO'. *See* 'Middle East Strategic Alliance' (MESA)
Arab Opinion Index, 37–8
Arab Peace Initiative (2002), 34, 59–60, 91
Arab Spring, 9–16
   calls for dignity, 9, 12
   camps, emergence of, 13–15
   failure of, 10
   and Israel's security, 9
   Israel's threat perception, 11–12
   'moments' of, 10–11
   social contract, 14
   uncertainty, 11–12
   unfinished, 3, 10
'Arab street', 10, 34, 39, 179
'Arab Winter', 10, 11, 44
Aron, Raymond, 246
Arsal, 238
al-Assad, Bashar, 207, 216, 218, 220, 224, 226
al-Assad, Maher (Assad's brother), 222
Assault Corps, 216

'Authority for National Jewish Identity', 157–8
al-Awdah, Ayman, 216
'Axis of Resistance', 13, 35, 96, 208, 209, 226, 250

Bab el-Mandeb, 29, 109
Baghdad Airport, 223
Bahrain, 34, 55, 72, 82, 84, 88, 95
Balata camp (Nablus), 133, 135, 136, 150
Banat, Nizar, 138
'Bani Fatima Six', 80
Barghouti, Marwan, 129–30, 143, 147–8, 149, 153
Basij, 211, 219, 247, 250
Bedouin communities, 167–8
'Beijing Declaration', 28–9
Beirut, 226, 235
Beitar Illit, 161, 162
Belt and Road Initiative, 28
Ben Gurion Airport, 151, 236
Ben Gvir, Itamar, 161, 167
Bennett, Naftali, 24, 55
Bennett–Lapid government, 166–8
Biden administration, 57, 62, 128
Biden, Joe, 41, 77
   and MBS, 94
   on MBS, 92–3
   Saudi Arabia visit, 41, 77, 93, 94
bin Farhan, Faisal, 77
bin Nayef, Mohammed, crown prince, 89, 92
bin Salman, Prince Abdulaziz, 99
bin Sultan, Bandar, 65
bin Zayed, Sheikh Tahnoun, 114

INDEX

'Blue Flag' aerial exercise, 70
Blue Line, 238
'Breaking Dawn', 227
'Breej Holding', 81
'Brother's Keeper', 185–6

Camp David Peace Accords, 93–4, 119
Çavuşoğlu, Mevlüt, 28
CENTCOM, 68–70, 77
Chevron, 107
China, 101, 212–13
    'Beijing Declaration', 28–9
    economic ties, 30
    influence in the Middle East, 21, 27–30, 31
    Middle Eastern officials visit, 28
Chinese Communist Party, 30, 212
Chollet, Derek, 20, 21
Christians, 220
Citizen Lab, 82
Cohen, Yossi, 81
Cold War, 20
COVID-19, 62, 79, 138, 164
Cybertech Global Expo (Tel Aviv), 80
Czechoslovakia, 10

Dagan, Meir, 65
Dahlan, Mohammed, 129, 189
Damascus International Airport, 222
Damascus, 208, 215, 220, 222, 224, 226
Daraa, 215
'Deal of the Century', 38, 39, 42, 58, 127, 192, 193, 197
Decathlon, 107

Deif, Mohammed, 184
Deri, Aryeh, 160
Dimona nuclear reactor, 236
drones, 71–2
Druze community, 164, 165, 171, 220
Dubai Airshow, 79
Dubai, 2, 5, 14, 75, 79, 104
Dweik, Aziz, 146

East Jerusalem, 55–6, 132–3, 143, 162, 186, 203
Egypt, 12, 39, 43, 44, 60, 73, 119, 160, 226, 232, 251
    exports, 46
    Israeli exports to, 111
    Khaled Saeed, killing of, 12
    police brutality, 138
    political activism, 45
    Sharm el-Sheikh meeting, 77
    Tiran and Sanafir islands, 93–5
EgyptAir, 2, 46
Egyptian army, 74
Egyptian Revolution (2011), 110
Eighth Brigade (Russia), 216–17
Elbit, 79
elections (2022), 161
'Enduring Lightning' exercise, 69
ENGIE, 107
Erdoğan, Recep Tayyip, 60–1

F-35 fighter jets, 59, 69
F-35 stealth fighters, 70
Faraj, Majed, 142, 144–5, 149
Fatah Revolutionary Council, 145–6
Fatah, 43, 44, 47, 128, 129, 130, 131–2, 134, 135, 137, 143, 144, 145, 146, 148, 150, 185, 186

263

Fatemiyoun (Afghan), 224
Fatemiyoun unit, 219
Fayyad, Salam, 131
'Firm Hand' (exercise), 231
Fisk, Robert, 180
Flag March, 55–6
France, 10, 74, 242
'Free the Galilee' (operation), 237

Gantz, Benny, 54, 63, 72, 75
Gargash, Anwar, 77
Gaza disengagement, 119–22, 194, 197
Gaza, 218, 225–7, 234, 238, 243, 253
   calls to 're-occupy' Gaza, 120
   death toll, 202
   demographics, 120–1
   Egypt's interest in stabilizing, 43
   Fatah/Hamas divide, 130–1
   Hamas governance, 182
   Israel withdrawal from (2005), 119
   Israeli bombing, 203
   Israeli operation in, 201–2
   series of escalations, 185
Gazan economy, 183
General Intelligence Service (GIS), 144, 145
Geneva Initiative, 197
Ghaani, Esmail, 232
'Golan File', 217
Golan Heights, 25, 217, 223
Golan, 232–3
'Good Neighbor', 215
'Great Satan', 208
Green Line, 150, 162–3, 176–7, 196–7

'Green without Borders', 238
"Group 42", 79, 81, 82
Guardian Council, 248–9
Gulf Cooperation Council, 28
Gush Katif, 119, 120

Haaretz (newspaper), 144, 145
Hader, 221
Haifa ammonia plant, 236
Halawa, Ahmad Izzat, 136
Hama province, 224
Hamas, 54, 102, 125, 137, 149, 170, 179, 226–7, 231–2, 234, 241
   arrests of Hamas cells, 134
   'Change and Reform' list, 146
   elections, 130–1
   Gaza under Sinwar, 182–5
   Israel declared war on, 20
   military capabilities, 181
   peace/quiet, notion of, 3, 122–4
   political role, 185–6
   representative of the Palestinians, 188
   rise to power, 44, 120, 122, 142
   self-portrayal of, 182
   series of border riots, 128
   takeover of Gaza, 149–50, 151, 152
   waves of violence, 186–7
   See also 7 October massacre
Hamdallah, Rami, 144
Haniyeh, Ismail, 129
Haram al-Sharif, 54–5
Hashem, Hajj, 221
Hassan, Jordanian crown prince, 104

INDEX

Herzog, Isaac, 60, 75
Hezbollah fire missiles, 236
Hezbollah, 25, 208, 217–19, 221–2, 225–6, 228, 233
   Israel's operations, 237–9
   Lebanon war III, 233–7
Homs province, 224
Hormuz Straits, 109
'House and Garden' (operation), 228
Houthis (Ansar Allah), 62, 75, 81, 101, 223, 234
   attacks against Abu Dhabi (2022), 64, 77
   Saudi energy facilities attacks (2019), 17, 18, 19, 20, 76, 95–6
Hubbard, Ben, 82
Hulata, Eyal, 83–4
Hussein, Saddam, 242

Idlib, 223
Independence War (1948), 169
India, 113
'International Maritime Exercise/ Cutlass Express' (IMX), 70–1
'interoperability', 74
Intifada, Second, 91, 134, 137, 148, 150, 152, 169–70
Iran, 14–15, 35, 63, 71, 72, 216
   'Beijing Declaration', 28–9
   borders expansion, 207–10
   Chinese partnership with, 28
   expansionism, 64–5
   on Israel's identity crisis, 176–7
   Israeli–Palestinian conflict, 226–9
   leadership, 64
   Lebanon war III, 233–7
   message to UAE, 75–6
   movement, 210–13
   nuclear program, 241–5
   policy of 'carrot and stick', 75
   Saudi energy facilities attacks (2019), 17, 18, 19, 20, 76, 95–6
   vs. Syria, 220–6
   weapons, 231–3
Iranian Revolution (1979), 110, 226, 249
Iraq, 12, 207, 209, 211, 231–3, 242
   Iran vs. Syria, 220–6
   Iran's growth, 231–3
   nuclear program, 242
Iraq–Syria border, 207–8, 223
Iron Dome missile defense system, 78, 79, 226, 236–7
'Iron Wall', 189–91, 194
Isfahan, 211
'Islamic Revolution', 15, 100
Islamic Revolutionary Guard Corps (IRGC), 1, 63, 211, 219–20, 222, 225, 245, 247, 250
Islamic State (ISIS), 11, 13, 96, 110, 144, 207, 215, 218, 220, 223
Israel
   budget, 172
   Chinese investments in, 30
   engagement with the Arab world, 51–6
   infrastructure project, 108–10
   integration into CENTCOM, 68–70, 77
   Iran's growth, 231–3
   Iranian nuclear program, 241–5

INDEX

Lebanon war III, 233–7
Lebanon, occupation of, 239–41
monopoly on imports, 106
operations, 237–9
peace treaty between Egypt and, 53
peace with Egypt, 2, 9
peace with Jordan, 2, 9, 54
pension funds, 114–15
political crisis (2018–22), 165
security sector, 114
supermarkets, 105
vs. Syria, 222–6
Syrian Civil War, 215–20
tensions with Iran, 63
Israel Aerospace Industries, 79
Israel Defense Forces (IDF), 69–70, 221, 228, 238
Israel's 'Basic Laws' (Knesset), 156–7, 165, 166, 174
Israel's identity crisis, 155–77
    Israeli Arabs, 158, 164–9
    Jewish state or democratic state, 156
    'judicial coup' (2023), 155, 162, 173–4
    ultra-Orthodox Jews (Haredim), 158–60, 161–3
Israeli Arabs, 158, 164–9
Israeli army training, 69
Israeli banks, 104
Israeli Central Bank, 113
Israeli Central Bureau of Statistics, 111
Israeli Declaration of Independence (1948), 156
Israeli Democracy Index, 176

Israeli Democratic Institute (IDI), 176
Israeli economy, 104–15
    clash with country's security needs, 106–7
    free trade agreement, 111–14
    pension funds, 114–15
Israeli elections (2019–20), 54
Israeli Ministry of Education, 157, 172
Israeli police, 132–3
Israeli Supreme Court, 155, 156, 157, 174
Israeli–Arab security relationship, 67–84
    air defences, 77–8
    CENTCOM, 68–70, 77
    cyber-security, 79–82
    defensive partnership, limits, 73–5
    intelligence agencies role, 67–8
    Israeli defense products, buying, 79
    joint exercise, 68–73
    'Middle East Strategic Alliance' (MESA), 73–5
    region's militaries, 74
    surveillance, 82–3
Israeli–Palestinian conflict
    legacy of, 33–4
    'Middle East Quartet', 33
    normalization agreements, 35–9
    Palestinians care for, 36
    radicalization of, 3
    solutions to, 195–9
Israel–Iran war, 231
Israel–Saudi relationship, 85–93

INDEX

Jabhat al-Nusra, 218
Jabotinsky, Ze'ev, 189–91
Jenin refugee camp, 133, 136, 228
Jerusalem Old City, 54, 180
Jerusalem, 208, 232
    tensions surrounding, 54–5
    as Israel's capital, 179–84
Jewish religious laws (Halacha), 156, 157
Jisr az-Zarqa, 169
Jordan, 12, 38, 44, 52, 82, 91
    foreign policy, 43
    free-trade zone, call for, 104
    Israeli exports to, 111
    Mossad and, 65
    transportation network, 109
    'water-for-energy' agreement ('Project Prosperity'), 2, 108–9
al-Jubeir, Adel, 64

al-Kadhimi, Mustafa, 76
Kadima, 121
Kafr Kela, 238
Kahlon, Moshe, 106
Kaplan Force, 173
Katz, Israel, 109
Khalid bin Salman, 41
Khamenei, Ayatollah Ali, 177, 227–8, 245, 249–50
Khashoggi, Jamal (murder of), 90, 92
kibbutzim border, 238
al-Kidwa, Nasser, 129, 131, 132
Kinzhal ('Dagger') hypersonic missile, 26
'Knife Intifada' (2015–16), 186
Kushner, Jared, 18, 58, 59, 92
al-Kuwaiti, Mohammed, 80

Lapid, Yair, 55, 172, 173
'Law and Order', 169
Lebanon Civil War, 208
Lebanon War (2006), 65, 225, 231–2, 233, 240
Lebanon war III, 222, 233–7
Lebanon, 12, 15, 208–9, 211, 222–3, 231, 232, 235, 238
    Iranian nuclear program, 241–5
    Israel's occupation of, 239–41
    Syrian Civil War, 215–20
Levy, Ronan ('Maoz'), 68
Libya, 27, 209–10, 251
'Lions' Den', 137, 149
Lipstadt, Deborah, 87
Litani River, 217–18, 237
Livni, Tzipi, 121
Local Defense Force, 220

al-Mabhouh, Mahmoud, 65
Macron, Emmanuel, 74
Madad Institute, 106–7
Manama Dialogue, 83–4
Mansoor, Ahmed, 82
Mansour, Sheikh, 80
'March of Return', 128, 183
maritime trade lines, instability, 29
Mashhad, 211
Mediterranean Sea, 223
    gas fields, 27
    Ukraine war impact, 26–7
Meretz, 179–80
Merom Golan kibbutz, 215
Meshaal, Khaled, 102
Metula, 238
'Middle East Strategic Alliance' (MESA), 73–5

INDEX

'Middle Eastern Air Defense Alliance', 77
Mohammed bin Salman (MBS), Crown Prince, 18, 19, 77, 92, 97
   deal with Israel, 88–91, 92, 98
   domestic reforms, 98
   Khashoggi, murder of, 90, 92, 93
   relations with the White House, 92–3
   'Vision 2030', 87–8, 97
Mohammed bin Zayed (MBZ), 18, 80
Mojtaba (Khamenei's son), 249
Morocco, 34, 55, 63, 72, 85
Mossad, 42, 65, 67
Mosul, 208
Mubarak, Hosni, 10
al-Muhandis, Abu Mahdi, 63
Muslim Brotherhood, 13, 15, 45, 110
Mutually Assured Destruction' (MAD), 240–1

Nablus, 132, 133, 136, 145, 228
al-Nahyan, Sheikh Tahnoun bin Zayed, 64, 80–2
'Nakba' (Catastrophe), 169
al-Nakhalah, Ziyad, 226–7
Nasrallah, Hassan, 236–7, 244
Nasser, Gamal Abdel, 44, 94
Natanz fuel enrichment plant, 242–3
National Defense Force, 220
National Economic Council, 158
Nation-State Law, 156, 157
NATO, 72, 251
NEOM city, 87–8

Netanya, 91, 150, 151
Netanyahu, Benjamin, 23, 43, 52, 54, 56, 127, 151, 154, 157, 160, 183, 252
   economy and security issues, 107
   meeting with Mohammed bin Salman, 88, 90
   Putin and, 23
   on return of PA, 188–9
   strategy, 192–4
   ultra-liberal policies, 161
   vision, 191–2
Netanyahu-led government, formation of, 172, 197
New Middle East, The (Peres), 103
New York Times, 81, 82
9/11 attacks, 91, 251
90th Brigade (SAA), 221
Noble Energy, 107
'Noble Waters' (naval drill), 69
'Northern Shield' (Operation), 238

Obama administration, foreign policy, 22
Olmert, Ehud, 65, 121
'Opera' (Operation), 242
'Operation 'Black Belt', 227
Osirak', 242
Oslo Accords (1993), 2, 9, 103, 104, 121, 122, 126, 132, 142, 152, 153, 174, 181, 199
al-Otaiba, Yousef, 51–2, 53, 59, 252
'Outside the Box' (operation), 242
Ovadia Yosef, Rabbi, 159, 160

Palestine Mandate, 190

INDEX

Palestinian Authority (PA), 54, 121, 125–39, 142–3, 151–3, 183, 185, 188, 196
   creation of, 126
   crisis of legitimacy, 133–4, 139, 141–2
   elections, 128–32
   financial crisis, 132, 135, 138
   internal crisis, 135–8
   leadership, loss of, 127
   return of, 188–9, 203–4
   security control, 132–3
Palestinian Basic Law, 146
Palestinian courts, 134
'Palestinian fatigue', 33–47, 100, 253
   Arab Opinion Index, 35–9
   internal divisions among Palestinians, 44
   leadership, lack of, 35
   Palestinian leadership, 43–4
Palestinian Islamic Jihad, 133, 137, 147, 149, 151, 186, 226–8
Palestinian Legislative Council (PLC), 131, 146
Palestinian Preventive Security Force, 134–5, 139
Palestinian state, creation of, 91
Palestinian Supreme Constitutional Court, 146
Palmachim, 70
Palmyra, 222
pan-Arabism, 39
'Passover Massacre', 150
peace/quiet, notion of, 3, 122–4
Pegasus affair, 82, 83
Peres, Shimon, 103–4, 115
Phoenix Insurance Company, 114, 115
'pirates', 71

Popular Front for the Liberation of Palestine, 147
'pragmatic' states, 13–14, 15
Prague Spring (1968), 10
Precision-Guided Missile Project (PGMP), 235
pro-democracy movements, 13–14, 15–16
Putin, Vladimir, 23

Qalamoun, 222
Qatar, 13
Quds Force, 232
Quneitra border, 215
Quneitra Province, 221
Qusayr, 219, 221
Qusayr, battle of, 238

Rabin, Yitzhak, 121, 159, 174
   assassination of, 103, 120
Radwan force, 241
Radwan unit, 219, 239
Rafael, 79
'Railway for Peace', 109
Raisi, Ebrahim, 211, 249–50
Raisi, Ebrahim, 63–4
Rajoub, Akram, 136, 143–4
Ramallah, 129, 130, 132, 135, 138, 139, 149, 151, 184, 186, 193
RAND, 195
Red Sea, 70, 71, 233
'regionalization', 61
Ritz-Carlton affair, 89
al-Rumaithi, Hassan, 81
Russia, 216
   bilateral relations between Israel and, 23, 24
   influence in the Middle East, 21

INDEX

intervention in Syria, 23
Ministry of Defense, 26
naval force deployment in Mediterranean, 26
shooting down Israeli planes, 25
Russian air force, 26

al-Sa'adi Bassem, 227
SAA. *See* Syrian Arab Army (SAA)
Saban, Haim, 59
Saied, Kais, 10
Salman, King of Saudi Arabia, 89, 92, 97
Sana'a, 208
Sarea, Yahya, 75
Saudi Arabia, 25, 59, 113, 207, 234–5
  against Iran, 64–5
  airspace access to Israel, 64–5, 72, 95
  anti-Palestinian rhetoric, 35–6
  Arab Peace Initiative (2002), 34, 59–60, 91
  'Beijing Declaration', 28–9
  Biden administration and, 87, 92–3, 100–1
  Biden's visit, 41, 77, 93, 94
  defense contracts with US, 19–20
  Iran's series of talks with, 63–4
  Islamic alliance, 73
  Israel–Hamas war impact, 101–2
  Israeli-made spyware, 82
  jihadist threats, 96–7
  MBS's domestic reforms, 98
  normalization agreement and risks, 98–102
  normalization agreement, 41–2, 86–9
  relationship with religious elites, 97
  religious power, 86–7
  Ritz-Carlton affair, 89
  rivalry between Iran and, 17–18
  Saudi–Israeli economic ties, 87–8
  tensions with Iran, 76–7
  Tiran and Sanafir islands, plans for, 93–5
  transportation network, 109
  US disengagement, 18–19, 20–2, 31, 61
  US–Saudi, 99 civilian nuclear program, 99, 100
  'Vision 2030', 87–8, 97
Scientific Studies and Research Center (SSRC), 224, 235
Sderot, 151
sectarian riots (2021), 168–9
Senate Armed Services Committee, 77
7 October massacre, 2, 4, 29, 101, 119, 120, 181–2, 188, 196, 197, 201–4, 231, 234, 241, 251, 253
Shach, Rabbi Elazar, 159–60
Shaked, Ayelet, 167
Sharon, Ariel, 119, 121–2
Shas party, 160
Sheikh Jarrah, 169, 186
al-Sheikh, Hussein, 130, 143, 144
'Shield and Arrow' (operation), 227
Shiite community, 207–8
Shuafat, 133
Silver, Vivian, 202

INDEX

Simchat Torah massacre. *See* 7 October massacre
Sinai Peninsula, 53, 60, 93, 160
Sinai Province, 11, 43
Sinwar, Yahya, 128, 182–5
al-Sisi, Abdel Fattah, 10, 36, 60, 74, 93
Six-Day War (1967), 55, 92, 94
small and medium-sized companies, 115
Smotrich, Bezalel, 161–2, 169, 197
Soleimani, Qassem, 18, 63, 221, 223
Southern Lebanon Army, 15
southern Lebanon, 208, 217–18, 225, 228, 233, 237, 239–40
Soviet Union, 240
Sudan, 57, 59, 68, 85
Suez Canal, 29
'Sword of Jerusalem', 184
Syria, 207–8, 211, 231, 232, 242
    Daraa protests (Mar 2011), 12
    Iran vs., 220–6
    Iran's growth, 231–3
    Israeli–Palestinian conflict, 226–9
    Lebanon war III, 233–7
    nuclear program, 242
    Russian threats, 25
Syrian Arab Army (SAA), 216, 220–1
Syrian chemical weapons program, 224–5
Syrian Civil War, 11, 110, 215–20, 221
Syrian Golan, 215

Tahnoun I, Sheikh, 76
Tanzim, 136
Tehran, 208, 212, 219, 220, 226, 232, 244
Tel Aviv, 226, 234
    flights, 1, 2, 3, 80, 81, 105, 150, 179
Tiandy, 212
Tiyas air base, 222
Torah, 161
ToTok, 81–2
Trump administration, 58–9, 127
    Israeli–Palestinian conflict, 42, 43, 58
    peace plan, 192
    and Riyadh relationship, 18–20
Trump, Donald, 34, 61, 90
    against Iran, 63
    'America First' policy, 19
    'Deal of the Century', 38, 39, 42, 58, 127, 192, 193, 197
    foreign policy, 57–9
    'Middle East Strategic Alliance' (MESA), 73–5
    isolationist policies, 18–19
    Jerusalem as Israel's capital, recognizing, 179–80
Tunisia, 9, 10, 12, 251
Turkey, 13, 27, 78
    China's diplomatic ties with, 28
    Israeli–Palestinian conflict involvement, 60–1

Ukraine, invasion of (2022), 23, 24, 26, 62, 93
    impact on supply chains, 112
    Israel's stance, 24–5, 27
ultra-Orthodox Jews (Haredim), 158–60, 161–3, 171, 172, 173

Umm al-Fahm, 169
'Ummah' (the Islamic community), 39
UN Interim Force in Lebanon (UNIFIL), 216
UN Security Council, 179
UNIFIL, 238
United Arab Emirates (UAE), 22, 25, 47, 55, 87, 95, 193
 al-Dhafra air base, training, 69
 anti-Iran alliance, 77–8
 cyber-security, 79–80, 81–2
 F-35 fighter jets, sale of, 59
 free trade agreement, 111–14
 investments in Israel's pension funds, 115
 Israeli companies moved to, 79
 Israeli exports to, 111
 on Yemen conflict, 81
 population, 105
 See also Abraham Accords
United Arab List (Ra'am), 56, 165, 170
United Nations Special Envoy, 33
United States (US), 25–6, 29–30, 74, 216, 240, 246, 253
 bond between Saudi Arabia and, 18–20
 disengagement from the Middle East, 18–19, 20–2, 31, 61
 era of American overconfidence, 22
 investments in Israel's pension funds, 114–15
 involvement in Abraham Accords, 61–2, 64, 66
 Iraq, invasion of, 207
 Jerusalem as Israel's capital, recognition of, 179–84
 military budget, 73–4
 missile, 223
 Saudi demands, 99–100
 Washington–Israel relations, 31
'unity Intifada', 169–70
unmanned vessels, 71–2
Unna, Yigal, 80
US embassy, 124, 128, 180
US Fifth Fleet, 69, 71
US military Central Command (CENTCOM), 68–70
US National Security Strategy, 20
US–Israeli relationship, 61, 62, 128
Uyghur minority, 212

Velayat al-Faqih, 211, 249

Wall Street Journal, 77, 99, 232
Washington Institute, 37, 98
West Bank, 120, 121, 126, 131, 134, 149, 163
 annexation of, 51–3, 54, 127, 193–4, 195
 escalation in Palestinian attacks, 137
 geography of, 150
 Hamas operation in, 183
 Israelis population in, 196–7
 protests, 180
 reoccupation, 152
 security collapse in, 150–1
 security control, 132
 'twilight zones', 133
West Bank, 227–8, 232, 245, 252
WhatsApp, 58

INDEX

WikiLeaks, 64
'Women, Life, Freedom', 211

Yated Ne'eman, 162
Yedioth Ahronoth (newspaper), 51–2, 252
Yemen conflict, 62, 75, 81, 207, 223, 231–4

Yom Kippur War (1973), 218, 233, 244

Zainabiyoun unit, 219
Al Zeyoudi, Thani, 112
Zionism, 159, 190, 191
Zogby Research, 37